Menzies versus Evatt

The Great Rivalry of Australian Politics

Anne Henderson

Connor Court Publishing Pty Ltd

Published in 2023 by Connor Court Publishing Pty Ltd.

Copyright © Anne Henderson

All rights reserved. Not to be reproduced without the permission of the Copyright holders.

Connor Court Publishing Pty Ltd.
PO Box 7257
Redland Bay QLD 4165
sales@connorcourt.com
www.connorcourt.com

ISBN: 9781922815606

Cover Design by Paige Hally

Printed in Australia.

For Gerard – intellectual street-fighter and lifetime companion.
Thanks for the ride.

Contents

Foreword	vii
1. Battle Lines	1
2. Two Lives	17
3. The Banks	35
4. Communism and Political Realities	55
5. A New Age of Cold War	73
6. Groundwork for a Showdown	91
7. Referendum Campaign 1951	111
8. An Election Win by Hook or by Crook	129
9. The Petrov Fallout	145
10. Endgame	167
Endnotes	187
Select Bibliography	201
Acknowledgements	209
Index	211

Foreword

Paul Kelly

The political battle between Robert Menzies and Herbert Vere (Bert) Evatt is remarkable in Australia's history for its ideological conflict, its personal spite and its length. Menzies and Evatt were giants on the Australian stage as leaders of the Liberal Party and the Labor Party but also as adversaries in the struggle over the nation's direction in the postwar era. Their rivalry became an engrossing study in personality – two men with much in common yet divided by temperament and character.

Their battle was about power but it was also a morality tale about the capacity of leaders to unite their parties and find the balance between self-interest and the nation's interest. Over the past two generations Australians have witnessed monumental political contests – Gough Whitlam against Malcolm Fraser, Paul Keating against John Howard and, within the same party, Tony Abbott against Malcolm Turnbull.

Yet the Menzies-Evatt encounter transcended such tussles – these leaders were bonded by their professional legal prowess yet were viscerally divided by personal antagonism. Superimposed upon the personal element was a political contest over what sort of nation Australia would become in the postwar world. Their rivalry had few limits and was often waged with an elemental cruelty.

Born in the same year 1894, Menzies and Evatt had parallel lives. They won scholarships and thrived in the law – but politics was in their bloodstream. With restless energy Evatt championed working class causes before being elevated to the High Court in 1930 aged 36 years. In 1934 Menzies switched from Victorian to federal politics, his intellectual command bringing him to the office of prime minister in 1939. With Menzies a wartime PM, Evatt's ambition saw him enter federal parliament at the 1940 election with his undisguised aspiration being the Labor leadership.

With Labor in office during the 1940s decade under John Curtin and Ben Chifley, Evatt served as both Attorney-General and Minister for External Affairs, won international recognition for his role leading to the formation of the United Nations and then as President of the General Assembly. He finally became Labor leader on the death of Chifley in 1951. Menzies, meanwhile, had been focused on political rehabilitation, the creation of the new Liberal Party and re-building the strength of non-Labor politics for the decisive battles over Australia's future. His victory at the 1949 election would become a turning point inaugurating an era of Coalition Government rule, yet this could not have been predicted when the competition between Menzies and Evatt reached its zenith in the early 1950s.

Their struggle was a brutal contest for power and a study in opposing leadership styles. It possessed a Shakespearean quality – both men had to master their demons within, arising from ambition and arrogance that always threatens successful leadership. Their battles culminated in three epic personal encounters. The first was Menzies' 1951 referendum campaign over the dissolution of Communist Party that saw Evatt vindicated with a narrow victory vesting his new leadership with immense status and the hope of terminating Menzies' hold on office.

The second was the 1954 election when Menzies thwarted Evatt's momentum, winning re-election with a shade under 50 per cent of the popular vote, in what proved to be Labor's final opportunity to halt the Menzies ascendancy. In the process Menzies had announced the defection of the third secretary at the Soviet Embassy, Vladimir Petrov, who requested political asylum. This ignited one of the most inflammatory mythologies in Australian politics with Evatt convincing himself of a conspiracy manipulated by Menzies to steal Labor's impending election victory. The conspiracy was never verified. While the Petrov defection did not figure in the campaign the event could only have helped Menzies. But Evatt had lost his golden chance and would spend years in a fatal obsession about the Petrov affair.

The third encounter was the emerging battle over the Cold War and the communist threat, abroad and at home, with cataclysmic consequences for Labor arising from the Petrov Royal Commission and the formal split in the ALP. Evatt insisted on appearing before the commission but his role as legal counsel disastrously undermined his role as political leader.

At this stage the iron entered Menzies soul. Aware of Soviet spying and fifth column operations he regarded Evatt as unfit to be prime minister. The personal enmity between the leaders reached new depths. The 1955 ALP split exposed Evatt's inability to manage his party and finished his hopes of becoming PM. In the end, Evatt was undone by two elements – Menzies and his own flawed character.

These leaders played for great stakes. The Menzies-Evatt battle has transcended their own time. It had been waged ever since between party loyalists and historians. It will be told and retold while ever our politics exists.

In this book historian Anne Henderson has brought the story to life for a new generation of readers. Her highly readable account opens the lens wide – Menzies and Evatt are painted in their strengths and flaws, with their shared endeavours and their irreconcilable differences and with their competing views of Australia and the world. Henderson's account is fresh and compelling, a study in the triumphs, tribulations and tragedies that are the nature of politics.

1

BATTLE LINES

Evatt wrote two long letters to Menzies, one when the latter became prime minister in 1939, and the other after his re-election in 1940. Both letters were egocentric and demanding and purported to indicate his tangible contribution and vision. The first ... was dismissed by Menzies with a brief acknowledgement, an insulting response to a High Court judge and former colleague of the bar ... These letters typified Evatt's conceit in using his authority as a judge to exercise influence by direct communication. Menzies stated that his detestation of Evatt began with Evatt's entry into the House of Representatives, but Sir Peter Heydon, who recalled both documents, considered Evatt's enmity to date from Menzies' reply to his letter of April or May 1939 – Peter Crockett[1]

In Melbourne, on 21 September 1951, the eve of the vote on the referendum proposing Australia's federal government be given powers to bring about the dissolution of the Communist Party of Australia (CPA), Prime Minister Robert Menzies was mobbed by schoolgirls seeking his autograph.[2] He had been presenting prizes at the Commonwealth Jubilee Schools Choirs Festival. After weeks of bitter campaigning, many of his meetings dogged by agitators and hecklers drowning out his masterful rhetoric, these schoolgirls must have lifted his spirits. Alas, as other Australian prime ministers would in time attest, schoolgirls do not vote.

Within 24 hours, the result of the government's referendum had delivered the Menzies government – not yet two years in office – a stinging defeat, albeit narrow. The referendum had gone down in three states and with a majority of voters. The result offered the new Opposition leader, Labor's Dr Bert Evatt, a glorious victory.

At the outset of the campaign a few months earlier, polls had put the "Yes" vote comfortably ahead on what some estimated as 70–80 per cent in favour. Evatt's strong opposition, traversing the states in just weeks, had swung the vote back to a narrow "No" vote in three states and an overall narrow loss for the government. Unsurprisingly, as the referendum results were counted, Labor's Arthur Calwell demanded Menzies' immediate resignation.[3]

The campaign for the Communist Party dissolution referendum was heated, excitable and divisive. The margin for the winning side was paper thin. Former prime minister John Howard, who was twelve at the time, recalls that it was the only occasion he knew of when his mother and father voted differently on voting day. His mother "No", his father "Yes".[4] Penelope Seidler, Bert Evatt's niece, was also a 12-year-old, attending Prebyterian Ladies College in Sydney at the time of the referendum. She recalls being an Evatt at school was not easy:

> *It was a shocking period for an Evatt to be at a conservative school in that time. Twelve year olds (and teachers too) can be thoughtless; I was branded as a communist by the other girls who although not fully appreciating what was entailed they knew it was evil! My comprehension of communism was not clear either, but through the media I knew it was wicked and to be avoided! The name Evatt was a RED flag; my father Clive Evatt QC was a NSW state Minister at this time. I was alone, the only girl who was branded this way, I was unaware of anyone else whose parents would have opposed this Bill.*[5]

Historian Russel Ward, a young MA graduate who had his posting to a teachers training college in Wagga Wagga rescinded in 1951 before he began a class, has written of what he perceived to be discrimination against anyone known to be a communist sympathiser, much less a party or former party member. Ward had been a member of the CPA since 1941 but had left the party in 1950. He blamed his CPA association for the reassessment of his appointment to Wagga. The job was eventually given to someone far less qualified. Writing of the win for the "No" case in the 1951 referendum, Ward hails Evatt as the hero of the day and fine libertarian generally, writing:

> *Apart from that on conscription for overseas service during World War I, no other political campaign affecting the traditional liberties of Australians had been so bitter, so long-drawn-out and so closely contested. Many of us liked to think it significant that the libertarians won both. They certainly could not have done so without the Herculean labours of that lifelong champion of civil liberty under the rule of law, H. V. Evatt. He fought every inch of the way in parliament, eloquently argued the bill's unconstitutionality before the High Court, and did more than any other hundred people to get a "No" majority in the referendum.*

Justice Michael Kirby was a boy of 11 when the Communist Party dissolution referendum was held. His family was Labor but not communist although his father's step-father Jack Simpson, who had married Kirby's feisty grandmother and proved a loving and kindly husband after her unsuccessful first marriage, was a committed communist and activist for the CPA. Jack's presence in the family collective softened Kirby and his father's view of communists; many were no different from other Australians and could be generous and peaceful. Kirby recalls being taken to help Jack put up election posters in 1949 with "Vote 1 L. L. Sharkey" the candidate for the Communist Party. His mother was furious when she found out – "she was incandescent that they had tricked their little prize boy into helping the communist cause," recalled Kirby. But she was still happy for Kirby to visit Jack and his wife regularly as part of the family.

This sort of personal relationship and its softening effect on Kirby's recall of communism at the time was probably true of other Australians who came into contact with unionists and others they knew to have radical views but who did not impose that on friends or colleagues. Being a pleasant or friendly person meant being no different from ordinary people – not recognisable as the stereotyped figures in anti-communist literature. Jack Simpson was a kindly member of the Kirby family who did not propagandise his young step grandson but was happy to let him peruse the piles of communist literature and propaganda to be found in his home when the Kirbys visited each week.

Kirby also recalls being quite an admirer of Robert Menzies in 1949, as was his mother. He remembers getting his mother to make cakes he could sell at school to raise money for "Mr Menzies" although cannot recall what he did with the money. Michael Kirby's experience of the 1951 referendum was quite different from that of Penelope Seidler. Going to a government school, he did not experience any talk of politics nor note any comment among students or staff on the politics of the day.[6]

The bitterness of the 1951 Communist Party dissolution referendum was mostly to be found in the rhetoric of the chief propagandists, in press and radio reports, in advertisements, pamphlets and placards for one side or the other, and in speeches from Robert Menzies denouncing communists and Bert Evatt proclaiming the horrors of the legislation which would bring an end to the notion of innocent till proven guilty. Amirah Inglis, recalling her time as one of the Australian communist comrades has recorded something of the feeling from within the party: "The USSR had become the enemy and in Britain Nunn May and Fuchs, scientists who wanted atomic discoveries to be shared with that country, were arrested as spies. In the USA … Julius and Ethel Rosenberg, were arrested and charged with selling atomic secrets. In Europe spies skipped over borders, and at home we communists were widely held to be traitors."[7]

The language in the debate reached new heights – the encroaching enemy of Stalinism on one side and the menace of Hitler style rule on the other. What the ordinary Australian made of it is hard to imagine decades later. While lauding Evatt as the hero of the referendum for his stand against the draconian measures of the legislation itself, Justice Michael Kirby has acknowledged that, in fairness to Robert Menzies, the legislation should be understood "in the light of the perils of the time".[8] In this he referred to Soviet atom bomb tests and the Soviet's conquest of Eastern Europe alongside the fall of China to communism and its advance through North Korea to the south. In Kirby's words, the understandable fear was that "perhaps we would be the next victims of 'the dictatorship of the proletariat'".[9]

The debate played out in the 1951 referendum was a reflection of the messy divide the world had entered in the half decade following the end of World War II. The defeat of Nazi Germany and its Axis partner Japan was meant to usher in a bright new age following a victory for freedom over dictatorship. A victory of democratic liberty over totalitarian repression. Instead, with the explosion of the atomic bombs dropped by the US on Japan, the new age to come was to be dominated by new forms of struggle between the totalitarianism of communism against the free world of Western Europe, the British Commonwealth and the United States, each side developing new and more dangerous arms and nuclear technology to defend itself against the other. With the control in Eastern Europe by the Soviets of satellite states such as Czechoslovakia, Hungary and Poland along with Albania, Romania, Yugoslavia and Bulgaria, conquest had moved from the field of armed combat to political entrapment, from tanks and bombs from the sky to fifth columnists and spies trading information. A new term entered the narrative – the Cold War.

The results of the 1951 referendum seemed for a short while to herald a quick comeback for Labor after its defeat by Robert Menzies' fledgling Liberal Party in the December 1949 poll. From 1941 to 1949, Labor had flung off its schisms left from the fallout following the 1929 financial debacle and the years in the wilderness after its split over conscription during the First World War. John Curtin and Ben Chifley had shown that, united, Labor could govern.

By the time of the Communist Party dissolution referendum in September 1951, in the less than two years that Robert Menzies had once again led Australia following the Coalition's landslide win, the Menzies government was facing global turbulence with the Korean War and genuine worry, from London to Washington and beyond, that a third world war was imminent – the West was now facing Stalin's communist forces in Europe and the newly formed People's Republic of China in what was then known as the Far East. The double dissolution election of April 1951 was easily won by Menzies but his large margin from December 1949 had been trimmed, closing the gap by 10 seats. By September that year, reports of inflation and price hikes filled page one newspaper columns and industrial unrest continued. *The Argus* concluded its 24 September report on the referendum result with the view, "if the next 18 months are as unproductive of Government activity as the last 18 months have been the Government is heading for a major defeat".

The referendum campaign of 1951 had finally brought head-to-head, in national and press focus, two giants of Australian politics in the 1940s and 1950s. True, John Curtin and Ben Chifley had dominated the leadership of Australia in the 1940s, but no two opponents so precisely matched off like Robert Menzies and Bert Evatt. Lord Carrington, as former High Commissioner to Australia, knew them both. He once opined that the only thing they had in common was a love of cricket.[10] For all that, both were distinguished barristers on entering parliament and, by mid-1951, each stood at the head of Australia's two major political parties. To this could be added that each had devoted and long serving partners in Pattie Menzies and Mary Alice Evatt (Mas).

Both Menzies and Evatt had battled demons; Menzies to have lost government as prime minister and leader of the United Australia Party in 1941 and to have considered giving up politics after the 1943 federal election;[11] Evatt to have ambitiously coveted the top political job from the time he had entered parliament at the 1940 federal election only to have been forced to support loyally those senior Labor giants, Curtin and Chifley. Evatt's occasional push for a national government, both in his long letter to Menzies soon after he entered federal parliament in late 1940 and, in approaches to Menzies again in 1941,[12] had been seen by some as prompted by his desire to take the prime ministerial spot. Like Menzies after losing the leadership and prime ministership in August 1941, Labor's defeat at the polls for Evatt, in 1949, had him consider leaving parliamentary politics.[13]

Domestic and international factors had propelled the Liberal and Country Party Coalition into government in December 1949. Robert Menzies had been deeply affected by the Liberals' failure to win or even make significant inroads against Labor's majority at the 1946 election. By mid-1947, a handful of Liberal Party figures were considering whether Menzies should be replaced as leader. The saying "you'll never win with Menzies" became familiar to insiders. And then Ben Chifley, after a hastily called cabinet meeting on Saturday 16 August that year, announced in just one sentence of around 40 words that his government would legislate to nationalise Australia's trading banks. Menzies bolted from the starting blocks. Bank nationalisation confirmed Labor's agenda for socialisation of Australian industry. The policy of international communism.

The battle for the banks would last until just months before the 1949 federal election, as challenges in the High Court of Australia and before the Privy Council in London were heard. In these challenges, Bert Evatt appeared for the government in his initial moves as Menzies' nemesis. But even as the legislation was declared invalid by both courts, 1949 also became the year Ben Chifley called out the troops to smash the disruptions caused by striking coal workers, largely stirred at the hands of communist unionists.

It would not be until faced with legislation to nationalise Australia's banks, however, that voters were able to connect warnings of communist inspired activity – such as the communist inspired unionist shut down of coal mining – to their actual lives. Jobs had been strong in the post war economy and peacetime, after war, had its own rewards. With the banking protest over nationalisation – as in any referendum campaign – ordinary citizens suddenly were awash with information overdrive as to how socialisation of industry and government control of the market would impact a free economy. Communism as a growing menace in post war Europe alongside home grown union disruption now had resonance in the nationalisation of the banks. Thus the 1949 federal election, that saw the defeat of the Chifley Government, set the parameters for what became a battle that eventually engulfed not just the nation but, more especially, the Australian Labor Party.

After the death of Labor leader Ben Chifley, in June 1951, Bert Evatt took his place as Opposition leader. His reluctant decision to stay in politics was now handsomely rewarded with a position within striking distance of his long held goal of achieving the prime ministership. With the parliamentary tussle to push through legislation to ban the Communist Party from 1950, Labor began to be faced with what would become a growing schism between its left and right flanks. Chifley held the team together as the Communist Party dissolution legislation was debated, wanting to vote it down in the Senate only to be overruled by the Federal Executive of the party to let it through. With the legislation next thrown out by the High Court and a loss for Labor in the subsequent April 1951 election, at which Labor also lost the numbers in the Senate, Chifley was becoming aware he was no longer physically strong enough to lead Labor. He hung on in the job simply in the hope of finding the right replacement. With the position going to Evatt, the challenge was on in what would become disastrous ways.

Evatt, as External Affairs minister had been seen as the hero of Australia's leading role in the formation of the United Nations. His time out of Australia at this stage possibly affected his failure to perform successfully in the appeals over the Banking legislation before both the High Court and the Privy Council. In Evatt's time at the helm of the External Affairs Department through the mid to late 1940s, concern had grown around leading Evatt advisors, such as John Burton – Evatt's chief of staff who became head of External Affairs in 1947 – and their soft attitudes to the Soviet Union at a time of increasing territorial Soviet expansion in post war Eastern Europe. Evatt, as Attorney General, had performed strongly in backing Chifley's tough action to deal with the communist controlled unions but his role in foreign affairs showed a tendency to respond to international tensions with an equal trust in all players.

The referendum campaign over the dissolution of the Communist Party in 1951, carried out over some weeks, provided Evatt with a comeback opportunity, a chance to establish his position as new Labor leader and score a win against the new Menzies Government, and this by coming to a narrow victory for "No" from a hefty losing position just weeks before voting day. With his win, Evatt was suddenly enjoying a pinnacle in the political cycle from where he would have expected to seize government for Labor at the next federal election. And as many major commentators opined.

Menzies and Evatt were very different personalities. They grated on each other and left colleagues sometimes entertained, and occasionally unsettled, by memorable exchanges. Howard Beale, a former Menzies Government minister after 1949 and ambassador to the United States from 1957, knew both Menzies and Evatt well. He also worked with a number of those who had experienced Evatt's time as External Affairs minister. Many in the US when Beale was there recalled how much Evatt had been disliked there; others, at home, observed how his erratic and suspicious personality as a minister had created division and resentment in his department.

Beale's description of the competition between Menzies and Evatt, while admiring their distinguished legal minds, is an acute summary:

> [Evatt] and Menzies disliked each other without bothering to conceal it, and when he [Evatt] succeeded Chifley as leader of the opposition the rivalry intensified. There was something slightly unpleasant in the spectacle of these two outstanding men struggling

> bitterly, pitted against each other in the political arena, Menzies with his sharp tongue scoring most of the points, and Evatt on the other side of the table in the House, looking for all the world like a bull in the arena hunched up as the barbs struck home.[14]

Evatt was very much a public persona, using the media to push his image, both as a family man and public leader in a style decades ahead of his time, as and when he could. Meanwhile, Menzies kept his personal life and preferences very much away from public scrutiny, even from colleagues. As Sir John Bunting has reflected, he was a mixture of confident advocate and public leader and a strange personal shyness. Paul Hasluck who knew Menzies well saw this too.[15] He was not one to sound his own trumpet, believing his record would speak for itself. In presentation, Menzies could be both formal and relaxed – with all the timing of an experienced barrister. His repartee at the microphone facing hecklers became a legend. His public appearance - a large man in his double-breasted suits - was commanding and often seemed pompous to ordinary folk. Yet he could, when away from his public duties, let the guard slip and appear as dishevelled and ordinary as any. He could at these times relate easily to waiters, staff or electors as he found them.[16]

Opposed to this, Menzies was often derided, accurately, as arrogant in the presence of less well educated colleagues, a trait which he needed to overcome in the years he sought to form the Liberal Party and win back government. Once in the position of prime minister a second time, lessons learned over decades saw Menzies become a careful strategist using a solid amount of consideration and thinking before a next move. For all that, his manner of governing was of a first minister among parliamentarians rather than using a strict cabinet government style, believing in a style of delegation that left his ministers free to deal with their departments without interference.

By contrast, Bert Evatt was a chaotic manager, relying on minders and staff to tidy up after him. His brilliance came with an indifference to order – from documents, whether confidential or otherwise, to personal appearance. He exhibited the ways of an eccentric genius always in a hurry. He thrived on those in his wake paying deference to his status and superior intellect. He expected to be central to all business. As a minister he was very much the man in charge, the man of ideas, presence and performance with his retinue expected to get him through the tedium of lesser matters and the mundane details of administration. Peter Crockett writes of Evatt looking down on "the lower echelons of the legal hierarchy, ill-equipped as they were, in his view, to address the philosophy of the law".[17]

Unlike Menzies, Evatt was not a polished speaker. His grating voice meant that his triumph as a public performer came more from his persuasive argument and legal mind than the wit to reduce an opponent. Undoubtedly, his ability to master a brief quickly and tackle arguments was his strength, such as at the San Francisco Peace Conference in 1945, out of which came the United Nations. Evatt's capacity in preparation for the Conference meant he was able to comprehend and absorb, in days, details that officials had been working on over years. Evatt's presence and mastery at the Conference led historian Peter Edwards to opine, "No other man has dominated the making of Australian foreign policy for a substantial period quite so single-handedly, except perhaps Hughes at Versailles."[18] Robert Menzies, even as he sketched Evatt's unravelling in the Petrov case, acknowledged his resilience saying, "persistence had always been a notable characteristic of his advocacy, whether legal or political".[19]

While Evatt's intellectual capacity was great, with a record of wins at the bar, international recognition and an impressive array of scholarly writings, his eagerness not to miss an opportunity often gave the impression of a cascade of achievements that missed a defined or strategic direction. He was a true believer in liberalism, in civil rights and freedoms of the individual, but at a very theoretical level and his devotion to the United Nations, in the end, would leave him floundering as the tide turned in the 1950s with defence, security and the Cold War dominating notions of peace in our time. There was often something naïve about Evatt's faith in collective goodwill.

In the tussle of minds between Menzies and Evatt, ironically, Evatt's referendum victory in September 1951 over Menzies would, in the end, be a last hurrah of sorts, an aberration in an ideological battle over some decades. The aloof man of pragmatic dominance, with his belief in combatting the evils of communism, would outplay the man of genius with his devoted but erratic belief in a better world. Moreover, Evatt's victory at the 1951 referendum would, ironically, save Menzies from any heightened US McCarthyist style witch hunt of communist leaning Australians. Meanwhile, Evatt's triumph would tag him with being soft on communist subversion whatever his arguments that free speech was the core of his opposition to the Communist Party dissolution legislation. With the defection of KGB officer Vladimir Petrov from the Soviet embassy in Canberra in April 1954, Labor's loss in the 1954 federal election soon after and Evatt's mishandling of his appearance at the Petrov Royal Commission which followed, Evatt's victory for the "No" case in the 1951 referendum faded, proving that much in democratic politics can be momentary.

The twentieth century division across the world stemming from the power and persuasion of socialisation, its acolytes and theories, thus would be played out in Australia in a drama led by Robert Menzies and Bert Evatt. Each man would become defined in history by this drama and its repercussions, one to remain the much-loved hero of the left cut down in his prime by the so-called conspiracies of his opponents, the other to dominate Australian politics for two decades.

Bert Evatt would end his life in the political shadows having had to resign from his post as New South Wales Chief Justice because of failing health. His moment of triumph in the 1951 referendum appeared to have been his swan song. The loss for Labor under

Evatt in the 1954 election and his appearance at the Petrov Royal Commission had overtaken in the public mind his achievements as External Affairs Minister and Attorney-General in the Curtin and Chifley governments. Menzies, on the other hand, benefited hugely from the Labor split of the 1950s, much of the cause of which would be laid at the feet of Evatt. Menzies retired as prime minister at the top of his game in January 1966. He would go on to a post prime ministerial life of writing, travelling and lecturing and being consulted as an elder statesman into the 1970s.

Yet, Evatt would make something of a comeback in the last two decades of the twentieth century. As the years after his death in November 1965 passed, Evatt followers became an energetic collective of scribblers, turning out pages in his memory. Among Labor heroes he stood tall as a man of intellect and substance. One who had stood for the principles of human rights and equal opportunity, cut down in his prime by the connivance of his arch enemy Robert Menzies. His failure to keep the Labor Party united in 1955 would be written up as another conspiracy, hatched by the followers of the sinister B. A. Santamaria. The non-Labor side of politics was no match for this, leaving the Menzies legacy to make its own way in the records until the revival of interest in the Liberal Party after the success of the Howard years of 1996–2007. By then, historians began to tackle the myths spread by the opponents of Robert Menzies. They set about recording the achievements of the Menzies years and peeling back some of the mystique and stereotyping of Menzies.

There was much of the negative about Menzies to unpack. The admiration for the "Doc" by left wing intellectuals had been matched only by their dislike and distrust of Menzies. The left view of the Menzies years would dominate the public memory in the 1970s into the 1990s. Even the use of "Doctor" before Evatt's name seemed to signal how much he stood head and shoulders over the brain power of others. For many in the Evatt fan club, it was a tragedy that he had been bettered by a man like Menzies. But there was one victory that stood above all in the Evatt trajectory – his victory over the lordly Menzies in the 1951 referendum to ban communism in Australia.

A few months short of the fortieth anniversary of the Communist Party dissolution referendum, in April 1991, the Evatt Foundation held a two-day conference to discuss the campaign, its implications and the achievements of its man of the moment, H V Evatt. The gathering and the speakers brought together senior judges, leading academics and some of the participants of the campaign itself.[20] The Evatt Foundation produced a book from the papers given, titled *Seeing Red*. In it, most authors eulogised Evatt's intellect and courage. Clem Lloyd's even-handed account of Menzies and the legislation to ban the Communist Party still seems to put Evatt's political demise after the referendum win down to bad luck, and timing, as if his own failings had no part in it.[21] Such writings and memorials to Evatt, by the Australian left, raised Evatt's memory to new heights for a decade and more.

In *Seeing Red*, Arthur Gietzelt extolled Evatt's contribution to Australia in a chapter titled "Principle Before Power". He also referred to a "personal antagonism between Evatt and Menzies" which remained for two decades.[22] The "Doc", in Gietzelt's view, was robbed by Menzies and the anti-communist paranoia of the 1950s, especially at the hands of Labor's industrial Groupers in which the Catholic Church and B. A. Santamaria's Movement were a strong force, manipulating Labor to support their efforts. Touching on the Petrov defection in 1954, which so ruined Evatt politically, Gietzelt argued the conspiracy line, promulgated by Labor and long since shown to be false, that Menzies had lied to parliament and used the Petrov defection to help win the 1954 election.

Gietzelt's chapter, replete with rationalisation of the ways in which Evatt was left a victim, presents the anti-communist forces within Labor as the enemy. Evatt, for Geitzelt, is the great Australian prime minister Australia never had. At the time of writing, Gietzelt was a former Labor Senator who had often denied he had any links with the Communist Party of Australia, much less been a member. However, with the publication of Mark Aarons' *The Family File* in 2010 and Stuart Macintyre's *The Party* in 2022, the evidence from ASIO files and personal recollections shows that Arthur Gietzelt was a member of the CPA from as far back as the 1940s until, possibly, 1983.[23]

Revelations, in hindsight, from those who published what they knew of the CPA from the inside plus the release of evidence from the Venona papers of communist infiltration in the West have long since re-evaluated Evatt's place and the CPA in the Australian political trajectory. Menzies, without a doubt, acted on justifiable grounds in opposing the activities in Australia of the CPA. As history has shown, he was unwise to try to ban the CPA, but his instincts about the subversive activities of the Australian Communist Party would in time carry the day.

It was left in *Seeing Red* to Justice Michael Kirby, an Evatt supporter, to get the legacy of the 1951 Communist Party dissolution referendum into perspective, writing:

> *In accordance with the Constitution, the referendum amendment was defeated. Evatt told the subsequent meeting of the Labor Caucus that it had been more important to defeat the referendum than to win a series of federal elections. Given what might have followed, I agree. But the result undoubtedly helped nail Evatt's political ambitions. The label "defender of communists" stuck. It was reinforced during the Petrov affair and the Royal Commission on Espionage which followed. It precipitated the bitter split in the Labor Party, partly along sectarian lines.*[24]

Constitutional lawyer George Williams has agreed, writing: "Evatt's victory in the *Communist Party Case* was a personal triumph. However, he soon reached his watershed for his success undermined his burning ambition to become Prime Minister and relegated the Labor Party to the Opposition benches until 1972."[25]

In the years that followed, whether Labor Party members would have agreed with Evatt about the importance of the referendum win above federal election wins is debatable. That assessment of the referendum outcome also underlines some of the essential differences between Evatt and his arch rival Robert Menzies. And perhaps explains why one man, in the end, was the ultimate winner.

2

Two Lives

What does one say to these young men who dream of national leadership? My advice would be that they are less likely to come to a position of leadership by proving that they are better than their fellows than by making themselves acceptable to their fellows; that they do not advance by learning the arts of command but by practising the techniques of support. – Paul Hasluck[1]

Born within eight months of each other in 1894, Robert Menzies and Bert Evatt were fostered in a British world at the edge of an empire. Their respective families were loyal to church, monarch and community even as their colonial order saw rapid change to become a federation just as the long serving Queen Victoria ended her reign and the indulgent and, by then, aging Prince of Wales became King Edward VII. Neither boy could have imagined how that act of federation would impact each other's world; how the centre of federal government, as it widened its powers, would involve them both at the highest level – politically and judicially.

In colonial New South Wales, Bert Evatt began his early years in the Hunter Valley's Maitland where the drama of historic floods hardened locals amid their isolation. Bert was the fifth born son and third living child of Jeanie and John Evatt who ran a hotel in the main street of East Maitland. Three younger brothers had followed Bert quickly, so that the Evatt siblings resembled a divide of two eldest brothers, who soon left to work in Sydney, and four much younger siblings. When Bert was seven, John Evatt died. Within a few years, Jeanie had resettled on the lower north shore of Sydney at Milsons Point near to her sisters and older sons. Extended family would be important in supporting Jeanie as she raised her younger boys. Their future, Jeanie determined, would be secured by the best education she could offer them. In Bert Evatt's trajectory, Sydney's Fort Street High stands tall.

As the winner of scholarships and prizes, the young Bert Evatt was a star pupil. His mother Jeanie instilled in him the need to excel. Various contemporaries noted how Evatt was desperate to succeed. For his mother, it was not enough to bring home eight "A"s if you sat nine subjects – where was the ninth "A" would be her response on being told.[2] At Sydney University, Evatt took out a Master of Arts in 1917 and a Doctorate of Laws in 1924, lectured in English, philosophy and law, went on to establish a lucrative legal practice specialising in industrial and defamation law and developed a particular expertise in constitutional law. His legal interests also brought him close to the causes and politics of the labour movement in its earliest decades.

Some 1200 kilometres to the south west of Maitland, just across the New South Wales/Victorian border, young Robert Menzies spent his earliest years in the rural town of Jeparit, a one street town in the northern Wimmera, an area known as the Mallee. Where the Evatts knew floods, the Menzies family endured droughts and dust storms. Young Robert, born the fourth of five children to James and Kate Menzies, enjoyed a strict but loving family. His parents, like Jeanie Evatt, determined their children would get the best education on offer and, for some years, sent their children to live during school terms in Ballarat with their grandmother. Here they attended intermediate school after their earliest primary years in Jeparit. From there, Robert won a scholarship which saw him spend his secondary years boarding at Wesley College in Melbourne. He later won scholarships to study law at the University of Melbourne where he excelled and won prizes. Unlike Bert Evatt, however, Robert Menzies would benefit from a father who, in spite of his stern command, would live to offer a guide for his son in the ways of politics. James Menzies was not only a shopkeeper in Jeparit but would also be elected to the Victorian Legislative Assembly in 1911, after which the family moved to Melbourne.

Lives in parallel, as bright young things, Menzies and Evatt made their way to professional success through their outstanding scholarship and early attainment of prestigious positions in the law and academia. But where Menzies was the man enriched by a Presbyterian faith and largely brought to adulthood in "marvellous Melbourne", the stronghold of a prosperous middle class protecting its control of a city untainted by convict origins, Evatt entered the world of pragmatic and egalitarian Sydney where deals and enterprise ruled the day, where it was enough to make good from what you achieved rather than who you knew or what group you belonged to. Menzies never resiled from his "blushing Presbyterian" origins and was apt to quote from the Bible to support his arguments. He spoke often at the Wesley Church's "Pleasant Sunday Afternoons", on one occasion using the New Testament to support his views of democracy. As such he saw the essence of democracy in terms of service: "We become master in this life by service. ... We can be masters of the State only by being servants and builders of the State."[3] In contrast to this, Evatt became an early convert to the socialist inspired notion of human rights. He would emerge quickly as a secularist seeking reform of the human condition through the courts.

Biographers of Bert Evatt have long grappled with the mercurial character of their high achieving subject – from the hagiographic portrait of Kylie Tennant for whom Evatt was a Labor hero to the more cutting assessments of Peter Crockett that emphasise Evatt's vanity and narcissism. In his political memoir *Against the Tide*, B A Santamaria gives an acute account of Evatt's duplicity in the lead up to the 1954 federal election, describing intimately how Evatt had duchessed Santamaria to gain his influence on the Catholic vote through The Movement only to turn in vengeance on the members of The Movement after Labor lost the election.[4] In 1954, B. A. Santamaria had headed both the Catholic Social Studies Movement (a select organisation at the time which Santamaria referred to as The Movement) and the Australian National Secretariat of Catholic Action (ANSCA). While the hierarchy split these two organisations in April 1954, Santamaria remained at the head of The Movement and ANSCA was wound up. Critics of Santamaria's Movement referred to the organisation as Catholic Action.

Santamaria's memoir carries a comment from English writer Malcolm Muggeridge on its back cover that captures Evatt's feelings at the effect of this leading Catholic on the Labor leader's political career: "In his last years, [Dr Evatt's] mind was not at its most lucid, but there was one thing that would arouse him in a kind of frenzy – it was the word 'Santamaria.'" Evatt biographer John Murphy's objective conclusions isolate six prominent characteristics that governed Evatt as both public and private figure. For Murphy these were ambition, overweening self-regard, suspicion of the motives of others (at times paranoia), a sense of self shaped by the law, liberalism and a lack of self-awareness.[5]

Those who worked with and knew Evatt invariably attested to his hot and cold emotional responses depending on circumstances – an intemperate and unconstrained dark mood could just as easily be followed by generosity and warmth. Peter Crockett illustrates Evatt's unpredictable and irascible manners in a brief account he gives of a departmental officer who met Evatt as Labor leader, straight off the plane in London in June 1953 for the Queen's coronation. Evatt had asked one of the Australian officials meeting him if the diplomat had heard from Evatt's Labor colleague (and rival) Arthur Calwell whom he disliked. The official told a colleague later that it was the sort of question where he could not have given a correct answer: "If he said yes, E. might conclude that he was plotting with Calwell against him; if he said no, it would invite the response 'Well, think of that! After all you've done for him'. Such was E's reputation amongst many officials."[6]

One acute observer of Bert Evatt, who worked with him when Evatt was Australia's External Affairs Minister, but also knew him after entering parliament as the Liberal Member for Curtin in 1949, was Paul Hasluck. Published posthumously, Hasluck's detailed notes and recorded observations about some of the leading political figures he had known over his career include a summary of Evatt's strengths and weaknesses as Hasluck witnessed them. While recognising Evatt's achievements and the energy he expended in this, Hasluck found Evatt to be "emotionally simple and intellectually complex" and "often like a naughty child" to the point where Hasluck "developed for him the odd sort of liking that one has for the naughty impulsive child in preference to the well-behaved pet". Hasluck excused Evatt his tantrums and simplicities, and his naïve calculations, as being the result of "an emotional life shackled to a complicated mind". And while it was not a creative mind, Hasluck recognised Evatt's "considerable mental powers" which "had great absorptive capacity".[7]

Hasluck also saw in Evatt a boy who needed mothering. Others, though, might have wondered if his father's death when Bert was just seven, and the lack of a father in his later school years might have deprived him of a way to those various levels of maturity he lacked. In adulthood, he would marry an enduring partner in Mary Alice Sheffer (hence "Mas") whose adoration of Bert and intellectual companionship provided the emotional buffer he needed.

This boyishness in Evatt is captured in Gideon Haigh's *The Brilliant Boy*, a close record of Evatt's professional achievements prior to his years as a minister in the Labor government of John Curtin and Ben Chifley. While rising parallel with Menzies as stand out barrister before the High Court and in chambers at a very young age, Evatt had less of Menzies' acumen in organised party politics. Where Menzies, while similarly attracted to a life among the silks and justices, moved quickly into leadership with the Nationalist Party, Haigh captures Evatt as a boy in a hurry, seizing at scholarly pursuits in law, history and even the arts as if enjoying an Aladdin's cave of opportunities for a clever mind with no particular end point decided.

In spite of a heavy workload later, as a justice of the High Court, Evatt could turn out books and monographs – among them *Injustice within the Law* on the Tolpuddle martyrs, *Rum Rebellion* as a revisionist account of Governor Bligh and a biography of NSW Labor premier William Holman. Evatt's orbit remained soloist in nature, the "Doc", a boy in pursuit of dreams notching up wins in court alongside being a noted Labor MP with acclaim for publications and even naïve enough to write to US President Franklin Roosevelt, in 1938, a long epistle on his observations after an initial visit to the US, including advice to the president in his selection of a new appointment to the Supreme Court.[8] It was all about Evatt.

Evatt's friendship from university days with socialist and pacifist Vere Gordon Childe, to whom he continued to write, helped him develop political views that began to challenge the nature and causes of the First World War, and reverse his support for wartime conscription. In May 1920, Evatt joined his local Mosman branch of the ALP, formed just months before.[9] In the state election of May 1925, Evatt won a record victory to become the Labor MP for the working class seat of Balmain in Sydney. After a rocky couple of years in the Lang Government and clashes with its leader Jack Lang, in 1927 Evatt retained his seat as an "Independent Labor" candidate. In December 1930, Evatt left state politics and became one of two Scullin Labor government appointees to Australia's High Court.

Reviewing Bert Evatt's biography of NSW premier William Arthur Holman, *Australian Labor Leader*, in 1940 for *The Australian Quarterly*, Evatt's friend American journalist C. Hartley Grattan praised the work's study of not just its subject but as a "document of great significance" in explaining the nature and workings of Australia's early Labour movement.[10] From reading Evatt's biography of this successful Labor figure Holman, who had dominated NSW Labor, as Grattan understood it, Australian Labour/Labor - while resting fundamentally on its union base - aspired to political power best when it was "weak on the industrial side" and its program "far from socialism as the Marxists think of it". Evatt had explained in his biography of Holman that, in Australia, political Labor's socialism when dominant was much closer to liberalism. And, in a prescient interpretation of radical unionisation within Labor, Grattan singled out Evatt's analysis of the effect of radicalism on political Labor:

> *Political Labour, as this study of Holman shows, ordinarily opposes Labour's radicalism; and this book also shows that if driven into a corner by union radicalism, parliamentary Labourites will "rat".*

Looked at from decades into the future, Evatt could have been analysing his own demise as Labor leader in the 1950s. For all his brilliance, when Labor split in the 1950s, Evatt would not be able to strategise around such "ratting" when it truly mattered to him and his ability to prevail.

Evatt and Menzies, after glittering prizes won at university, both established careers in the years following World War I. Neither had gone to the war. Evatt was rejected for call up because of his weak eyesight and his family would be affected by having two brothers, one older and one younger, lost in action. Menzies would not enlist because his family prevented him. The fact that he had not enlisted dogged him for years in public life as, in loyalty to his parents, Menzies would not explain the reasons he had stayed home. Menzies' two older brothers had signed up and Menzies' parents insisted he stay behind believing the family had given enough in sending two boys.

World War I changed the world in unforeseen ways. The death toll was some 20 million, with a similar number of casualties. It would claim the lives of 60,000 Australian men. It altered global boundaries, ended empires and spawned revolution and the rise of the radical reformist ideologies of communism and fascism. It handed the government of Russia to a Marxist dictatorship and soon saw an internationally focused communist push, under Moscow's Comintern, to overturn Western democracies as agents of capitalism. It, equally, spawned the rise of right wing and fascist opponents of the communists, forces that in time took power in Italy and Spain. The defeat and humiliation of Germany, in turn, gave way to a revived German nationalism, soon to be hijacked by Hitler's National Socialists.

In Australian politics, the post war years saw the Australian Labor Party damaged by a war-time split over conscription with its leader Prime Minister Billy Hughes and his followers linking up with the non-Labor side of politics to form the National Labor Party and retain office. The remnant Labor Party would battle through the 1920s, besieged by new and radicalised elements in the unions and its ranks, imbued with militancy echoing from European communism. The Communist Party of Australia took shape in these years, feeding into union activists and further radicalising Labor ranks.

Robert Menzies, like Bert Evatt, took to the law after university as an unchallenged bright young thing. He read with legal heavyweight Owen Dixon and, at the age of twenty-five, made a name for himself by winning the landmark Amalgamated Society of Engineers case before the High Court. Ironically, Bert Evatt appeared as a junior in the same case for the opposing side.

The Menzies clan was a diverse group. On his mother's side, her father John Sampson had been president of the miners' union in Creswick and left Menzies with fond memories of a man who did not speak down to children.[11] But while it was often said Menzies' temperament reflected the family's Sampson Cornish traits, it was his Scottish heritage on the Menzies side that he always acknowledged. With the Scots influence strong among the elite of Melbourne's business and legal circles, this may well have facilitated Menzies' rapid assimilation into Nationalist Party ranks.

It is not closely recorded how Robert Menzies became interested in public affairs sufficient to stand for parliament. Menzies' biographer Allan Martin explains how, in the 1920s, the non-Labor side of politics was inspired by the sacrifice of World War I and Australia's allegiance to Britain and the empire.[12] This stirring of national feeling among the middle classes saw a burgeoning of public spirited groups – some with sentiment that was narrow, even sectarian, but others genuinely interested in stirring debate as to how to legislate for a better society. The growth of these loyalist groups also increased in reaction to the mounting and strident calls from leftist Labor activists. The Communist Party of Australia had invaded Australia's union movement and was standing candidates at elections with policies urging the overthrow of Westminster style government. An early form of disruptive politics.

It was through friends and colleagues in the Constitutional Club, in particular Wilfrid Kent Hughes, that Robert Menzies was elected to Victoria's Legislative Council in October 1928 as a Nationalist and in 1929 won the seat of Nunawading for the Victorian Legislative Assembly. He was a rising star in a party desperate for rejuvenation after years of tension with radical elements in the Victorian Country Party. By 1932, Menzies had been made Attorney-General and Minister for Railways in the Victorian state government. At the federal election in 1934, Menzies switched to federal politics taking the seat of Kooyong for the United Australia Party and becoming Attorney-General in the Lyons Government.

While the older Menzies would write that law was his great love and politics his duty, the role Menzies came to play in the formation of the United Australia Party (UAP) in 1931 and the formation of the Liberal Party of Australia in the mid-1940s suggests that Menzies was addicted to political activity. He was a natural leader. His father and grandfathers had been politically involved. He had inherited their thirst for political action. As a young politician, Menzies stood high above colleagues in his learning and accomplishments. His hauteur in manner was often the cause of friction with some. It was said of his early years in the United Australia Party governments of Joseph Lyons and later as prime minister himself that "if he felt that he had an equal on the political scene, he never acknowledged it".[13] Percy Spender has written of how when PM first time around, Menzies intimidated his ministerial colleagues often sending them away like a bad-tempered headmaster. Spender wrote of an evening when Menzies had dined with a small number of colleagues in "top form". So much so that one senator suggested to him he should be more like that all the time. His problem was that he did not suffer fools gladly. Menzies ruined his good impression in just a few words replying, "And pray, what do you think I am doing now?"[14]

This contrasted with the inspiration to be found with Bert Evatt whose academic and intellectual interest in working class causes, albeit sincere and a constant motivation, lacked the hands-on political machine networking of most hard-edged political aspirants. Labor icon and party operative Jack Lang could not have been more different in aspiration from Evatt who saw his political appointments more as prizes awarded for his brilliance at the law and in his contribution to legal battles won. And later his ministerial role and responsibilities as the forerunner to the top prize, whether president of the United Nations Assembly for a year or the failed cause of becoming prime minister.

Bert Evatt's commitment to labour causes against the might of capitalist enterprise developed out of his legal work in areas of law just beginning to flourish. As a student and budding intellectual fresh from university, Evatt admired statesmen like Alfred Deakin and reformer jurists such as Henry Bournes Higgins and Issac Isaac, men who were known as liberals in a world yet to experience the radicalism of an organised Labor Party. Writing in 1915, in what became the Beauchamp Prize Essay at Sydney University for that year, Evatt made an early joust at pragmatic politics, writing:

> *We must see to it that empiricism does not get too secure a hold on us and that the new form of government will be based on the principles of liberty and equality. If that ideal can be achieved one more victory will have been won by Liberalism in Australia.*[15]

Evatt's convictions as a liberal were heavily dependent on theoretical assumptions such as the view of Henry Broadhurst that liberalism did not seek to make all men equal but rather remove impediments to equal opportunity.[16] With the growing strength of Labor in political action, Evatt soon saw Labor as the next step up from the liberalism of those early federation leaders he admired. In time, however, having sought to join the ranks of the Labor Party, some of his political theorising would clash with Labor realities. This was especially so with Evatt's recorded view that Labor's preference to unionists did not commend itself to liberalism. And, in the drawn-out coal strikes of 1949, as Attorney-General, Evatt would be responsible for freezing union funds and the legislation that gaoled communist leaders.

Workers compensation litigation and industrial law offered Evatt a more accessible answer for his theoretical leanings. In his work as a professional advocate, Evatt saw himself standing in support of the oppressed against the privileged. With Labor taking office increasingly such as in NSW and Queensland, Evatt also acted for Labor government administrations making him recognised politically as well as at the bar. He was the brilliant young lawyer making a difference for the labour movement in the courts alongside their industrial action.

Evatt became known for his passion for civil liberties – a notion still to gain traction in wider political circles. He also branched out to more aesthetic interests defending the off-beat saucy *Smith's Weekly* against action for libel.[17] It entertained him and added to his bank balance. Where Robert Menzies was a traditionalist, quoting the Bible liberally and affirming his loyalty to the Crown, Bert Evatt was breaking out of the barriers. In time, Evatt and his wife Alice would link up with John and Sunday Reed and their artistic set in Melbourne enjoying their designs and their society and buying their merchandise. Paul Hasluck records that the raffish painter Sam Atyeo, whom Evatt came to know through the Reeds, eventually accompanied Evatt when he was External Affairs minister on overseas trips as a sort of personal attendant.[18] Evatt was the modern against the conservative Menzies. Gideon Haigh captures some of this in an account of reactions to a 1936 exhibition by avant-garde painter Adrian Lawler in Melbourne.[19]

In spite of a grandfather mentor who had been part of the pioneer labour struggles, Menzies' political persuasion and endeavours were underpinned more by a British mixture of Edmund Burke and John Stuart Mill - the protection of individual and citizens' rights and responsibilities under the Westminster system and the Crown. But Menzies' political stances and his notion of liberalism, unlike Evatt's, were developed out of the realities of contemporary political systems. Menzies' antagonism to state control of either the left or right never wavered. With the Young Nationalists, Menzies joined discussion groups, and speeches on street corners, that pushed for balanced budgets, law and order, financial security for small and large businesses, loyalty to the empire and unity for the fragmented non-Labor side of politics.

While federal Labor would fall into government in October 1929, the stress of the stock market crash soon after, a global credit squeeze, divisive figures like NSW Labor leader Jack Lang and extremist views among some Labor MPs over handling financial meltdown soon divided Labor ranks once more. Out of this would come the United Australia Party which, with the help of Robert Menzies and a group of businessmen known as the Group of Six, would be led by what Evatt would label a Labor "rat" in former Scullin minister Joseph Lyons. The UAP under Lyons would win a landslide in December 1931, and Lyons would remain Australia's prime minister until his sudden death in April 1939. It would also be a decade where Robert Menzies came into his own as a non-Labor parliamentary leader while Bert Evatt excelled on the High Court.

In a decade on the High Court, little Evatt did suggested that he was other than a Labor appointee. Of twenty workers' compensation claims he found for the applicant in ninety per cent of them;

in twenty-nine arbitration cases he sided with the employee in twenty-seven. He was often antagonistic to litigants in a way that disturbed Owen Dixon. But unlike his fellow judges, Evatt was an activist judge out to use the law as he saw fit to change societal mores. In many instances, he would be vindicated over time such as with his dissenting opinion in *Chester v Waverley Corporation*.[20] In the case of the so-called peace activist and Comintern connected writer Egon Kisch, brought to Australia by the Comintern-funded World Movement Against War in November 1934, Evatt found against the Lyons Government in the attempts to deport Kisch that went before the High Court. Kisch's time in Australia was seen as a loss for Menzies, Attorney-General at the time, a great win for Evatt and, with Menzies' defeat, a win for the Opposition.

As the radicalisation of left and right politics increased in the 1930s, Menzies' opposition to communism sharpened. His natural Christian bent was to see communism as emanating from a godless movement hell bent on crushing freedom. His views on fascism were equally repugnant. Historian David Furse-Roberts has noted, "his [Menzies'] Scots Presbyterian faith was real and he did not conceal the fact that his views on politics, culture and ethics were informed by Judeo-Christian precepts … [and] his anti-communism was largely driven by the hostility of the ideology towards religion and Christianity".[21] In a speech for a broadcast entitled "Is Democracy Doomed?" given in the mid-1930s, Menzies challenged the view that new forms of radical ideology offered any sort of alternative to representative government as Australians knew it:

> *In a word, a good democracy wants good democrats, and the good democrat is not the man who shouts loudly of his own rights and thinks of government in terms of individual or class interests but the man who realises that the social contract which binds any society together is one expressed in terms of duties and obligations.*[22]

He would go on to develop this further in a broadcast in October 1943, defining his "liberal" fundamentals:

> *The choice is not between the extremes. The choice in practical*

> *truth is between communism and fascism on the one hand and an enlightened liberal system on the other, which has no desire whatsoever to go back to unrestricted and ruthless competition, but which does see in the system of individual initiative, a driving quality, a motive power, an instrument of progress which is of such great value to mankind that to destroy it would be to inflict almost untold hardships upon future generations.*[23]

Liberalism then was a core belief for both Menzies and Evatt, a belief that reflected their enlightened education and middle class sense of fairness and fair play. However, Menzies looked at the world and saw it dominated by clashing political and social philosophies in a fight that had debilitated Western democracy in the Second World War and threatened it from within with the operation of communist fifth columnists. Menzies' views would only harden on this after the war with the rise of the Soviet Union. For Menzies, it was a battle between Western democracy underpinned by Christian fundamentals and materialist totalitarianism. Speaking in the House of Representatives on 5 August 1954, Menzies evaluated the changing and communist threatened situation in Vietnam, along with radicalised self-determination in post-colonial Asia:

> *It is ... foolish, superficial and dangerous to speak of the conflict in the world as a contest between two economic systems, capitalism and communism ...It is desperately important that the world should see this as a moral contest, a battle for the spirit of man. There can be no easy or enduring compromise between peoples who affirm the existence of a divine authority and the compulsion of a spiritual law and those others who see nothing beyond an atheistic materialism.*[24]

Against this, while Evatt would be regarded as on the right of the Labor Party, he was unreliable on the matter of opposing communism. Evatt too often sought to argue for moral equivalence such as in his response to Menzies in the House of Representatives on 5 August 1954. While conceding the dangers of communism, he contested Menzies' singling out of communist aggression while not mentioning other non-communist aggressors. Kim Beazley senior offered a view, while seeing Evatt's part in legislation to end the communist-inspired coalminers' strike and the Australian Defence Projects Protection Bill as an exception, that Evatt "was much softer on international dangers posed by communism. He did support a United Nations debate on human rights abuses in the Soviet Union but he drew back when the Soviet ambassador, Molotov, counter-attacked by presenting photos of Western Australian Aborigines in chains, under arrest by the police."[25] And, in the Petrov defection affair, Evatt's gullibility at Soviet Foreign Affairs Minister Molotov's response that the Petrov documents were forgeries showed he held Moscow in higher respect than he had for leading democratic powers such as the Menzies Government.

With the death of Lyons in April 1939, and after a bitter contest with Country Party leader Earle Page making a personal attack on Menzies in the House, Menzies was sworn in as the new United Australia Party prime minister on 26 April. Just four months later, on 3 September, Menzies declared Australia was at war in support of Britain against Germany and, within weeks, Australia had joined New Zealand in announcing it would send an expeditionary force to the Mediterranean. The federal election on 21 September 1940 was held following a year under wartime regulations in which the Coalition had suffered division and after, just weeks before voting day, a plane crash that killed six including three cabinet ministers and the Chief of the General Staff and shook the Menzies government.

Labor leader John Curtin, meanwhile, had steadied his divided caucus with the war effort. Across the parliamentary table, a battered UAP was looking tired and frayed. Menzies, in particular, was worried he was not being heard in London while Australian troops were readying for action in North Africa. Weeks out from the election, Justice Bert Evatt announced he was standing down from the High Court and would be the Labor Party candidate in the seat of Barton in Sydney. He had taken his decision carefully, canvassing the move with friends and associates over months, but eventually sure in the knowledge he was a standout candidate to boost Labor's vote.

Such was the press interest in the Evatt candidature, his announcement was treated much like a celebrity moment in Australian politics. In an era where the press did not generally devote space to personal spreads on the lives of leading public figures, Bert Evatt and his family scored a full page in the *Women's Weekly* a week out from voting day where a half page photo of the Evatts and their two children was headed "A breakfast-time interview with Dr. Evatt" with a short article beneath highlighting how much salary Evatt was giving up to go back into politics, their charming light filled living room adorned with modern pictures, their delightful children, Evatt's mother's struggle to give her son the education his brilliance deserved and some of the attributes of the wonderful partner he had in Mrs Evatt. Readers half a century on would find nothing exceptional here but in 1940 such exposure was gold. A week later, *Women's Weekly* offered another full page spread almost entirely taken up by opposing photos of Bert Evatt and Bob Menzies – Evatt striding confidently forward, Menzies more laid back and described as having a surface "complacency". The heading – "Dr Evatt and Mr Menzies …. a camera contrast" - said it all.

The political contest between Menzies and Evatt would last some two decades, beginning with the two sharing personal attacks in the press the morning after Evatt had announced his candidature for Barton. Evatt's stepping down from the High Court was labelled "a most regrettable precedent" by Menzies, with Evatt returning a sharp "I venture to predict that not only will Mr Menzies be a loser but that he will be a sour-tempered bad loser".[26] The press now had a new hero, a potential new leader of Labor and quite possibly one who could unite the "two Johns" – John Curtin and Jack Beasley (a supporter of Lang Labor) – leading the opposing factions of Labor.

Ironically, what the press still had not factored in was that if anyone divided Labor thinking it was Bert Evatt, the member without a faction, the one in the team that seemed not to fit and who stirred resentment among colleagues. Campaigning in Gosford a few days out from the 1940 election, Evatt spoke at length in support of a National War Council with the confidence of a party leader about to become the new prime minister. Referring to resolutions decided at a Special Labor Conference in June 1940, Evatt outlined moves a Labor government would make if elected to govern. He then posed the question of national government under Labor, saying: "Would there be any nearer approach to a government that would be truly national? This is a fair question and I shall answer it unequivocally. I answer it Yes, and I do so with the fullest sense of the special responsibility which weighs upon me because of the probability of Labor's success."[27] The outcome of the election was to return the UAP, albeit holding power with the votes of two independents. It did not stop Evatt speaking out on Labor's role in war decision making.

Hoist on his petard, Evatt spoke to the press within a couple of days of his election in Barton, yet again, as if making decisions on behalf of the Labor Party and continuing to air his views on Labor needing to be part of a national voice in government alongside the Menzies team. This in spite of John Curtin, months before, having rejected Menzies' offer to Labor of a role as part of a national government, as had happened in the United Kingdom. Significantly, in a brief *Sydney Morning Herald* report set directly below Evatt's statements, acting Labor leader Frank Forde put paid to Evatt's ideas saying that while Labor would consider any offer from Mr Menzies, it would not accept minor representation in a War Cabinet where it had no real executive power.[28] The signals were there early - the "Doc" would need to be handled with care, and most adroitly, by leaders John Curtin and Ben Chifley in the administrations they led up to December 1949. As late as September 1942, Churchill in a meeting with Owen Dixon, then Australia's Minister to the USA, at the White House spoke of Evatt's "transparent manipulation to keep open the door to a National Ministry" which Churchill supposed Evatt expected to lead. He asked if Curtin was in any way concerned. Dixon had replied that "Curtin understood Evatt perfectly well, and kept good control."[29]

For Curtin, trying to keep a divided party together, Evatt was a spanner in the works. Evatt was the soloist as so many historians have noted. His entry into federal politics saw him engage the media as a personality even to overshadowing his party leaders. Evatt spent much of his first year as an MP travelling across Australia to speak in Labor electorates as if he was about to become the new leader. Menzies, nonetheless, saw Evatt as a challenge - principally as his lack of a faction and high profile professionally with the middle class made him a voice to draw the support of middle income voters. As it had in Barton, where Evatt had won with a landslide victory.

The contrast in how each man approached organised politics sheds light on their respective careers. For Menzies, party was always his first step. He was a master at collective action from his time with the Young Nationalists through to spearheading the formation of the Liberal Party. For Evatt, politics was about how he, himself, could make a difference and wear down an unequal status quo, whether in conflict abroad or equal opportunity at home. He spoke and acted as if believing the world operated on universal principles, and that these could be debated and changed for the good, simply by consultation.

The Menzies-Evatt parliamentary tussle would be short lived in 1941, however. Within a year, the UAP government had collapsed after Menzies stood down as leader at the end of August 1941, and John Curtin became Australia's wartime prime minister with Bert Evatt assuming the roles of Attorney-General and Minister for External Affairs. It was Evatt's time to soar politically while Menzies entered his own dark night, eventually emerging in 1944-45 to spearhead a new political party to be called the Liberal Party of Australia. Menzies would win back government at the 1949 federal election but only after the first of his notable clashes, in the law and on the hustings, with Bert Evatt. This would happen with the battle for the banks.

3

The Banks

The forty-three word statement rocked the political world for the next three years and is accepted as the greatest single factor in the defeat of the Chifley Government. – Fred Daly[1]

It was a pleasant late winter Saturday afternoon in Melbourne – date 16 August 1947. Record snowfalls across the Victorian Alps meant there was a chill in the air on this cloudy day in Melbourne. Robert Menzies was attending a friend's lawn tennis party when, over the radio, he heard reports of Prime Minister Ben Chifley's very brief press statement, a statement of just over 40 words which had been handed nonchalantly to the pressmen waiting outside the hastily called Cabinet meeting in Canberra.[2] The statement read:

> Cabinet today authorised the Attorney-General and myself to prepare legislation for submission to the Federal Parliamentary Labor Party for the nationalisation of banking, other than State banks, with proper protection for the shareholders, depositors, borrowers and staffs of private banks

Menzies' first reaction was to think the move would not be unpopular.[3] He recalled the anger felt towards banks for their refusal of credit in the Depression, then of not-so-distant memory. Ben Chifley, likewise, remembered this but with a longstanding resentment at the banks, seeing them as a major reason for the failure of the Scullin Government 1929-1931.

Notions around nationalisation of Australia's banks and the belief that private banking lay at the heart of greedy and exploitative capitalism had existed from the earliest labour days in the 1890s.[4] After the debacle of the Scullin Government and its failure to manage the credit and financial crisis, not least from its own schism, in 1932 the ALP State Executive in NSW produced a report that exonerated Scullin's Labor government and claimed that the solution in the future was the nationalisation of all Australian banking business.[5] Chifley himself, as a member of the Lyons United Australia Party government's 1935-37 Royal Commission into Monetary and Banking Systems, had submitted a minority report that advocated the nationalisation of all private banking.[6]

The Prime Minister was confident in his move that Saturday, as the manner of his announcement seemed to indicate. His confidence came with the solid victory Labor had won under his lead just under a year before, at the September 1946 federal election. Chifley had found himself finally in charge of the nation in his own right, not just as John Curtin's successor. As 1947 opened, Chifley had pondered his chance to put his imprint on the nation in more significant ways. Federation somewhat rankled Chifley – especially how the states could make the national government defer to them under the Constitution, a constitution drawn up in the days of jealously guarded colonial divides. In his move to nationalise the trading banks, Chifley also had the unanimous agreement of his Cabinet colleagues.

True, the September 1946 referendum had increased the Commonwealth's power in social services, as various decisions of the High Court since Federation had done in other areas. The federal takeover of uniform taxation during the war years remained in place with Chifley refusing to bend and return those powers to state control, telling the states in July 1947 that the "High Court had confirmed that the Commonwealth had prior taxing rights".[7] Meanwhile, the *Banking Act 1945* had extended wartime regulations on state and local banks, forcing them to continue to bank only with the Commonwealth Bank. But Chifley still believed more could be done to have investment with the private banks work in support of the federal government. And, while the private banks had gone quiet after the extension of the wartime regulations, fearing bank nationalisation if they protested, the Act was open to challenge under the constitution.[8] Balancing the odds, Chifley had made his move.

In May 1947, with his treasurer's cap in play and with a large increase in the number of Commonwealth Bank branches open across the nation, Chifley and the federal treasury had advised that under section 48 of the Banking Act, some 200 local governing authorities were to cease trading with the private banks. In other words, banks aside from the Commonwealth Bank (or, necessarily, state banks) were prohibited from conducting banking business on behalf of the states or their authorities.

At the time, Australia had nine major private trading banks, of which three were controlled from London – the Union, the Australasia and the ES&A – with head offices in Melbourne. The Bank of New South Wales - oldest and largest – had a head office in Sydney. Brisbane was home to the head office of the Queensland National Bank and Adelaide the Bank of Adelaide. There was also the Commercial Banking Company of Sydney along with the Commercial of Australia and the National Bank of Australasia, both with head offices in Melbourne.[9] These banks represented a significant slab of the Australian economy.

Chifley's decree stirred an upheaval of thinking. Apart from the dismay within the banking fraternity, from local shires to metropolitan councils, there was widespread objection among many long-time customers of the trading banks. Loyalty and familiarity combined with indignation at being ordered as to where they should bank.

The wealthy Melbourne City Council, a National Bank customer, was having none of it and took a challenge to the High Court. Its challenge, however, objected not only to section 48 of the Banking Act but, more broadly, to sections 15 to 22 or the core of the entire legislation, under section 55 of the Commonwealth constitution. Should the MCC win, all sections of the Act would be invalid. In the end, just the challenge to section 48 would go forward, but the arguments by the National Bank's Leslie McConnan and his supporters against other parts of the Act encouraged thoughts that the *Banking Act 1945* was flawed.

On 13 August 1947, with only Labor appointed Justice McTiernan dissenting, the High Court handed down its decision that local and state authorities and municipalities could bank wherever they wished. As Professor Cheryl Saunders has put it, this case is now "taken to stand for the proposition that the limits on the scope of express Commonwealth legislative powers can be implied from the federal character of the Constitution"[10] Ben Chifley's move to advance the Commonwealth's powers, vis à vis the states, had been trumped. What happened next began one of the most protracted legal battles in Australian constitutional history.

Chifley, weighing up the odds that the Act might be further challenged and having for months mooted bank nationalisation among advisers and close colleagues in retaliation for the banks' resistance, now acted swiftly. Various historians and biographers have noted that hubris and pique could be said to underpin his move. Or this combined with a long held personal desire to bring about bank nationalisation of Australia's banks. He was also emboldened by the opinion of Labor's in-house legal guru Bert Evatt, who had just returned from meetings in Japan.

Evatt's work with the United Nations General Assembly and as Minister for External Relations saw him, between early 1945 and the end of 1949, out of Australia in foreign parts for a total of 27 months. Evatt biographer Kylie Tennant relates how Evatt, reuniting with Australian politics as the High Court's decision on section 48 of the Banking Act was received, and distracted by preparations for a Commonwealth conference to be held in Canberra in late August, "explained to his attentive colleagues in Cabinet that the actual powers of Labor's banking legislation had not been touched, the structure had not been undermined" by the High Court's judgement in favour of the Melbourne City Council.[11] He also assured Chifley that under the Constitution the federal government could nationalise the trading banks.[12]

With the threat of more challenges to the Banking Act, Evatt's opinion seems to have been the spur for Chifley to sort out the matter once and for all. Three days later, in a Cabinet meeting called at random the day before in Canberra and after two days of consultations with Treasury officials and heads of the Commonwealth Bank, Chifley staggered his colleagues by announcing he had a mind to nationalise the banks. He asked Bert Evatt to outline for Cabinet colleagues the arguments in its favour. Jaws dropping, each man was then required to offer his thoughts. This was Chifley's way of getting what he wanted; in reality, the PM was asking for support. Around the table, every minister gave it. Thus came the weekend announcement that the Chifley Government would legislate to nationalise Australia's banking system.

As Opposition leader and leader of the Liberal Party in 1947, Robert Menzies and his close supporters were fending off a quiet rebellion within the party against Menzies' leadership. The results of the 1946 federal election had not convinced many that this high minded legal professional had the right style to win back government. In March, a meeting of the Victorian Council of the Liberal Party had heard critics speak of Menzies' "conceit" and others allege he had a head "too up in the clouds" before a motion for a change of leadership was voted down.[13] Chifley's move to nationalise the trading banks handed Menzies a cause not just to solidify his leadership but in time one that would bring down the Chifley Government.

Within a day, Menzies had taken up the fight. *The Argus* in Melbourne on Monday 18 August led with a front page screamer "'Totalitarianism!' says bank's spokesman" under which the sub heading "Menzies declares: 'To Russia for a parallel'" completed the hard point. Further into the paper, a longer piece added, "Australians were now called to a great battle to defend their freedoms against dictatorship at home, Mr Menzies said last night when attacking the Government's decision to nationalise the trading banks."[14] A week later Menzies appeared before huge rallies in Sydney and Melbourne where his case against nationalising the private banks had taken on a distinct and warlike tone. Appearing before a lunchtime crowd of 6000, many munching on sandwiches, held at the Sydney Town Hall on Monday 25 August, *The Sydney Morning Herald* reported:

> *He recalled that when he was Prime Minister he declared war on the Fascist dictators abroad from the Town Hall platform. Now, he said, he was declaring war on the Fascists within Australia. He warned his audience that if the war was lost the result would be no less dire than if Hitler had marched through London or than if the Swastika had flown from the Town Hall.*[15]

Three days later, on Thursday 28 August in Melbourne, 3000 packed the Princess Theatre as well as on the kerb of Spring Street outside, across the road from the State parliament, to hear Menzies and Victorian Opposition leader Tom Hollway attack the Chifley Government's bank nationalisation proposal. Menzies told the crowd that the plan was "a further step towards totalitarianism by a government already drunk with power". He added, "It is clear that this action was taken in a fit of bad temper by the Prime Minister, who set out to destroy the whole of the banking structure so far as it is made up by private banks because the High Court told him that he could not take the banking of the Melbourne City Council away from a private bank."[16]

The shock waves refused to abate as the drafting of the banking legislation began. Attorney-General Bert Evatt was overseeing the bill and within days was facing queries about what its ramifications might mean. The position of British banks operating in Australia such as the Bank of Australasia, the Union Bank and the ES&A. had multiple questions and there were few answers. All were anticipating even before a bill had been drafted that there would be challenges in the High Court and even to the Privy Council. Then there was the vexed question of compensation for loss of shares and assets by the private banks. As with any big new project, the unknown allowed for speculation. It was soon reported that federal unions were pressuring the federal government to extend its nationalisation policy to other key industries such as mining, steel, transport and insurance.[17]

In spite of the challenges, the Chifley Government was confident it could have the legislation working by the end of the year and settled in well before the next federal election in late 1949. Dr Evatt, Labor's legal overseer, was on the case with the Prime Minister's faith in him to deliver. Meanwhile, the Menzies opposition along with the private banks led by the National Bank's McConnan continued their saturation campaign against nationalisation. At one meeting in Sydney's Domain on 14 September a crowd of 10,000 protested, petitions with hundred of thousands of signatures were taken to Canberra and on 16 September, the night the federal Labor caucus accepted the policy formally, the federal president of the Liberal Party Richard Casey spoke against the policy on 88 commercial radio stations.[18] This was but the tip of a huge campaign that would continue until the legislation was challenged in the High Court and again as the 1949 election approached.

Bert Evatt, with his usual routine as Minister for External Relations, was absent overseas for most of the debates in the House of Representatives over the banking bill. Menzies' arguments that the new banking policy should be put to a referendum were dismissed by Chifley. Speaking for the second reading of the Banking Bill in the House of Representatives on 15 October, Chifley crisply summed up the justification for the legislation thus:

> *The Labour party has maintained for many years that, since the influence of money is so great, the entire monetary and banking system should be controlled by public authorities responsible through the Government and Parliament to the nation. On this principle the Labour party has held further that since private banks are conducted primarily for profit and therefore follow policies which in important respects run counter to the public interest, their business should be transferred to public ownership.*[19]

It was as simple as that.

But, by the time of the second reading of the bill, an election had been forced in the state of Victoria after the Opposition had blocked supply in the Legislative Council and brought down the Cain Labor Government. The Liberals' election campaign under leader Tom Hollway focused entirely on the Chifley bank nationalisation legislation. Mid-point in the Victorian campaign, in the House of Representatives on 14 October, Menzies used an extract from Bert Evatt's *The King and His Dominion Governors* not only to justify the Liberals' bank nationalisation focused campaign but to make a point against the Chifley Government. Referring to Labor complaints that the Victorian election was out of order in being an Opposition vehicle against the federal banking legislation, Menzies said:

> ... [I would like] to make a reference to the legal adviser and law officer of the Crown - the Attorney General - who, unfortunately, is not with us, but who obligingly has left behind him one of his books ... I shall read an extract from page 199 of the first edition of this valuable book; I do not know whether there has been a second edition. The passage at page 199 of the Attorney-General's book reads:
>
>> It is sufficient to make the point that, in the interests of the people, and because of the absence of controlling constitutional provisions requiring great changes to be endorsed by vote at a referendum, some reserve authority may have to be exercised to prevent the abuse of legislative power, and to require great changes to be submitted for popular approval.
>
> That is a very cogent justification for the taking of extraordinary measures to force some consultation of the people - a very appropriate justification of what has recently occurred in Victoria, and an unanswerable argument, because it is based upon the one thing which the Attorney-General's colleagues now forget, namely, that all power within the term of a parliament, as distinct from the organic law contained in the Constitution, comes from the people.[20]

Menzies had scored a point – not recognised as he spoke – when, on Saturday 8 November, the Victorian election saw the defeat of the Cain Labor Government largely as a reaction to the federal Labor government's banking legislation which was still to be passed.

The *Banking Act* was assented to on 27 November, with Owen Dixon of the High Court granting an injunction the next day to prevent the government from going forward with the Act until the High Court had met to consider the challenge in the early months of 1948. In an unprecedented move, even before the Act was passed, eleven trading banks had issued a writ with the High Court on 17 November seeking an injunction.[21] Throughout the months of debate over the Banking bill, Attorney General Evatt had been overseas even as his advice on the strength and validity of the bill was under extreme pressure.

John Murphy has written of how the years 1945 to 1949 represented the zenith of Evatt's career making his presence noted on the world stage, a stage he saw as more important than the Australian domestic scene. "His urgent drive to be recognised and to have his voice heard was being realised," writes Murphy, "in London, at the San Francisco conference, and at subsequent UN meetings in Paris and New York."[22] In the weeks the Banking bill was debated, Evatt had been at the UN chairing the Committee on Palestine as the new state of Israel took shape. By mid-December, Evatt had picked up the government's Banking Case brief on his way back from the US and returned to Canberra to prepare for his appearance before the High Court just weeks later.

For Menzies and Evatt, the end of 1947 saw them both appearing tired and somewhat worn even while both were enjoying an uplift in their careers. Evatt was the Australian dashing about on a world stage as none before; Menzies had found a cause to carry him high on Opposition shoulders in the protest over the Banking Act. On the evening of Menzies' address to the House on 23 October during the second reading of the Banking bill, in spite of a foregone conclusion that the government had the numbers and nothing Menzies could say would make a difference, hundreds were turned away from the public gallery with the press and diplomatic galleries uncharacteristically full. But while Menzies would opt for a private trip to Britain and a six month health break after the rents and prices referendum campaign in May 1948, Evatt took on even more as the Commonwealth's barrister in the record breaking legal tussle over the Banking Act which would be argued before the High Court of Australia through most of 1948 and then before the Privy Council in London for a large part of 1949.

The most entertaining account of the legal challenges to the *Banking Act 1948* is to be found in David Marr's *Barwick: The Classic Biography of a Man of Power*. Barwick led the defence for the banks both before the High Court and before the Privy Council in London. Writes Marr: "He [Evatt] had not argued before a court for 17 years yet advocacy is an art which demands practice or its edge is lost. He was rusty. Nor was that the only consideration which might have made him pause. He was returning to the High Court which had been happy to see him go seven years before and the animosities had not subsided with time."[23]

Evatt's erratic behaviour from day one suggested that he was either at the time emotionally taxed or simply in the early stages of the mental deterioration he would later become well known for. In February 1948, as a former member of the High Court, from 1930 to 1940 when he resigned to stand for parliament, Evatt was appearing before a number of former colleagues, some of whom had reasons to find him irritating. It was not a good look then when Evatt began by requesting two of the judges – Dudley Williams and Hayden Starke – disqualify themselves on the grounds Starke's wife held shares in two of the banks while Williams' sister was the interest beneficiary of shares Williams held in two banks. Chief Justice John Latham rejected Evatt's submission.

The hearings in February took place in heat wave Melbourne (the court would adjourn at one point until there was cooler weather) and in an unairconditioned chamber. And yet, Evatt developed a fear of getting a cold and dying. At one point he demanded the windows be opened which caused untold interruptions. Then he demanded they be closed and called for a rug to be brought from a nearby department store.

Evatt's technique was to laboriously repeat the facts as he saw them, stretching arguments beyond constitutional precedent and monotonously droning on in an irritating voice – in all for 18 days of the 39 days of the hearing. As Marr puts it: "The days were marked by even more intense monotony from Evatt, and fresh abuse from Starke." When the court handed down its decision in August 1948, the six judges delivered five separate findings which resulted in uncertainty. In essence, however, the government's Banking Act was found to be invalid in part. The government could have tried to amend the legislation but, on 13 August which was a year to the day of the High Court's decision against the 1945 Banking legislation, Chifley announced his government would seek appeal in the Privy Council.

Far from Australia's shores, by August, Bob Menzies had settled into Brown's Hotel in London with wife Pattie and daughter Heather. Their voyage to London from Melbourne on a Norwegian cargo ship which offered accommodation for a small number of private passengers had passed with sufficient amusing moments to fill letters to family and lots of time for a healthy recuperation for the Menzies trio. By October, Menzies was writing to his brother Frank that "the little symptoms that I had before leaving Australia have entirely disappeared".[24] In meetings in Britain, France, the US and Canada, Menzies found the common theme was concern at the rise of Soviet Russia with overtones of fear of an approaching war. In discussions, Menzies spoke up for the strength of the British Commonwealth and the need for Britain and the US to be the global force to counteract the Soviets.

From late June, the Berlin Blockade by the Soviet Union had

prompted the Berlin Airlift with the US and Britain flying in supplies by the tonnage to West Berlin. In Menzies' view, the United Nations was too weak an organisation to have any real effect.[25] This contrasted with Evatt, then spruiking for the UN and in London deputising for Chifley at a Commonwealth Prime Ministers conference in October. In November, Evatt tried to use the United Nations to find a solution to the Berlin Blockade, fearing like most it could develop into a war. Evatt was a supporter of the view of John Burton, then Secretary of the Department of External Affairs, which held that the Soviet Union was not alone to blame for Cold War tension – there was fault on both sides. Nothing came of Evatt's proposal – when the matter was referred to the Security Council it was blocked by a Soviet veto.

In February 1949, Menzies and Evatt clashed in the House after a speech by Evatt on Australia's foreign policy. Lauding the United Nations' importance to Australia's foreign policy, Evatt placed it front and centre in Australia's foreign policy settings in any negotiations for peace and security. Menzies replied a day or so later, accusing Evatt of a theoretical and legalistic approach that ignored realties, saying:

> We must face the fact that until the ideal, happy state of affairs can be brought into existence, we must first deal with the enemy as we find him and deal with problems which may be solvable only by expediency, as the problem of the Berlin blockade has been solved. Do not let us become too high and mighty about the contrast between justice and expediency when we contemplate that blockade, and the expedient that it has evoked from the people of the Western powers. … the world is in a ferment and peace at this very moment hangs on a thread. The Minister for External Affairs himself exhibited quite unreal optimism and even, I think, once or twice, some measure of boasting, but let us face the facts quite bluntly. In spite of all these things, the Soviet Union, which is a subscriber to the Charter of the United Nations and is, in fact, a member of the United Nations … has by aggressive action, by march, threat or bluster, overrun countries like Poland and Czechoslovakia and

> has committed an unprovoked and unparalleled act of war in relation to Berlin. By indirect methods, the Soviet has attacked the self-governing sovereignty of France, Italy and China, and is at the moment – although this is sometimes forgotten – by means of bluff, infiltration and fifth column activities, threatening Western democracy and the peace of the world.[26]

Those who listened to Menzies in this speech would have heard a message that would become increasingly common in the Opposition leader's speeches in this election year. Returning from Europe, the UK and North America after months of meetings, against a backdrop of rampant Soviet incursion and the fragile if not alarming situation in Berlin, Menzies was firm in his resistance to any fellow travelling of the left, fellow travelling that believed accommodation with communism and socialism was any sort of answer in a parliamentary democracy.

Evatt may well have been simply a believer in international congress and the right of all nations to a fair hearing. To be a believer in his ability always to be able to argue and deliberate a peaceful solution across a table. As he reasoned in the House in 1948, in a debate on banning the Communist Party: "Communism can be suppressed, not by coercive means but in open encounter. We can deal with communism by applying the famous maxim of ... John Milton: Let truth and falsehood grapple. Whoever knew truth to be put to worse in an open encounter. Let the encounter be free and open."[27] But Evatt's bent would also be often to appear to go soft on the left in a somewhat naïve way – as his later involvement in the Petrov defection affair would attest.

The validity of the Chifley Government's Banking Act was still to be argued before the Privy Council in London but already Menzies had Evatt's peace message and work with the UN in his sights. Menzies, in his response to Evatt's speech in the House, had signalled he would be going in hard against Soviet third columns infiltrating domestic politics in a year that would necessitate Chifley bringing in the troops to break the actions of communist inspired strikers.

Beginning in mid-March 1949, the UK's Privy Council hearing on Australia's Banking legislation lasted 37 days during which Evatt spoke for 22 days. Two judges died before it finished. In the end, the government's appeal was once again lost - the Privy Council handing down its decision on 26 July. Chifley's banking legislation lay in tatters. Evatt had helped deliver an inevitably dark reality for the Chifley government. His legalistic approach to the issue of bank nationalisation, and the way he had argued to himself, the government and the courts that it could not fail, meant that Evatt had ignored the wider political ramifications of socialism in the community.

At a time when the Soviet Union was encroaching in Eastern Europe as Hitler had done in Western Europe in the 1930s, the Chifley government's banking legislation heralded a move to the left that worried the general population. In September 1949, the Catholic Church in Australia distributed two hundred thousand copies of a Social Justice Statement on socialisation that declared the policy "repugnant to Christian social principles".[28] The Labor Party might object to the church's interpretation, but it touched a raw nerve in those who read the Statement, thanks to the government's *Banking Act 1948*. All this and the federal election, by then, was just months away.

Not one to take a win for granted, given failures in the past, Menzies now worried that the Opposition would not be able to sustain the banking campaign with the legislation finally rejected. Menzies also had his doubts that the banks could deliver. Although the banks continued to argue they were not safe while Chifley and Labor retained government. It was clear that if the banking issue could be kept alive, the Coalition would defeat Labor. The National Bank of Australasia's McConnan made a deal with Menzies that if he and the Opposition could keep up the momentum of positive hope for change, the bank officers' campaign would be re-energised to defeat Chifley on the banking issue.[29] And it was.

In 1949, the banking issue became front and centre of Menzies' campaign – both as an issue on its own or rolled together with arguments against any move for the Chifley Government to increase government control over enterprises. *The Sydney Morning Herald* echoed the line at various times such as in its editorial for 24 November against socialisation where it poked at Chifley over the Banking legislation with: "What he has been careful not to say at any stage is that he will bow to public opinion, and abandon his cherished scheme of establishing a banking monopoly." In another piece on 2 December, the same newspaper ran the headline "Socialisation is a major election issue" adding "After the shock of the attempted bank grab are not electors entitled to assume that Labor means business with its socialisation objective?"

In his opening address for the campaign, Menzies referred to socialism as "an alien and deadly undergrowth". His government would repeal the *Banking Nationalisation Act* and appoint a Commonwealth Bank board.[30] At Labor's campaign opening, the left leaning *Argus* highlighted Chifley as saying he would not nationalise "farms and ships". Adding that "industry is primarily a field for private enterprise". Which left banking hanging in the air.[31] A major opinion piece by Donald Mackinnon, President of the Victorian Liberal and Country Party, written for *The Argus* and published on 10 November, was headed "Liberals believe the basic issue is Socialism or free enterprise." Even cartoonists had a say. *The Argus* captured some of it pictorially on 9 November with a cartoon that had the figures of Bert Evatt and Eddie Ward as officers on the deck of a gunship with a sailor in between. Evatt says: "And we'll never, never nationalise the banks." "What? Never?" responds the sailor. "No, never," answers Evatt. But Ward on the other side of the deck mutters: "Hardly ever." All a wonderful re-use of Gilbert and Sullivan's lines from *H.M.S. Pinafore*. And so it went.

Historian David Day has written that, in view of the anti-bank nationalisation campaign waged by Menzies and the Opposition, "the adverse vote [federal election] was … a rejection of further socialisation and a poll on Chifley's plans for bank nationalisation".[32]

The 10 December 1949 federal election saw the Liberal/Country Party Coalition win a solid majority. As with any change of government, it was shock, joy and tears all round. Menzies, at his first press conference after the win, was captured in three photos by *The Argus* on 12 December looking down with his eyes closed in one and another his chin propped on one hand. "I'm in a bit of a coma today," said Menzies, such was his exhaustion and almost disbelief at what he had achieved. For Evatt it was shock of a different kind. Kylie Tennant quotes him telling a friend: "Do you remember you told me at the Wagga aerodrome that we wouldn't win the election? I was affected by it in my calmer moments, but the shock – not from what you said but when it happened – telescoped me".[33]

Bert Evatt KC as a brilliant young barrister before his appointment by the Scullin Labor government to the High Court of Australia at age 36.

Bert Evatt as he appears on the High Court of Australia website – he was a justice of the High Court between December 1930 and September 1940.

Robert Menzies as a brilliant young barrister. He was the principal advocate before the High Court in the Engineers Case in 1920 at age 25.

A confident Bert Evatt, Attorney-General and Minister for External Affairs in the Chifley Labor government, at the United Nations in New York. Dr Evatt was President of the UN General Assembly 1948-49.

Dr John Burton, then head of the Department of External Affairs, with his minister Bert Evatt at the United Nations – circa late 1940s.

Attorney-General Bert Evatt and Prime Minister Ben Chifley. Evatt appeared for the Chifley government in the bank nationalisation cases.

Cartoonist Mick Armstrong takes an irreverent scene from the Gilbert and Sullivan opera *HMS Pinafore* to mock Labor's promise never to nationalise farms and ships and other forms of private industry. *The Argus* (Melbourne), 9 November 1949.

Prime Minister Menzies introduces the Communist Party Dissolution Bill in the House of Representatives on 27 April 1950. In the front row behind the PM are Richard Casey (second from left), Arthur Fadden (third from left), Percy Spender (fourth from left) and John McEwen (fifth from left). Paul Hasluck is third from left in the second row.

4

COMMUNISM AND POLITICAL REALITIES

The creation by the Chifley Government of the Australian Security Intelligence Organisation (ASIO) in 1948 was part of the price that Australia had to pay for the inclusion in the West's intelligence network ... the Department of External Affairs did not escape critical attention. Some of those recruited to the department during the 1940s, including some in posts of high authority, were regarded in Defence as being at best woolly-minded liberals, at worst dangerously left wing. – Peter Edwards[1]

Keith McEwan grew up tough in Melbourne's inner north Coburg neighbourhood during the bleak depression times of the 1930s. His mother kept the family in food by earning small amounts doing people's laundry; his father had joined the ranks of the unemployed as a result of injuries sustained in the First World War and was at a disadvantage, because of his age, when jobs returned and unemployment numbers dropped. Aged fourteen, McEwan worked in an engineering plant and eventually joined the Ironworkers Union. After coming under the influence of a man called Bernie who called at the family's front door selling copics of the *Guardian*, in 1947 McEwan joined the Communist Party aged twenty-one.

Joining the Communist Party, as McEwan later recorded, led to something akin to a religious conversion. He found his life took on new meaning, becoming filled with activities for the party; he gave up old friends and now spent his free time attending party meetings and helping organise campaigns, and reading literature to guide him in his communist commitment. The party took McEwan over, re-educating him and re-energising him, as it did with others who joined its ranks. He was in a sense reborn; he moved to work at the large General Motors Holden assembly lines where he hoped to recruit new members for the party. Like communist cadres everywhere, he was an apostle, a man with a mission:

> *Marxist books answered many of my questions. Complex issues became simple. Life took on a wonderful new meaning ... Things became defined into blacks and whites... I could understand the causes of exploitation of man by man, of wars and poverty... I accepted as an inevitable process that socialism would replace capitalism as capitalism had replaced feudalism and feudalism had replaced slavery as a social system. ... For me and other Party members Communism was a glorious goal. The repressive state machine would wither away and men would live in peace and brotherhood suffering no injustices, but instead a life of creative endeavour and freedom.*[2]

Like all faiths, however, such fine communist principles were infected by the frailties of the human condition. Especially so with regard to the teachings of Karl Marx. Whatever Marx had intended in his theories about the advent of the dictatorship of the proletariat, by 1947, communism and the Marxist revolution meant the activities of the network of believers and party members held together across the world by directives coming from the Communist Party of Russia's Josef Stalin in Moscow. Mark Aarons, son of the CPA's Laurie Aarons and nephew of the CPA's Eric Aarons, has recorded how members of the Communist Party of Australia were "entirely blinkered in their support of Stalin's Russia", concluding "such idealism was misplaced and masked terrible political mistakes, excesses and blindness to the crimes committed in communism's name".[3]

The history of the communist regime in Russia after the 1917 uprisings and the ensuing civil war had been excessively bloody. Vladimir Lenin had led the Soviets until his death in January 1924, after which Josef Stalin assumed sole leadership by eventually forcing out Leon Trotsky. Stalin's rule saw forced famine, terror and purges. Terror had become part of the Soviet system of management as revolution and civil war established Soviet rule. By the 1930s the Cheka (All-Russian Extraordinary Commission for Combating Counter-Revolution and Sabotage), with operatives numbering in the hundreds of thousands, had been responsible for the forced collectivisation resulting in deaths in the millions throughout the USSR. The accurate figure is debated through lack of definitive statistics – Stalin is said to have told Churchill the numbers of deaths from forced collectivisation was 10 million.[4] In 1936-38 the Cheka launched the Great Terror which would be responsible for executions, and deaths from its extensive gulag of exiles, likewise in the millions. In the establishment of communist power, McEwan's "blacks and whites" of belief and control had taken on a brutal meaning.

A communist propaganda machine and with Russian society being mostly closed off from the outside world may have kept followers like McEwan ignorant of its horrors until publications, drawing on evidence from witnesses and culminating in the 1970s with Aleksandr Solzhenitsyn's *Gulag Archipelago*, exposed the Stalin reality. Mark Aarons does not go along with that theory in the case of members such as his uncle and father who were at the top of the CPA movement in Australia. He believes, they could not have been unaware of stories of the upheavals in Russia and the wider Soviet where conflict and starvation, not to mention terror, were abundant. As Aarons explains: "Along with all other communist parties affiliated to the Comintern, the Australian party blindly supported Stalin's policies, ignoring growing evidence of his crimes."[5]

Visits to the Soviet Union such as those made by Australia's Manning Clark in 1958, out of which he wrote *Meeting Soviet Man*, or that which produced the UK's Aneurin Bevan, George Strauss and John Strachey's 1931 *What We Saw in Russia* and Sidney and Beatrice Webb's visit and recollections in 1932 were controlled and sponsored, with the visitors hailing the communist society they experienced in hearty and positive reports when they were back in their respective Western democracies, having avoided seeing or experiencing the realities of repression under which a majority of Soviet citizens lived. Or simply rationalising what they knew of it as part of the great communist revolution.

Australian writer Katharine Susannah Pritchard fell for Marxism heavily in her early adulthood, so much so that after a visit to the USSR in 1933 she later wrote that what she saw convinced her that "Marxist principles for the construction of a state …were sound". She proclaimed her belief that only communism would bring peace by ending "the horrible mania for war which Capitalism uses as a profitable investment" and that this was endorsed by what she had seen in Russia.[6] Pritchard saw what she wanted to see. Her beliefs, detailed and promoted in a small booklet, read like those of a religious missionary. Likewise, Ian Milner, Australian foreign affairs officer and spy for the Soviets in the late 1940s, visited Russia in 1934-35 and wrote glowingly of what he found there – "impressive evidence of a successfully working socialist order … the people by and large do seem happy and quietly confident. You feel they know their place in the new order and are happy with it… we have much to learn from the Russians".[7]

Pritchard's booklet *Why I Am A Communist*, in praise of Russian communism, was published in 1953. Just three years later, Soviet leader Nikita Krushchev made his secret speech denouncing the USSR's regime of terror under Stalin that Pritchard and others refused to see. Accounts over the years, from refugees, had contradicted such praise and described a gruesome reality. These were largely ignored or countered by the left as right wing or fascist propaganda. Malcolm Muggeridge's 1934 fictionalised description of Stalin's USSR in *Winter in Moscow*, after his own trip to Russia in 1933, satirised the farce of the reports from Marxists who visited the Soviet Union and offered a piercing insight to the realities of Stalinism. Muggeridge's work was condemned as biased. For the faithful, the USSR, could do no wrong. This blinkered attitude, in the view of long time Australian communist Bernie Taft, contributed to the Australian Communist Party's eventual demise.[8]

While Marxism and its theories of overturning a capitalist order in favour of a workers' paradise underpinned much of the labour movement in the late nineteenth century across the Western world, a political party serving the aspirations of a representative government and its people could never satisfy the ambitions of faithful followers of communism.

The First World War not only gave rise to the Bolsheviks, having overthrown Russia's Provisional government in October 1917, but for Marxists it also exposed the weakness of the trade union backed new Laborite MPs as having sold out to capitalism. For true communists of the time, capitalism was the root of all war; only by overthrowing the capitalist order could peace and a Marxist society be established. As communists saw it, the Australian Labor Party in signing up to the war effort had betrayed its Marxist principles. Militant Australian communist leader Lance Sharkey opined: "The attitude of the Australian Labor Party to the imperialist war which broke out in August 1914 was in every respect similar to that of the parties of the Second International which betrayed Socialism. In its election manifesto (September 1915) the ALP stated: 'War is one of the greatest realities of life and must be faced … if returned with a majority we will pursue with the utmost vigor every course necessary for the defence of the Commonwealth and the Empire.'"[9] From this point on, the far left of the labour movement was looking for a new front.

The Communist Party of Australia officially began its existence on 30 October 1920 at a conference of left wing groups and socialists in Sydney. However, in the nature of dogmatic politics, the groups split their allegiance and two parties emerged, neither accepted by the Communist International (Comintern) in Moscow. It would be a decade of division and attempts to infiltrate and influence the Australian Labor Party before Lance Sharkey would wrest control of what became the continuing Australian Communist Party, then called the Communist Party of Australia.

In 1929, party headquarters in Moscow instructed all national communist parties to cut links with social democrats, i.e. Labor parties, and Sharkey made his move. On the Labor side, larger than life operator and New South Wales Labor leader Jack Lang had already convinced Labor that CPA operatives should not be ALP members. Looking back, Lang's opposition to communists being part of the Labor Party is supported by long since released Comintern archives. Documents published by David Lovell and Kevin Windle demonstrate how the Moscow Comintern (or central authority for international organisations) played a large role in communist activities in countries like Australia. It held the party together and instructed them as to their strategies so much so that Lovell and Windle argue that the CPA's subservience to Moscow "justified the Australian government's decision to declare the party unlawful in 1940".[10]

By the 1930s, communism in Australia had been established as a subversive, secretive and fifth column operation bent on bringing down social democracy Western style. The Lyons Government's *Crimes Act 1932* meant the CPA went underground disguising its activities in popular fronts such as peace movements and groups supporting the rights of minorities. Comintern activist Egon Kisch's visit to Australia in 1934 under the sponsorship of the Movement Against War and Fascism caused great embarrassment for then Attorney-General Robert Menzies and is a good example of how communist agitation slipped the noose in democracies like Australia. Shielded by the catch cry of peace, Comintern cadres spread dissension. Representative government was at a loss as to how to handle it.

Meanwhile, in the CPA, repression and totalitarian methods abounded. Former Communist Party member and historian Stuart Macintyre described the culture as one of local purging and suspicion. As he described it: "A comrade who resented the authority of another, or allowed personal duty to come before duty to the party, or attributed his own treatment to malice, was succumbing to the heinous sin of petty-bourgeois individualism. ... the cumulative effect of its beleaguered condition and the iron discipline was to remake the Australian Communist Party into a party like no other in the country's experience of radical movements. Demanding absolute obedience, it treated anything less as treachery."[11]

This secrecy and fifth column activity would continue. It would intensify with the outbreak of war in September 1939 and the Menzies Government's declaring the CPA illegal in June 1940. In August 1939, the non-aggression pact signed between Germany and the Soviet Union divided Poland between them and allowed the Soviet Union to take the Baltic states of Latvia, Lithuania and Estonia along with an easy conquering of Finland all of which made Hitler's advance to the west and south smoother.

The Nazi-Soviet Pact should have awakened national communist parties to the double standards applying back at Moscow's party headquarters; instead the move by Stalin was interpreted as a necessary step in the ultimate defeat of Germany. As life-time Communist Party of Australia member Eric Aarons has explained: "Unaware of the secret agreements, we declared that it was all necessary to gain time to strengthen the Red Army ... we accepted the line of the Communist International that the war was now one between imperialist powers."[12] In June 1941, Germany attacked the Soviet Union and Russia became allied with Britain. In December 1942, Attorney-General Bert Evatt lifted the ban on the CPA. In his statement issued at the time, Evatt was at pains to point out the move did not suggest any support for the CPA but only that circumstances had changed and the CPA had given undertakings to support the war effort.[13]

Communist Party candidates who stood at Australian elections had little success. It was in the trade unions where communist influence grew. Communist Bernie Taft estimated that at the end of the Second World War, "the party had a decisive influence in over one third of trade unions – among them some of the most important and strategically placed".[14] The rise of an anti-communist trade union opposition to the Communist Party of Australia's influence in the trade unions – known as the industrial "Groupers" – was not surprising. More surprising, in the early 1950s, was Labor ill-feeling towards the Catholic Groupers such that it led to the debilitating Labor split that left the ALP in Opposition for two decades. In this, Bert Evatt would play a leading role and Robert Menzies would be the beneficiary.

With the end of the Second World War and the territorial movement of the Soviet Union into territories liberated from the Germans, Stalin's true motives for Soviet expansion and global influence became apparent. The Red Army had found its moment. These immediate post war years also saw fresh challenges for Australian Communist Party comrades.

With the dissolution of the Comintern in May 1943, local communist parties were free to develop socialist objectives of their own. In January 1944, Australia's party changed its name to the Australian Communist Party (ACP) to emphasise its national character and began considering what tactics would be best for this new phase in the coming revolution. However, no successful direction evolved and, from 1946, as Alastair Davidson explains, "for the next five years it continued to work along international lines in theory, and in practice for the next ten years. In the final analysis its policies emanated from Moscow." Davidson adds, "It was almost impossible for all these [Communist Party of Australia] leaders to adjust to a communism that was not monolithic and which did not follow international directions."[15]

In fact, such was Australian communists' adherence to Moscow, in 1956 when new Soviet leader Nikita Khrushchev denounced Stalin and spoke specifically of Stalin's crimes in the murder and execution of so many Soviet citizens, Eric Aarons has written of how he accepted the validity of Khrushchev's speech of "self-correction". However, Aarons then offered a disturbing afterthought:

> *I made the point at the Central Committee meeting which decided the matter that our outlook was such that, had we been in power [in Australia], we too would have executed people we considered to be objectively, even if not subjectively (that is by intention), helping our enemies.*[16]

Fortunately, the Communist Party of Australia was never in power in Australia to confirm Aaron's reflection. Post war, in the federal election year of 1946, such was the perceived ineffectiveness of Australian communists in their struggle to disrupt what they termed the capitalist system, even under a Labor government, both Robert Menzies as leader of the Liberal Party and Bert Evatt as Attorney General expressed views that echoed each other in their public tolerance of the Australia Communist Party as a legitimate social institution.

Menzies, in a speech in February 1946, opined that he believed his party would be extremely reluctant to put a ban on the Communist Party as times were different from those of the days early in the war when his government had banned the CPA which was opposed to the war effort. He argued that the Communist Party instead must be "brought into the open and met by strength of argument against it" and by the education of people against "its false doctrines".[17] Similarly, during the September 1946 federal election campaign, Bert Evatt argued, "Communists are fellow citizens. Let them have freedom of expression, unless they break the law of the country. That is the same as Mr Menzies' policy."[18]

As the Soviets made territorial gains in Eastern Europe following the fall of Berlin and Nazi Germany in late 1945, Soviet thought as expressed from the new Communist Information Bureau (Cominform) divided the world into two - the peace loving anti-imperialist bloc led by the Soviet Union opposing the warmongering nations led by the USA. Alongside this, the Cominform developed a new theory that the "people's democracy" could be achieved through the activities of a new people's front rather than by revolution. To this end, local communists should aid and support a people's front through the growth of organisations devoted to various causes. In Australia, these blossomed from the late 1940s through to the 1950s, many replacing older organisations of similar bent – groups such as the Australian Peace Council, the Australian Soviet Friendship Society, the Australia-China Society, the Union of Australian Women, the Australasian Book Society and the New Housewives Society.

These front organisations, however, would prove to have little impact on government policy. The real strength for Australian communists lay within the trade union movement. Here, by agitation and support for action, communists worked to make a difference via a new people's front. Their action not only disturbed industry and civil society, it also provoked the Labor government of Ben Chifley where divisions that would haunt Labor for the next two decades had taken root. As Alastair Davidson explains it: "Organised ALP opposition to communism began after 1945 because of the strength that the communists showed at the 1945 ACTU congress ... It is significant that the Industrial Groups were set up soon after ... Another reason for ALP opposition was the generally held belief that the communists were responsible for a series of stoppages in 1945 and 1946 [and] ... the ALP was threatened with electoral unpopularity if so many of its trade union leaders continued to associate with communists."[19]

From 1947–49, Australia experienced some of its worst industrial strike action. Australian communism after the war, as party member Bernie Taft has written, "reverted to its traditional extreme 'leftist' position [and] resumed its hard-line oppositionist attitude to the Labor Party".[20] Industries where workers belonged to communist influenced unions saw regular strike action - coal mining, stevedoring, transport and Ironworkers Union operations. While the war time removal of price controls had meant sharp inflation, genuine claims by workers were exacerbated by communist influence inside unions.

In 1947, with the announcement that the Chifley Government would construct an experimental range for rocket missiles, unions where communists held influence threatened to boycott the project. In the debate to pass the *Defence Projects Protection Act* on 6 June, Attorney General Evatt made clear that both he and the Labor Party regarded the Communist Party opposition to the missile project as part of a communist attempt to impede government defence policy "in the interests of a foreign power".[21] Communist influence in the trade union movement was no longer seen simply as disruption but had become linked to the motives of its leaders in Moscow at a time of international tension and fears of another war. The Berlin Blockade would begin just a year later.

In a lengthy speech to the House of Representatives on 9 February 1949, at the height of the Berlin Blockade, however, Evatt missed his opportunity to target the real concern growing in global affairs. While he could single out local CPA disruption of government, he was unable to confront real communist pressures abroad. Instead, in making his significant statement on Australia's security at the start of that election year, in the midst of growing tension and confrontation with the Soviets in Europe, Evatt chose to focus almost entirely on the work and service of the United Nations Security Council, arguing its importance to world peace and stability.

The United Nations had absorbed Evatt's energies in the post war years; as the President of the United Nations General Assembly from July 1948 to June 1949, Prime Minister Ben Chifley took on the role of Acting External Affairs Minister. Evatt saw his role at the United Nations as his greatest achievement and it seems to have distracted the Chifley government from the importance of huge and growing post war developments in international affairs that had political strategists speaking of a "Cold War" from as early as 1946. Defence alliance was the order of the day. At heart, though, Evatt was a neutralist. Ric Throssell, the son of Katharine Susannah Pritchard and one of Evatt's young officers in the Department of External Affairs recalls a night at Evatt's home where he admitted he was. As Throssell recalls it, in response to his having declared that Australia should stay out of wars and remain neutral, Evatt replied: "I agree with you – in principle – but it is just not politically practical. We would have to go to the people. They wouldn't agree'. Not now."[22]

Historian David Lowe has written of how "the Chifley Labor Government resisted the Cold War as a framework for understanding change, whether overseas or at home. Australia's two major allies, the governments of Britain and the United States, provided much of the Cold War's definition and status; and Chifley's reluctance to accept their views prompted animated exchanges with both London and Washington. Within Australia, there also flew heated words between Melbourne, where the Department of Defence accepted a view of the world polarised by the Cold War, and Canberra, where External Affairs did not."[23]

Evatt was no doubt the influence on Chifley's reluctance to accept the new world view of the dangers of encroaching Soviet communism. Kim Beazley senior has written of how when given letters of introduction when he went to the Coronation in 1953 by Evatt's staff and other associates, the people he met were often those who had a stronger allegiance to the Soviet Union than their own democratic government. Beazley also described how Evatt too often aligned himself with the left writing, "Evatt would become almost hysterical if anyone attributed to the Soviet Union the massacre of several thousand Polish officers in the Katyn forest. Against all the evidence, he swore the Nazis had done it."[24] Beazley went on to say that he thought Evatt saw himself as the person who could bring the great powers together again. What he could not accept was that Britain and the USA had fought Germany to win a war while "Stalin had been aiming to win a world".[25] Bert Evatt, as External Affairs Minister would become a weak link in the Chifley Government with regard to Australia's foreign affairs standing with its most important allies.

Evatt's 9 February 1949 speech to the House of Representatives gave lengthy examples of UN success in negotiations, such as developments in the settlement in Palestine. As if this new body of nations had exceptional global power, Evatt argued that the United Nations was the way forward to future peace - nations could be brought together under its charter to avoid hostilities. Conferencing would replace armed conflict. The United Nations would be fundamental to Australia's foreign policy as a middle power in the world's peaceful progress. Evatt also expressed surprise that a gulf had developed between the UN's major powers on the Security Council – as reflected in the Berlin Blockade and other tensions. In many ways, the speech sounded as if from a parallel universe to the one experiencing Soviet confrontation in Eastern Europe or the growing strength of communism in mainland China and widespread international analysis of the developing Cold War.

Evatt seemed to reflect no appreciation of communism as a global force or of its territorial ambitions. He made little, if any, specific comment on the most concerning matters for global peace and security. He spoke as if believing that leaders of countries where totalitarian regimes ruled were of equal readiness to resolve conflict peacefully as countries ruled by representative governments. He concluded:

> *The effect of the presence of the leaders of the great powers at these conferences is beneficial in the long run. They meet. You cannot meet human beings, the leaders of nations that have been your allies in a great war, without having a hope in your heart that disputes will be settled on a basis of justice. I do not mean that they should be settled on a basis of ridiculous appeasement and yielding always to the other side, but on a basis of justice.*[26]

Evatt spoke with the avidness of the recently converted. His crystal ball, however, could not imagine how this would be tested in coming decades, even by the end of that year. In February 1949, the growing fear of a new outbreak of European hostilities was something Evatt should have referred to, if not made the focus of his address. But his fixation was the United Nations which showed a personal obsession alongside a refusal to confront the reality of the spread of communist disruption, in Europe especially but growing in other parts of the world. This gave Menzies all the ammunition he needed.

In his reply to Evatt on 15 February 1949, Menzies demonstrated how different the two were in their approach to the issues of defence and foreign policy. Even perhaps to politics in general. From the outset, in his speech, Menzies was on the attack, belittling Evatt as being legalistic and theoretical in his arguments about the importance of the United Nations, even somewhat boastful as part of its formation. Then Menzies moved straight to an analysis of the dangers of communism and the failure of the UN to counter it, the UN being an organisation of so many members and with no international authority or powers to control nations with rogue ambitions. As such, the UN could never prevent war said Menzies; then he quoted from Evatt's own writings to this effect.

The bluntness of Menzies' message contrasted sharply with the high minded and wish fulfilment style of Evatt's extolling of UN virtues. Menzies went for the jugular, accusing the Chifley government of weakness in the face of communist activity, saying, "The Australian Government scoffs at the idea of the fifth column in this country... It believes that active revolutionary communists must not be dealt with harshly because they merely have a political philosophy of their own." In short, Menzies laid out a theme he would use effectively and often in the coming election year, saying:

> *Expediency matters in this world, and if we are confronted by a state of affairs in which we find thugs challenging the peace of the world and the security, safety and future of our own people, it is of no use stating airy fairy legalistic ideals. We must face the fact that until the ideal happy state of affairs can be brought into existence, we must first deal with the enemy as we find him and deal with problems which may be solvable only by expediency, as the problem of the Berlin blockade has been solved.*[27]

Menzies hammered home his critique of the United Nations as

an ineffective body in the face of real enemies. He was not simply attacking what he saw as a weakness in Evatt's arguments but sounding out genuine concerns about the way in which such a body could even stand in the way of concerted action by allied nations to overcome enemies of the West. He continued:

> *What are we to do about Russia in Europe? Here is a huge problem of which we have heard relatively little. The General Assembly for the United Nations took a hand in the German stalemate recently. It intervened. It demanded, in effect, of the great powers that they should negotiate. It did not say a word about the blockade. It was apparently unaware that there was a blockade. Its intervention was roundly condemned in Great Britain and the United States of America because, in effect, it was chiding or criticising the Western powers for insisting upon the lifting of the blockade before negotiations about the currency and other matters. That intervention, as I happen to know, produced great resentment in London and New York, although I dare say that it gave some gleams of satisfaction in Moscow.*[28]

On the domestic front, in 1949, Australia's industrial strikes and Communist Party involvement would link up with such discussions of the wider threat of communism, in Europe especially, and with a break down in international collaboration. But, even as the parliamentarians debated these issues, the Communist Party of Australia faced exposure and disruption of its own.

In February 1949, the defection of Communist Party State Executive member Cecil Sharpley in Victoria led to disclosures of union election rigging. He also outed numerous comrades, selling his secrets to Keith Murdoch's *Herald* newspaper. In his pamphlet "I was a Communist Leader", Sharpley wrote of meetings in "cold Party rooms high above Elizabeth Street" where he and other Party executives "dictated the policy of 'militant' union representatives on the Melbourne Trades Hall Council".[29] His defection led to the setting up of the Lowe Royal Commission to investigate the Communist Party in Victoria. That same month, CPA leader Lance Sharkey told a *Daily Telegraph* reporter that "If Soviet forces in pursuit of an aggressor entered Australia, Australian workers would welcome them as the workers welcomed them throughout Europe when the Red Army liberated the people from the Nazis."[30] In October, Sharkey was sentenced to eighteen months jail for his sedition leaving communists to protest injustice and most Australians to concur with the judgement.

Then came the coal strike. In the cold of winter, from late June to mid-August, weeks of privation and industry losses from a nation-wide strike by coal miners proved crippling. Provoked, Chifley turned to military forces to open the NSW coal mines and force workers back on the job. According to Bernie Taft, this strike was "the last, desperate attempt by the CPA to take over leadership of the working-class movement".[31]

By now, recognition of communist influence in the unions had become mainstream. Taft and communist colleagues might well look back and opine that the mood across the land was anti-communist hysteria but industrial disruption, revealed as organised and promoted by communist influence, was now sitting alongside Chifley's attempt to nationalise Australia's banks. That it was a Labor government tackling the communist infiltration in the unions did not solve Chifley's dilemma. Communist influence was also apparent in Labor ranks. For a large number of Australians, this connected with the encroachment of Soviet communism in Europe and a Chinese civil war that, by October, had led to a takeover of China by Mao Zedong's communists.

Former Country Party leader and Menzies' colleague Artie Fadden recalled that when he had, in 1946, recommended that the Coalition parties advocate a ban on the Communist Party, Menzies had told him, "We must not let it be thought that they are such a force in political philosophy that we cannot met them."[32] By 1949, Robert Menzies had moved in his views on communism, influenced by developments in Europe and strengthened by his 1948 visit to the Britain. His attitude to the Communist Party was no longer so san-

THE GREAT RIVALRY OF AUSTRALIAN POLITICS

Dean Hewlett Johnson of Canterbury Cathedral did not distinguish between Christian teaching and the ideology of communism. He supported such communist totalitarian dictators as Josef Stalin, Mao Zedong and Fidel Castro. The Red Dean addressed the National Peace Congress – a Communist Party front organisation – at the Melbourne Exhibition building in April 1950. He won the Stalin Peace Prize in June 1950.

Katharine Susannah Prichard (1883-1969) was a life long Stalinist. She was the mother of Ric Throssell, a member of the External Affairs Department and mentioned at the Petrov Royal Commission.

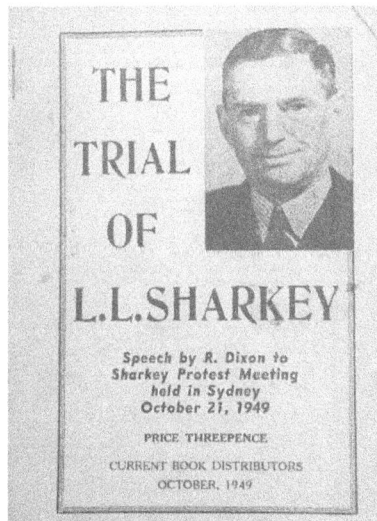

Communist Party functionary R. (Richard) Dixon spoke in support of CPA General Secretary L. L. Sharkey who was found guilty of sedition for saying, in March 1949, that Australians would welcome invading Soviet Union forces.

Wally Clayton (1906-1991) who was "Klod" in an Australian CPA network – was an operative who was the principal conduit forwarding Australian intelligence to the Soviet Union from communist spies in Australia

guine as his 1946 comments suggested. Opening the Liberal Party's election campaign on 10 November 1949 in Melbourne, he emphasised his party's rejection of socialism which he argued ran strongly in the Chifley Government's policies. This would be a major theme of his election campaign, taking his Liberal Party and the Country Party into government. Even more striking, alongside his attack on socialism in his opening speech, was Menzies' pledge to ban the Communist Party of Australia, as he put it:

> *Communism in Australia is an alien and destructive pest. If elected, we shall outlaw it. The Communist Party will be declared subversive and unlawful, and dissolved. ... No person now a member of the Communist Party shall be employed or paid a fee by the Commonwealth; nor shall any such person be eligible for any office in a registered industrial organisation. The laws with respect to sedition or other subversive activities will be reviewed and strengthened. Conviction under such laws will disqualify from employment under the Crown or from office in a registered organisation.*[33]

What happened next would, in time, surprise the pundits.

5

A New Age of Cold War

During the war the threat to the Western world came from the dictatorships of the right and public opinion swung left. By 1951 the threat to the Western world was coming from the dictatorships of the left and public opinion swung right. – Kim Beazley senior[1]

The mornings of 6 August 1945 and 9 August 1945 (US time) brought an end to World War II. On day one, a US plane named Enola Gay dropped the first atomic bomb to be used in war on Japan's city of Hiroshima – exploding 1800 feet above its target, it reduced five square miles of the city to ashes. Three days later, a similar bomb devastated two square miles of the nearby city of Nagasaki. The nuclear age had begun and, more importantly for the 1950s, not long after so did the Cold War. International conquest would henceforth go underground in new ways. Atomic secrets and advances in weaponry its new goals.

From the discovery of nuclear fission in 1938 by two German scientists, the race to beat the Germans at developing an atomic bomb was on. From this had developed the Manhattan Project connecting up US, British and Canadian technology. After the war, the mission was to stay ahead of the Soviets in weapons development and prevent new discoveries and technological advances falling into Soviet hands. What Ian Fleming created by way of entertainment out of espionage with James Bond, in reality, was a nasty subterfuge, the secrets of which have taken decades to unravel. Menzies and Evatt would clash heavily in this campaign – and each face consequences neither could have foreseen in the 1940s.

Undercover intelligence operations had taken on new meaning with the rise of the Soviet Union and, by 1950 as the new Menzies Government took office, had become a growing enterprise for Western allies. With it came intelligence advice, collected through the then highly secret US Venona Project intercepts of Soviet communications, that Australia was harbouring a number of Soviet spies. This, coupled with a mistrust of External Affairs minister Bert Evatt and his chief of staff John Burton, had led the US to withhold top secret information from Australia in the latter years of the Chifley Government. It was also the impetus for the Chifley Government to set up the Australian Security Intelligence Organisation (ASIO) in 1949.[2]

Menzies was first told of the Venona program and its secrets relating to Soviet agents working from within Australian institutions on 3 January 1950 when he met with the then head of ASIO Sir Geoffrey Reed.[3] Menzies' beliefs about the insidious nature of communism and communists in Australia were at once confirmed as staggeringly accurate. Chifley himself had only learnt about the Venona information on Australian Soviet agents in 1948, which had explained, to some extent, why the British and US had a mistrust of Australia which they had given a security grading at the same level as India or Pakistan.[4]

Leaks from Australia had been going back to Moscow from as far back as the early war years through the Soviet embassy in Canberra. In addition, leading figures in the UK's MI5 and Foreign Office, such as Esler Denning, head of the Far Eastern Section, found John Burton, who headed Evatt's Department of External Affairs from 1947–50, to be something of a Soviet fellow traveller, albeit no agent, and far too open about what he discussed with the Soviet Legation in Canberra. MI5 had multiple concerns with regard to Australia's weakness around some of its foreign affairs operatives.[5]

Along with his boss Bert Evatt, Burton had an almost evangelical belief the United Nations could create a new world order where peace would replace war through trust between east and west and the voices of smaller nations would prevail over the superpowers. In this, Burton believed in "open diplomacy" where information should be shared rather than kept secret. Like Evatt, he also had little time for security operations. Stories of Evatt's office being left with top secret files abandoned on desks and files carelessly left lying about wherever he travelled are numerous. Burton also opposed any suggestion communism in the Far East, as it was then called, was a negative. Burton believed that communism was what under-developed nations needed, saying "the spread of Communism in China, Korea and throughout other Asian areas must be regarded as inevitable".[6]

Menzies' very different messages about communism had resonated in the 1949 election. The Chifley Government's position in international affairs of wanting no division between east and west and a belief – derived much from Evatt – of an international liberalism that could be managed by the United Nations where middle powers could override the dominance of superpowers gave off a tone of softness towards communism. This flew in the face of increasing tensions in the east-west divide and as Winston Churchill spoke of an "iron curtain" descending on eastern Europe. Evatt at the UN Security Council would not allow Australia to join the British and US in opposition to the Soviet Union.[7]

As, increasingly, the news came of Soviet encroachment in eastern Europe, Menzies' views on communism made gains in political debate. While the Chifley Government had gone in hard against communist inspired union action in the national coal strike and with the *Approved Defence Projects Protection Act 1947*, Labor links with the trade unions and with Evatt's department of External Affairs showing signs of being the source of Soviet leaks meant the US continued to lack trust in Australia under Labor.

As early as 1948, Defence Department head Sir Frederick Shedden, with Chifley's sanction, had singled out External Affairs officer Dr Ian Milner, as a possible agent leaking documents to the Soviets.[8] This would be confirmed a few years later but, until that time, the department was under a shadow. The cell of Soviet agents revealed by the Venona intercepts was nicknamed the "Klod" network after the central figure Wally Clayton (Klod). It involved a network of informers from writer Katherine Susannah Pritchard to anthropologist Professor Fred Rose to typist in Evatt's office Frances Bernie to External Affairs officers Jim Hall and Ian Milner. They were connected by one individual, long since identified as Communist Party operative Wally Clayton. In total, eleven Australians were in the network plus Clayton. Some were actual agents, others simply informers for Clayton. The best summary of the network is depicted in Des Ball and David Horner's *Breaking the Codes*.[9]

Australia's relations with the US would improve after 1950 with the Menzies Government and the appointment of Colonel Charles Spry as head of ASIO. But the network had still to be formally identified. Wally Clayton, originally from New Zealand, was a long time Communist Party organiser "handpicked" by the CPA leadership for the "dangerous work early in the Second World War", as Mark Aarons tells it. Clayton's "patient work and attention to detail" was the reason the banned party "continued to function effectively with the help of secret members and anonymous supporters". Aarons also confirmed, using his father's experience in the RAAF, how the CPA was able to infiltrate Australia's military services during the war, something the party had done since the 1920s.[10]

The communist problem, as now outlined to Menzies in 1950, went far beyond the disruption caused by trade union activity. The information about agents in Australia confirmed his views but also complicated them. Just who were the individuals working in secret and spying for the Soviets? How to flush them out would be a difficult task, as governments across the Western world would find in coming years. And, in trying to do so, what names would be tainted by association with such investigations and what careers would be upended in the hunt? These were considerations that would affect the debate over the Communist Party of Australia which Menzies was about to begin. And all before an unknowing public who could never have the full information revealed by the intercepts but known to government.

Banning the Communist Party had been an election promise from Menzies and as such it was top of government priorities as much as protecting the banks from nationalisation. Moreover, international developments had pushed the rise of communism closer to home. China had become a communist country just months before and, in February 1950, Stalin signed the 30-year Sino-Soviet Treaty of Friendship, Alliance and Mutual Assistance with Communist China. Meanwhile, the Soviets had tested their first atomic explosion in August 1949, sending Western allies into a state of apprehension regarding atomic secrets leaking from the West to Russia. In addition, Malaya, Vietnam and the Philippines were experiencing communist inspired violence connected to independence movements. At the end of 1949, the Dutch East Indies had become the Republic of the United States of Indonesia. The old order was breaking up.

For Robert Menzies and his wife Pattie, their return to the Lodge was a sweet triumph. But the Lodge had not been lived in by a prime minister's wife for some years owing to Mrs Chifley choosing to reside in her home town of Bathurst. The Curtins, as first couple for most of the war years, had also not used the house very often for entertaining. Curtin himself resided at the Kurrajong Hotel. There was much to be renewed with Sir John Bunting recalling that there was "decay all over the building itself and, as to the internal arrangements, such as fittings and furnishings, the kindest words for them was meagre".[11] But Patti Menzies expressed her delight at what she found. No doubt for all the Menzies family, the second chance at prime ministerial life opened up new possibilities; the war had long gone, they belonged to a new and successful political party and the tide was going their way.

Menzies found his work load to be exacting, part of what his biographer Allan Martin found in his correspondence of the time to be a "relearning" of the ways of government.[12] Foremost in the legislative program was the banking legislation and the move to ban the Communist Party. Support for the latter was around 70 per cent; in June after debates over the bill in parliament support had risen to 82 per cent. Foreign affairs and domestic affairs had become intertwined with developments abroad impinging on fears at home.

Outlining the directions for the Menzies Government in its foreign affairs, External Affairs minister Percy Spender touched on the new focus of Asia and the Pacific for Australia in a speech in the House of Representatives on 9 March 1950 where he said:

> *The birth of new members of the Commonwealth, Pakistan and Ceylon and the Republic of India, the creation of new national entities in the form of the Republic of Indonesia, and the States of Vietnam, Laos and Cambodia in what was previously known as French Indo China, are developments which have helped to shift the centre of gravity of world affairs more and more to this area. Our policy must be to ensure, to the full extent we can, that these new States co-operate with each other and with us in meeting positively and actively the new problems created in this area by the emergence of a Communist China, and by the ever-increasing thrust of communism, which endeavours to ally itself, in the pursuit of its ends, with the national aspirations of the millions of people of South-East Asia.*[13]

In the same speech, Spender also acknowledged Australia's obligations to the United Nations adding, with a swipe at former External Affairs minister Evatt, that "there is a danger of exaggerating, not the importance of the aims or purposes or principles of the United Nations, but the extent to which in present circumstances it can exert real influence for the maintenance of peace in the world. It must never be forgotten that, as its membership includes representatives of all the groups of the world, it may contain those who are working to disrupt the order we believe in, as well as those who support it, although of course all are pledged to support the principles of the United Nations." There could be no doubt that Australia's foreign policy settings had taken a 180 degree turn under Menzies, who dominated cabinet.

The Liberals with the Country Party had won a commanding

victory in the 1949 federal elections. The number of senators in the upper house had increased at the 1949 election from 36 to 60 but, due to the Senate being elected by half senate elections, Labor retained a majority in the upper house. Getting legislation on banning the Communist Party through both houses was the task ahead. And if it passed both houses, there was always the chance of a High Court challenge. The legislation had many corners to cover.

Given the unsettled state of international affairs, fears of a new world war dominated global thinking. The left of politics justified the USSR's moves into Eastern Europe as developing a defence buffer against the newly established North Atlantic Treaty Organisation (NATO). In the years following the war, communist parties had taken control of Poland, Czechoslovakia and Hungary, closely aligning their regimes with the Soviet Union. The work of communist supporters was to deny that war was any aim of communists; only fascists were warmongers. To that end, a visit to Australia by Hewlett Johnson known as the "Red Dean of Canterbury" in mid April 1950 saw 10,000 pack the Exhibition Building in Melbourne to hear the message that it was a wicked lie that Stalin's USSR had any intention or motivation to bring about a war. "The truth is they that plan, think, desire and speak peace," Johnson told the crowd, along with the message that he had just visited the Soviet Union and found no religious discrimination and that "English press men" who had spent years there had told him there was no evidence of "millions thrown into gaols".[14] Menzies was unmoved.

Faced with a rearguard action of rolling strikes on the waterfront against the installation of his new government, Menzies invoked the Crimes Act. With industrial tension the background, the Communist Party dissolution bill was introduced to parliament on the evening of Thursday 27 April. Anticipating protests, parliament was closed to all but those who had admission tickets. A crowd opposing the legislation of some 250 men and women arrived at Parliament House in varying groups but did not cause any disturbance and a small number were allowed into Kings Hall as a deputation to meet politicians. These were reported to have spoken to Labor MPs only. *The Age*, running photos of the protest visitors walking towards Parliament House across the lawns and packing the corridors inside, headed the photo spread "Communists 'Invade' Capital".[15]

In order to justify such an extreme step as banning a political party, a step which Menzies referred to as "novel", from a legal perspective, under the defence power in the Constitution, the government needed to prove that Australia was in a state of war - one different from the normal notions of hand-to-hand combat but a war none the less being fought against an enemy, both within the nation and linked to international forces. The Cold War would need to be accepted as a new form of war, one fought to save the West from being overtaken by communism and its agents. As for precedents, only in war had any Australian political party been banned – in World War I, Prime Minister Billy Hughes had outlawed the International Workers of the World and in 1940 the Communist Party was banned by Menzies.

In his first words to the House, Menzies made clear the bill was "to outlaw and dissolve the Australian Communist Party" and that it was a proposed law relating to "the safety and defence of Australia". The enemies that Australia was being defended against, said Menzies, were "the King's enemies in this country" adding "We are not at peace today, except in a technical sense".[16] In Menzies' view, Australia was at war with agents in its midst seeking to destroy it. This was an essential component of the bill.

From the outset, Menzies' speech was laden with the phrases of war. It was a war to retain liberty and the choice was there – to "attack these communists" or "adopt inaction". (No doubt a reminder of appeasement in the late 1930s.) Which he followed with "Why then did we fight the Germans? Because they sought to overthrow liberty!" Menzies went on to point out it was "the power of the Commonwealth of Australia to make laws with respect to the naval and military defence of the Commonwealth and of the States" and that the government was acting on two principles which he defined as: "The first is the defence of this country, and the second is our right and duty to maintain the Constitution and the laws against any wrecking attack whatever." This was not a bill about conciliation and arbitration – not about disruptive union activity in other words – but about the defence of the nation.

For much of the speech, Menzies referred to the writings of well known communists from Stalin to Australia's CPA leader Sharkey emphasising that communists had no intention of bringing about reform of Western democracy but only the complete overthrow of government: "'Revolution' means what it says. It means guns, rifles, bayonets". Australia was under attack. And to the argument that banning the ACP would send it underground, Menzies countered that a significant and destructive part of communism's work was already being carried out underground and in secret. Full knowledge of which, of course, he could not share nor speak of. Then he turned to words from the Australian Labor Party condemning communism, challenging Labor to come clean and not oppose the bill on grounds it might entangle some trade unionists. Defence of Australia's freedom was a higher priority than a few trade union leaders' jobs.

Before outlining the specifics of the bill, Menzies closed his war defence strongly:

> *The security and defence of Australia are dependent not only upon the valour of our troops in time of war and upon the industry with which they are supported in the factory and on the farm, but also upon the continuity of those great industries that are vital to a national effort should war come ... We would not have tolerated a fifth column in Australia from 1939 to 1945. We certainly do not propose to tolerate one in 1950, at a time when militant communism, checked for the time being in Western Europe, is moving east and south-east to carry out its plans to put down democracy and to usher in the revolution. Coal mining, iron and steel, engineering, transport, building and power are key industries. ... it would*

> be an act of criminal folly to leave revolutionary Communists in key positions in those industries so that with all their smallness of numbers they may achieve destructive results which five army corps could hardly hope to achieve.[17]

Significantly, Menzies' speech received front page news in local dailies. And further comment deeper into the papers. The words "Reds" and "Communists" were splashed across headlines in unflattering phrases. But Menzies's appeal to the sense of war was overtaken by summaries in the press of what the bill actually would mean to individuals in the Australian community. In a list of "six main provisions" of the bill *The Argus* singled out seizure of communist property, the proscribing of affiliated bodies of the CPA which would have "a right of appeal to the High Court; but must accept the onus of proof", officers and members of unlawful associations who would be "under penalty of imprisonment to cease their activities", declared persons who would be "disqualified from employment under the Commonwealth" and individuals in "key industries". All would be "declared".[18] The enemy was truly within.

In the heat of battle, so to speak, Menzies and his colleagues had not considered the extent of the bill's assault on, possibly, ordinary Australians. Two incidents quickly suggested worrying possibilities. The complexities of the bill's implications were immediately illustrated when Menzies was forced to advise the House of Representatives on 9 May that among the list of 53 communist union officials he had given names for in a speech to parliament on 28 April there were five persons who were not communists. This led Labor Opposition leader Ben Chifley to interject that the government could not be relied on for its information in the hunt for communists, lending credibility to criticism by the Melbourne University Dean of Law, Professor George Paton, of the bill that it was "a very dangerous procedure" in resting of the "onus of proof" on the "declared" person.[19] In other words a reversal of the onus of proof.

An exchange in the House of Representatives on 4 May between Menzies, Chifley and Labor's Eddie Ward also challenged Menzies' argument that the bill was fundamentally a defence of decent Australians against a faceless enemy. In a debate over proposed changes to voting for the Senate after a double dissolution and after a jibe from Menzies' bitter opponent Ward, Menzies suggested he could, if provoked, "declare" a couple of Labor Senators. This led Ward to respond, "the Fuhrer has spoken". To which, Menzies replied, "I can think of one member of this House who might escape only by the skin of his teeth." When Chifley interjected that this was dangerous ground for Menzies who should not make threats, the PM responded, "I never make a threat that I do not carry out."[20]

Chifley's response to Menzies' speech, given in the House of Representatives on 9 May, made full use of these two damaging aftershocks of the announcement of the bill to ban the CPA and its details. Menzies had not only demonstrated that information on communists could be flawed but had suggested he could use the legislation to attack his Labor opponents. As Chifley summed it up:

> ... where does the Government and the Prime Minister stand in relation to the matter of whether or not Labor members of Parliament or persons other than Communists are intended to be covered by this act? If the Prime Minister is honest he will say at once that there are members of the Labor party who may be declared under this bill, even though they are not Communists.[21]

The bill to ban the Communist Party of Australia would cause divisions within Labor. After years of attempts by Labor – principally the Industrial Groupers - to fight off the growing influence of communists in the union movement, Labor was not in a position electorally, or as a party, to show signs of weakness in the face of action against the CPA. However, the bill was extreme and had potential to split the party should the Labor leader appear to stand with the party of what Labor members saw as capitalists against the rights of workers. *The Age* reported that Labor's reaction to the bill was "one of worry and indecision" and wrote of it as bringing about "one of the greatest decisions of its history".[22] The following week's reports of Labor indecision continued. Caucus had met on

3 May in Canberra for three hours with no conclusion on how it would react to the bill. Labor firebrand Eddie Ward was quoted as having attacked the bill "bitterly" and calling it "an assault on the basic freedoms of Australians" and that it "should be fought to the last ditch".[23]

For all that, as Labor leader Ben Chifley spoke in the House of Representatives on the evening of 9 May, he announced that Labor would not oppose the bill but instead seek to have changes made to its details. Percy Spender immediately accused Labor of not having the courage to oppose the bill outright. Labor was fearful that Menzies could use the bill, if rejected by Labor, to call a double dissolution election at which the Liberal/Country Party Coalition could take control of the Senate. Chifley's speech, one of his finest, called the bill "monstrous and a complete abrogation of the principles of justice". He argued that injustice was against ordinary Australians and said Labor would seek amendments to give accused persons the right to various compensations if shown to be innocent as well as prevent random searches of property by forcing only those authorised by the Attorney-General and with a warrant from a magistrate.[24]

After Chifley spoke, it was Bert Evatt's turn to attack details of the bill in a more legalistic manner. It was a speech that Menzies' biographer Allan Martin has described as "the most sustained and intellectually reasoned argument" against the bill.[25]

Evatt had taken the loss of government badly. He had been ready to quit politics, and spoke to Labor heavy Jack Ferguson, then president of both the NSW and federal branches of the ALP, about his desire to leave politics and move to the NSW Supreme Court. He knew Ferguson could smooth the way for him. Ferguson, however, opposed the idea. Ferguson told Evatt it was not proper for him to leave – no doubt worried not only the party could lose another seat but also because he was one of the party's most prominent MPs. As Evatt biographer John Murphy puts it, "If Ferguson had brought his power to bear, Evatt's career would have run a very different course, and possibly the trajectory of post-war Australian politics would have been different too."[26]

Evatt had initially thought Labor would be foolish to oppose the banning of the Communist Party bill. No doubt the results of the 1949 federal election had left him fearful of the party being seen to be soft on communism. It had cost them government. But, being a lawyer and a barrister, once he had been asked to take the brief, so to speak, he swung behind the party line to defeat the bill.

In his speech to the House of Representatives on 9 May, Evatt did not avoid an attack on the work of communists in Australia. Activity which he argued had been opposed and condemned by Labor over years. In office, Labor had invoked the *Crimes Act* to resist communist activity in Australia, and more besides. Evatt's main thrust against the bill was in the matter of the onus of proof, saying:

> *This bill is directed very largely against persons, and the consequence of declaration is that the person concerned will lose his livelihood if he is an employee of the Government or holds trade-union office in certain industries. The bill proposes that it shall be enough to show that the person declared was a member or officer of a declared association. That will include hundreds, perhaps thousands of people who have no personal connection with communism, are not Communists, and are not members of the Communist Party.*[27]

Evatt, following Chifley's line of attack, turned the argument back on the government as designing legislation that could produce witch hunts against ordinary and innocent Australians. In any attempt to ban the Communist Party, under the bill as offered, individual Australians could fear unjustly being "declared" to be communists and suffer loss of employment and much more.

Labor, Evatt said, had never refused to fight back against communist inspired disruption in Australia. The Chifley Government had boycotted communist unions over the guided weapons testing range by passing the Defence Projects bill to make attacks on the project subject to the law and a punishable offence. In Evatt's view "that principle ... should be adopted in all our dealings with bodies of the character of the Communist Party". Individuals who break such laws can then be prosecuted, with the onus of proof of their offending, in a court and accordingly punished. Such laws, unlike a ban on the Communist Party, applied to all members of the Australian community and did not discriminate on the grounds of opinion or attachment.

In the case of the national coal strike, likewise, a bill was passed making "it an offence for the funds of organisations to be used for the purpose of promoting or continuing that strike ... Certain people defied the court's orders, and ten were imprisoned". Evatt argued that nefarious activities by communists could and should be dealt with by the courts without a bill to ban the CPA which would enact a law "the like of which was unknown in any British community". The reason, he continued, that the government had resorted to a ban on the CPA rather than use legislation such as with the Defence Projects Bill, was because under such legislation "it involves application to the courts of law ... [and] it is obvious that the intention of the government is to avoid and evade legal processes"[28]

Evatt proceeded to take apart the bill's details, illustrating possible cases of where individuals could be "declared" with no membership or attachment to the CPA and their lives destroyed - ordinary Australians caught in a net of suspicion. Chifley had referred to pimps, liars and perjurers being given licence by the legislation; now Evatt was drawing up scenarios based in law from the details of the bill.

All manner of employees of the Commonwealth could find themselves stripped of livelihoods on the suspicion of being communists. And then there were other associations where communists were active. "It is terrible to think that people who take part in any crusade for peace," said Evatt, "... are to be suspect and may have their names placed upon a list of proscribed persons merely because communists are associated with the movement or because communists are trying to run it." Taking up Menzies' use of the recent war, Evatt then himself reached for parallels with the Nazi experience, albeit from another perspective. Where Menzies used the war with Germany as an analogy to support his argument that the ban on the CPA was in defence of Australia's liberty, Evatt used the war analogy to suggest the government, in the legislation as constructed, was seeking to strip Australians of that very liberty:

> ... this bill is the apotheosis of tyranny in respect of individuals because it says, in effect, "You are a secretary of a trade union. By a power of a government to "declare", you hold your office at the pleasure of the government of the day. Judging by some of the arguments that have been advanced, some people may consider that active pursuit of a union's interests in an industrial dispute means that a man's activities are prejudicial to the defence of the country. ... That kind of thought was the rule under the regime of Hitler in Germany from 1933 onwards.[29]

With the government using the guillotine, the bill passed its second reading on 16 May. It next moved to the committee stage where Labor attempted to have it amended and succeeded only in gaining the right of a declared person or association to appeal to a State Supreme Court rather than the High Court and that search warrants must be obtained on reasonable grounds from a magistrate before any searches could be conducted. However, since Labor had the numbers in the Senate, the bill had a more difficult hurdle still to face.

At the 1949 federal election, the increase in numbers of the House of Representatives to 121 seats (plus two non-voting from the territories) had necessitated an increase in the seats for the Senate due to the nexus regulating the balance of the two houses of parliament. In addition, and more importantly, in 1949 the system of voting for the Senate had been changed by the Chifley Government to a proportional voting system. While this had increased considerably the numbers of non-Labor senators for half of the Senate, those senators elected for six years in 1946 – a large majority of whom were Labor – still meant that Labor had a majority until the 1946 senators were up for re-election at the next federal poll.

Inevitably, with the Communist Party dissolution legislation, the ball was in Labor's court. It presented Labor with something of a rock and a hard place choice as, with the atmosphere against communism such as it was, to simply reject the bill and create grounds for a double dissolution of the houses of parliament could result in Labor losing its majority in the Senate as well as the House of Representatives. Caucus and the party haggled over it for months while the bill went back and forth between the Senate and House of Representatives over amendments. At the end of the parliamentary session on 22 June, Menzies moved that the bill be laid aside. While Menzies could accept a number of Labor's requests for change, he continued to stand firm on the need to reverse the onus of proof for anyone or association declared. He spent the parliamentary recess of July and August making a trip to Britain and the US. Meanwhile, on 25 June with the North Korean People's Army crossing the 38th parallel and invading the Republic of Korea, the Korean War began.

As parliament resumed, on 28 September which was the day the Australian ground force arrived in Korea, Menzies introduced into the parliament the Communist Dissolution Bill (No 2) guillotining its debate until 3 October. Evatt made loud protests but Menzies offered veiled threats he was prepared to go to a double dissolution election over the bill. The bitterness of the debate that day has been summed up by Menzies' biographer Allan Martin as producing in Menzies "a form of fanaticism" which enabled him to argue against the "basic element in the British system of justice, trial by jury" with Martin concluding it was to be "the nadir of the illiberal position to which obsession with security was finally driving him".[30]

With tensions running high in Labor, both within and without its parliamentary team, Chifley was under pressure to reverse his opposition to the bill which he had already declared he would be

THE GREAT RIVALRY OF AUSTRALIAN POLITICS

Cecil Sharpley, one time member of the Victorian CPA executive, broke with the party in 1949 and wrote a series of articles for *The Herald* (Melbourne)

The CPA's ideological "five year plan" for Australia, 1951

J. A. Maloney was a Labor Party member of the NSW Legislative Council who was appointed by the Curtin Government in 1943 as Australian minister to the Soviet Union. He became an outspoken critic of Soviet communism and published a series of articles following his return to Australia in early 1945. Australia-Soviet House (a CPA front) published this pamphlet in reply to Maloney – the lead comment was from Professor Max Crawford of Melbourne University.

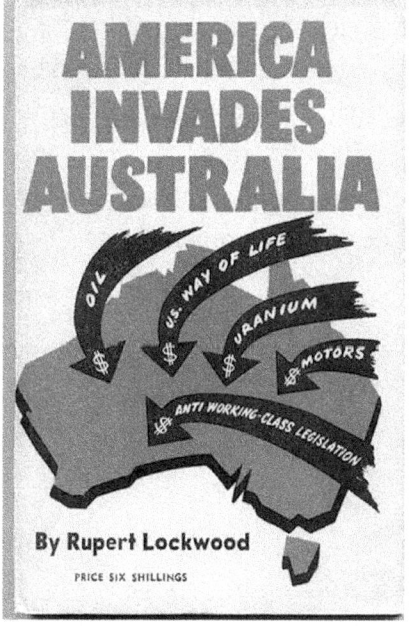

Communist Party member Rupert Lockwood, author of the infamous "Document J", wrote this series of articles at the office of the Communist Party Maritime Union, they were published after the Petrov Commission by Current Book Distributors, a CPA front organisation.

happy to fight an election on. Finally, it was the federal executive which broke the Labor deadlock by instructing the party to pass the bill in the Senate which Labor senators did on 19 October making the CPA illegal on 20 October. A few days later, the CPA and ten unions mounted a High Court challenge to the Act. When the news came that Evatt had agreed to act for the CPA's controlled Waterside Workers Federation, eyebrows were raised. Evatt had been hesitant to take the brief and needed a lot of pressure, as the clerk of the House Frank Green put it, having been informed of this by Waterside Workers unionist and PAA leader Jim Healy. Evatt was afraid it would harm him with the Catholic vote.[31]

There is division among historians as to whether Evatt had agreed with the decision to let the bill go through - as he believed it would be rejected by the High Court. Also, a time for him to star perhaps. But, with his record before the High Court in the Banking legislation, he could not have been so confident as to assume the legislation would fail before the High Court. Taking the brief was a gamble. But the step would be, for Evatt, a chance well taken. For all that, Evatt could not imagine how, whatever his success before the High Court, his move to appear for a communist trade union, in time, certainly would impact on his support among Catholic voters, among others.

6

GROUNDWORK FOR A SHOWDOWN

> *It is now generally recognised among members that Mr Chifley forced himself from his sick bed to lead his party to the last elections. He did this to maintain solidarity among members of the [Labor] movement and to stop difficult situations arising from suggestions that certain members of the Labor Party were assisting the Communist Party by indirect means. – The Canberra Times*[1]

Communism would prove to be the enduring disruptor of the twentieth century. Especially for governments, institutions and labour groups. The secular and antagonistic ideals of Soviet Marxism also challenged the teachings of Christian religions, in particular the Catholic Church which, from the late nineteenth century, had supported the work of groups of Catholic laymen around what was known as Catholic Action. This arm of the church promoted community action by the laity on behalf of workers and the socially deprived, but without any political party affiliation. Early versions of this lay activism were reflective of the distributist ideas of G. K. Chesterton and Hilaire Belloc who advocated a redistribution of property from large corporations to the people. This was a variation on communist themes but without the violence of overthrowing or destroying representative democracy or the antipathy to religious institutions or belief.

Robert Menzies, in defending parliamentary democracy against communism, often condemned its atheist nature in contrast to Christian values. In a broadcast he made in July 1943, at a time when the USSR was the West's ally in the Second World War, he said: "… a liberal democracy is the best because it alone recognises the infinite variations of human nature and the unlimited potentialities of the individual human being. Communism in this country is the enemy of these things. It is illiberal, pagan, violent and essentially dictatorial. It does not believe in parliament."[2]

By the 1930s, such was the influence of the Soviet Comintern especially after the Soviet Union's entry into the League of Nations in 1934, that Catholic Action groups world wide recognised a battle was looming against the influence of communist fifth columns within organised labour, principally the trade unions. In Australia, in 1937, the Australian National Secretariat of Catholic Action (ANSCA) was formed under the authority of the Catholic bishops. The newspaper, the *Catholic Worker*, with its inaugural young editor B A Santamaria spread the lay gospel and attacked both communists and capitalists.

Before long, however, Santamaria began developing his own lay group, centred around covert activities linked with Catholic trade unionists. This collective would become known as The Movement. Working in secret, it was developed out of a small faction close to Santamaria and sought to enlist Catholic workers from organised labour to fight communists within the labour movement. In 1941-42, The Movement was given the formal support of Melbourne's Catholic Archbishop Daniel Mannix who also gave some financial backing.

Santamaria had been encouraged and helped to develop The Movement by Herbert Michael Cremean, deputy leader of the Victorian parliamentary Labor Party.[3] Cremean also connected Santamaria with J. V. (Vic) Stout, a non-Catholic and Secretary of the Melbourne Trades Hall Council. Stout would work with The Movement's Norm Lauritz to place operatives inside union meetings to help balance the numbers against communist infiltrators.[4]

The Movement would become the strongest of the various grouper protagonists inside the labour movement, assisted by a Catholic network of parishes and Catholic sodalities where contacts and members could be sourced and finances raised. In time the various small local groups became a secret network connected as The Movement and would develop ideas and strategies through education programs and meetings and with publications such as Santamaria's *News Weekly*. In its operations, The Movement copied its arch rival the Communist Party of Australia, albeit devoid of instructions from an offshore headquarters such as the Comintern or Cominform.

Other Labor Party inspired Industrial Groups sprang up during the Curtin Government years, one group centred on the Boot Trades led by Mick Jordan and Gil Hayes and D Lovegrove of the Fibrous Plasterers Union. Others were encouraged by the Curtin Government itself. All were connected with Vic Stout. In Sydney, Groupers worked to hold off communist infiltrators in the unions organised by R. King, Secretary of the Trades and Labor Council.[5] By the time the Communist Party dissolution legislation was before parliament in 1950, divisions between Groupers and the left within Labor were an open sore. While not great in numbers as MPs, the Groupers had control in the wider party in Victoria where in 1949 they had forced out the big man Pat Kennelly as secretary. Groupers were also increasingly influential in New South Wales where they had made an alliance with AWU national secretary Tom Dougherty.

It was not that all the anti-communist groups in the Labor Party were in favour of banning the Communist Party. Archbishop Mannix did not favour the CPA's dissolution and stuck with that view. But The Movement changed position. In his *Against The Tide*, Santamaria explains that initially his Movement followers were in favour of supporting the "No" vote but that position changed as a result of the increased intensity of the Korean War and the fact that there was confusion in the group being so opposed to communism while arguing that the CPA should be allowed to continue its subversive operations. As Santamaria concludes of the outcome of the referendum, "Dr Mannix believed that we should not move from our original position…In retrospect, he was right and we were wrong."[6]

Labor's anti-communists within the federal executive pushed in favour of the legislation being allowed to pass. Articles in *News Weekly* strongly favoured a "Yes" vote, even after the High Court challenge. As well, sensing Menzies' tactic of dividing Labor with the legislation by threatening a double dissolution election – apart from his firm belief the CPA was a dangerous threat at a time of encroaching Soviet and communist disruption – many feared the possibility of yet another Labor split such as had kept Labor from office for so many years in the past. At the time, it looked like Labor had a good chance of winning back government at the next election, due in 1952. Inflation was eating at household budgets and argument over the Communist Party dissolution bill was an unwanted distraction. If Labor let the bill through, it could win back government and reverse the ban later.

Bert Evatt had taken a long time to come around to the view that Labor should oppose the bill. Ironically, considering how the debate would play out over the next few years, Evatt believed it would not serve Labor to be identified with the CPA. Then, having reversed his view to support Chifley, he became an ardent opponent of the legislation. Hence, it was a bitter blow for both Chifley and Evatt having to accept the federal executive's directive to support the bill when Grouper influence in the larger states and a last minute change in the Western Australia votes on the national executive, pushed by electorally threatened WA Labor MP Tom Burke, forced Labor to vote the bill through in the Senate on 19 October 1950.[7]

Evatt's sudden announcement in the days following the bill's passing that he would take the brief in the High Court for the CPA controlled Waterside Workers Federation challenge to the legislation was yet another of Evatt's moves made regardless of party solidarity. Moves such as he had made on entering parliament in 1940-41 with his personal push for a national government against party policy. Now, Evatt would swing the debate for Labor over the next few years to one in opposition to the Menzies Government's war on communism rather than inflation, cost of living and issues affecting daily lives. He would win some of his battles but also cause Labor to do what he himself had warned against – identify itself with the CPA.

Immediately Evatt's advocacy for the WWF was public there was uproar in the House of Representatives where the Minister for Labour and National Service Harold Holt accused Evatt of being at odds with the vote of his party, and indeed himself, in favour of the Communist Party dissolution legislation. He was also giving "a sympathy and support for the cause which he seeks to defend on behalf of those for whom he appears". Taking the argument further, Holt concluded that Evatt "took this course with the full knowledge of the significance which would be attached to his actions, and with a reckless disregard of its consequences to his party, or he believed that what he was doing was justified in the eyes of his party".[8] Chifley defended Evatt saying a barrister had no right to refuse a brief on the grounds of having a differing view from the client; Menzies in the House said that the matter was entirely one for Evatt but added he himself would be very embarrassed if asked to argue a proposition contrary to the beliefs of his party colleagues.[9] Evatt replied shortly after that he was determined to perform his duty as a member of the bar.[10]

Meanwhile, raids on CPA offices were being carried out with Commonwealth Investigation Service police seizing books, pamphlets, documents and files in Sydney, Melbourne, Perth, Hobart and Darwin. In some offices, secretaries screamed or refused to hand over filing cabinet keys but for most it was something the party had been preparing for over a couple of years and anything really incriminating would not be found in a party office or headquarters or any operative's house.[11] In one case, at the home of a former secretary of the Communist Party's Darwin branch, the wife of the accused had a pile of literature ready and waiting saying: "I think this is what you want."[12] The raids were more a symbolic statement that the government was back in charge. And Menzies had only to await the High Court judgement which, if the challenge was successful, he would then call a double dissolution election with the aim of winning the numbers he needed in the Senate.

While Menzies set off for his first Commonwealth Prime Ministers conference over the Christmas parliamentary break, the government waited for a decision in the case before the High Court over the Communist Party dissolution legislation. Argument before the justices in Sydney had not gone easily for the government's case, led by Garfield Barwick. Connecting the disruption of communist influenced trade unions and the defence of an Australia at war was the nub of Barwick's case. It was Barwick's job to make this connection. Barwick had to convince the court that the CPA, following the orders of its Soviet masters and as a revolutionary fifth column, was at war with Australia, and vice versa.

Barwick fell back on the "recitals" in the Act that defined communism as a revolutionary army set out to establish a dictatorship of the proletariat. He argued that the court should just accept that was a situation of war. As David Marr has described it: "Barwick was, in effect, trying to freeze the High Court out of the process ... The argument began to take on the appearance of a great demarcation dispute between the pretentions of the parliament and the powers of the High Court. Though the judges were at pains to play this down, their hostility to these implications became plain."[13] Evatt's appearance, which followed, continued his style of long-winded pedantry over unairconditioned days in the court during Sydney's intense heat. But Barwick had much to make up, even as China entered the fighting in Korea. And he failed to do that.

When the verdict was handed down in Melbourne on 9 March 1951, only Chief Justice Latham supported the Act. It was a case of the majority judges disagreeing with parliament that Australia was at war. The High Court majority had decided Australia was not at war against a communist enemy. Yet, had the dissenting judges been given reliable proof of Australia's "at war" situation, they would have found the Act to have been valid. Evatt had won, not on account of his arguments against the Act but more because Barwick could not offer proof of Parliament's definition of a state of war.

Emotions rode high in the days before and after the High Court's decision. In Parliament, as the government awaited the result after four months of judicial consideration of the arguments, the forthright anti-communist Liberal Bill Wentworth tackled Bert Evatt in the House, saying: "The delays which are the Communists' main weapon at this moment are being cleverly co-ordinated in the courts and in the Parliament by the right honourable member for Barton (Dr. Evatt), who acts for the Communists in both places." On the day of the High Court decision, Evatt was on the attack in the House denying the charge; in response, Wentworth declared he would repeat his comments outside the House. In front of a number of MPs and members of the press, Wentworth said he had not accused Evatt of being a member of the CPA but that he did accuse him of "having too often adopted policies and tactics which were in fact in the Communist interest".[14] This line of argument would dog Evatt in the years to come.

Robert Menzies took a more considered approach, telling reporters as he left Canberra for Sydney, after the news came through, that he had yet to read the judgements and had not consulted with the Attorney-General. He did add, however, that it was not the end of the fight against communism, merely the beginning.[15] He could not have known how true his throw-away line would prove.

Within days of the High Court decision the gloves were off in the House of Representatives. By 13 March, Menzies was challenging Labor to fight a general election and the chamber was in uproar. Chifley accused Menzies of not being able to "take it" and Menzies, on a roll, chided the Opposition with being out to frustrate the business of government in the Senate, a "farce" that had to end. He was ready to welcome the "verdict of the people" who had witnessed an Opposition bent on a preference for "shabby expediency to the vital interests of government". The government, Menzies said, was seeking constitutional power to deal with not just communists but with "communist wreckers"[16] In other words, as Menzies put it, Labor was in bed with the CPA intent on wrecking Australia's economy. Menzies had opened his election campaign before an election had been announced.

The wrecking, as Menzies described Labor's work in the Senate, would give him the opportunity he needed for a double dissolution election. When Labor referred the government's Banking bill in the Senate to a select committee, soon after, Menzies sought and was granted a double dissolution election from Labor appointed Governor-General Sir William McKell, to be held on 18 April. As former Labor MP Fred Daly has written, "McKell, so bitterly attacked by Menzies and his colleagues on his appointment as Governor-General, had now sent Labor to the people. It was a great shock and disappointment."[17]

Evatt's appearance for the Watersiders in the High Court had not enhanced Labor's stocks with the electorate. Menzies would fight the election on the Communist issue which would dominate the campaign and cloud Labor's arguments that the Menzies Government had sat on its hands for more than a year doing nothing to ease galloping inflation. The anti-communist, but Labor leaning, *News Weekly* had sounded a warning about Evatt in February saying that not only had his efforts for the WWF before the High Court shown sympathy for communists but his antipathy to the US over Manus Island and the rearming of Japan, in the face of a belligerent Communist China, were signs that "the line taken by Dr Evatt runs parallel to that pursued by international communism".[18]

Opening his campaign in the Canterbury Memorial Hall on 3 April, Menzies outlined how his government – if re-elected – would deal with the Communist Party. He described communism as "a set of ideas quite foreign to our civilisation" and spoke of his detestation of what communists stood for, which made the crowd cheer.[19] He also emphasised the need for the government to win a majority in the Senate. These would become his major themes across all states as he campaigned over the weeks ahead. Whenever he touched on the problem of the rising cost of living, he blamed the communists in the unions that blocked production. When referring to his Labor Opposition, Menzies invariably named Bert Evatt as an example of Labor's softness on communism such as in a packed hall in Hurstville on 23 April where he said: "It is very hard to believe after a few years that Dr Evatt and his friends should be able to stand up in public and say, 'You have nothing to fear from the communists.'"[20] It would also not have gone unnoticed by Menzies' team that the Catholic Archbishop of Melbourne, Dr Daniel Mannix, had told an Hibernian Communion breakfast on Sunday 1 April, just two days before Menzies launched his campaign, that "electors must do the right thing for Australia by returning a government that would deal with the menace of communism".[21]

The Government had called the election in some haste. *The Sydney Morning Herald* reported on its front page the Labor seats where the Liberal Party was still finalising the pre-selections of its candidates. The party was not necessarily expecting to win these seats from Labor but in this election the more seats the party contested the better its prospects in the Senate election. This was an election designed to break the stranglehold on Labor's majority in the Senate where it was opposing significant government legislation. Commentators following the election were wont to opine that the 18 months of the Menzies Government had been a waste with no ability for the government to overcome its lack of numbers in the Senate. The Communist Party dissolution bill was at the top of the list. It would become an election campaign lacking any real contest between the parties over the major concerns of ordinary Australians, many of which were economic. But the sense of frustration was also seen to come from the frustration of the Coalition government by the opposition. Evatt spoke out against Menzies' policy speech launching his campaign, calling it a "necklace of negatives", but the Government's answer that the key factor affecting the economy was the Opposition with its link to radical unions and their damage to industrial peace hit home.[22]

Chifley was fighting his third federal election as party leader, an election battle that would sap his health. Still, a press photographer managed a convivial shot for *The Sydney Morning Herald* on 5 April, taken at Eagle Farm airport where PM Menzies, Ben Chifley and the state Labor premier Ned Hanlon had crossed paths on the election trail. Chatting together, the suited group all in hats gave no sign of their political tussle. It was an image not to be imagined had the contestants been Evatt and Menzies – their body language could not hide their enmity.

Menzies had thrown down the gauntlet poking at Labor's soft approach on communism. A supportive press gave its approval. *The Sydney Morning Herald's* editorial on 5 April, began with "As the leader of a great political party, Mr Chifley has remained strangely impervious to the realities of the international situation." Chifley's ignoring of these realities was referred to as "smug provincialism" which could be seen from Chifley's comments on Korea and defence. He did not recognise the "dangers" of the times. It went so far as to add that the only "apparent support" for Chifley's stance on Korea had come from the British communist *Daily Worker*.

With Menzies' accusation against Chifley and Labor as being fellow travellers with much of the communist spirit, the Labor leader was left sounding defensive and was forced to emphasise that Labor had been tough on communists; in government, Labor had dealt with communists under the *Crimes Act* and had established what Chifley called the Commonwealth Security Service.[23] It had also eventually agreed to pass the Communist Party dissolution bill in the Senate. As the campaign wore on, Chifley also became a victim of sophistry when trying to define the difference between good and bad communists. Menzies derided the idea as a "kind of rubbish".[24] Chifley was forced to define "good" communists as those of Spain as opposed to the communism of the Soviet Union with its police state.

Menzies, undaunted and sensing he had a reasonable chunk of the voting population on side, ploughed on with his message – undoubtedly helped by the actions of Labor's deputy leader Bert Evatt with his forceful arguments before the High Court on behalf Communist unions. Here was an illustration of what the PM was arguing.

Evatt was Labor's weak link throughout the 1951 election campaign. On the eve of voting day, Chifley was obliged to mount a defence of Evatt, saying, "He has his human failings but down through the years he fought for the underdog ... for civil rights and the maintenance of justice for all the people in the community."[25]

The Menzies Government was returned to office on election day on 28 April 1951. A loss of some five seats still left the Government with a 17-seat majority in the House of Representatives. In the Senate, the Coalition achieved its aim and won a majority of seats which would break the deadlock of opposition to its bills in the upper house. It was a triumph of strategy on Menzies's part delivered to him by Evatt's win for the communist unions in the High Court. As Paul Hasluck once wrote, "The leader is the man with the better bag of tricks."[26]

Evatt would hold his seat of Barton by just 233 votes against war hero Nancy Wake who had a few days before the election appeared in a bumper Anzac Day parade in Sydney. Wake had trimmed Evatt's margin in the 1949 election to 2644 votes, a seat where the normal Labor majority was estimated at some 10,000. In 1951, Wake came very close to winning and changing Australia's political history in remarkable ways. Such was the feeling that Evatt had not helped Labor in the election with his defence of the Watersiders, a *Sydney Morning Herald* reporter who had accompanied Chifley during the campaign wrote that the poor showing in his electorate and his unpopularity with many Labor members because of his "association with the Communist Party litigation" who felt that "Dr Evatt was a handicap in the election" meant that he could face "a struggle to retain his deputy leadership of the Federal Labor Party".[27] Meanwhile, the anti-communist *News Weekly* headlined "Labor Definitely Threw the Game Away!! Evatt was too Great a Handicap for the ALP"[28]

Labor as a party was by now far from the united team it had been in the days John Curtin and Ben Chifley had led Australia. The defeat in 1949 had been followed by a significant acceptance by the Government that the global threats had moved left in ways that many in the Labor left were not prepared to concede. Menzies had driven a stake through the divisions and Chifley could see a new leader would need to be adept in ways unforeseen. Fred Daly recalls how he would stroll with Chifley through the gum trees near Parliament House in those days when Canberra was still very much a country town. He began to notice his leader was slowing down and after the 1951 election, Daly suggested to Chif (as he called him) that he should consider retiring. Chifley had replied, "I'll wait for a few months as I want the right man to lead Labor and he may turn up within that time. Evatt's a brilliant man but I don't think he will make a successful leader."[29]

With the death of Ben Chifley on 13 June, just weeks later, Evatt was elected Labor's new parliamentary leader with Arthur Calwell deputy. Fred Daly has written that they were an odd pair to be leading the party and as different as chalk and cheese. They were about the same age and both ambitious with the prime ministership their object. They were competing for the ultimate prize but at the same time while supposedly working together as a team. As Daly saw it, "From the start they were pulling in the opposite directions and Evatt got the impression that Calwell was not giving him full support." But he added, "It is difficult to imagine anyone being a successful deputy to Evatt because he did not trust anybody. Once he had the position of power, he was a law unto himself. From the start, in my position as [parliamentary] Whip, I found the difficulties immense. Ultimately, I gave the job away."[30]

News Weekly welcomed and complimented the new Labor leader on his handling of Labor during Chifley's illness in 1950 saying, "Under Evatt, justice was not only done in Caucus debates, but also appeared to be done." It added that, "if Evatt and Calwell played their cards right", they would pass the test of leading Labor back from the mistakes of the past few years. Clearly, the editorship of the anti-communist *News Weekly* looked forward to a Labor Party ready to recognise the worth of its anti-communist activists.[31] The newspaper would report moves by Evatt to heal divisions with the Victorian Labor Executive (anti-communist control) in its next issue. The peace deal would not last long.

On 5 July, the day that the new bill to ban the Communist Party by way of referendum was introduced into the House of Representatives, the Federal Executive of the Labor Party, meeting in Canberra, voted by eight to four to oppose the referendum. The anti-communist bloc or "Yes" faction had lost. And the Labor Party was increasingly divided with Labor's Victorian executive voting four to one the same day to support the legislation. On 6 July, the debate in the House on the new bill went over old ground except that, with the High Court ruling having exposed the weaknesses in the original bill, the Government now opted to seek a general power to deal with "communists and communism" while seeking a specific power to legislate re the invalidated old Act and amend it before or after a referendum. As Leicester Webb opined:

> *By doing so it gave the Labour Party a colour of justification for another* volte face *and enabled the Labour campaigners to lead their opponents into a maze of legal argument which could only leave the electors baffled and suspicious.*[32]

In the House, new Labor leader Bert Evatt was in strident form, reaching for fresh heights of hyperbole against the new bill. It was "a direct frontal attack on all the established principles of British justice" and went much further than the Act found to be invalid by the High Court, while being "one of the most dangerous measures that has ever been submitted to the legislature of an English-speaking people". Picking apart sections of the legislation, Evatt argued that the terms of the bill were so loose that there were no barriers to having trade unionists or labour groups caught up in the ban. All of which led to extreme accusations. Egged on by an interjection from Labor colleague Daniel Curtin MP calling, "Did Hitler do that?", Evatt spoke of concentration camps and the inevitable outlawing of Labor MPs by the Communist Party dissolution legislation.[33] While Hitler did not legislate to change Germany's constitution, Robert Menzies would legislate to set up his own dictatorship. The debate to come would be very raw.

Menzies had chosen to go to a referendum on the Communist Party dissolution legislation after two failed attempts to have it become law. There was nothing much to recommend his third attempt for success except that the polls taken of the electorate's view suggested that the legislation was hugely popular. A Morgan Gallup Poll conducted in June - just three months out from the referendum on 22 September - suggested that 80 per cent of voters were in favour of the "Yes" case. By August, polling suggested nothing much had changed with 73 per cent of voters in favour of the referendum question.[34] Unsurprisingly Menzies was ready to take the chance on a win rather than back down as a loser.

Bert Evatt, meanwhile, was carving out a line that would damage Menzies in the referendum campaign where the "Yes" case would became caught in legal specifics. A line that was plain and simple, if hyperbolic. But developed around legislation on the books that would deny natural rights. And legislation coming from a prime minister who, while erudite, commanding and a great orator was also perceived to be aloof and intimidating.

At the same time as the referendum legislation was being debated, with Evatt's hard hitting accusations of the government that Menzies, in particular, was seeking to install dictatorial rule, the Menzies Government was passing – eventually by using the guillotine - the Defence Preparations Act. This Act, as one report put it, would allow the government to "make regulations for the control and diversion of national resources – including money, materials and facilities".[35] Menzies had explained that the legislation was to give the government far reaching powers to strengthen the Australian economy and organise resources in preparation for a possible major war by the end of 1953. "Freedom," he had added, "must be purchased at a great price."[36] Some have since argued the legislation was to help combat inflation.[37] This may have been part of the background. But the hostilities in Korea and the Cold War had sent global tensions swirling and the argument of the possibility of another world war was reasonable, and in many quarters believed. For all that, the Act was barely given effect over the years it prevailed and no world war did eventuate even as hostilities in Korea threatened to broaden.

What the legislation did do, nonetheless, was give Bert Evatt another platform to rail against Menzies' rule as dictatorial and increasingly absolute. Speaking in the House, Evatt called the legislation a "power grab" which would "transfer powers of the vaguest and widest character to the Executive Government and also to unspecified persons to make orders which are really laws".[38] In other words, Menzies was using arguments about a third world war to usurp the authority of parliament. Evatt argued that the bill "foreshadows a new system of peace-time government without the checks and balances of the parliamentary system. ... If we accept this bill, we shall also accept the proposition that Australia as a nation is in a permanent or indefinite state of war."[39]

Without making any specific reference, Evatt had linked his opposition to both the Communist Party dissolution legislation and the Defence Preparations legislation by dismissing the government's definition of war. Even as he spoke in the House, Evatt reminded his colleagues that the High Court had dismissed the 1950 Act to dissolve the CPA on such grounds. Clearly, Evatt was starting to develop a key plank of his case opposing the referendum question. This was a government hell bent on using a false definition of war by which it would seek power to rule absolutely against the freedoms of the Australian people. The cartoonists were ready, the pamphleteers had set their letterpress blocks, the journalists were ready to file - Menzies and Evatt were about to face each other and the Australian people in a unique contest.

An unknown *Sydney Morning Herald* cartoonist has Evatt dismayed at the open support he is receiving in the Communist Party Dissolution Referendum campaign from a communist Hammer & Sickle flag-waving dog. (*Sydney Morning Herald*, 22 August 1951).

"Yes" and "No" posters and cartoons (above and following pages) in the 1951 Referendum campaign. The "Yes" campaigners focused on the threat to Australia from communists within and outside the country. The "No" campaigners portrayed Menzies as a fascist and a supporter of Hitler's Nazi Gestapo.

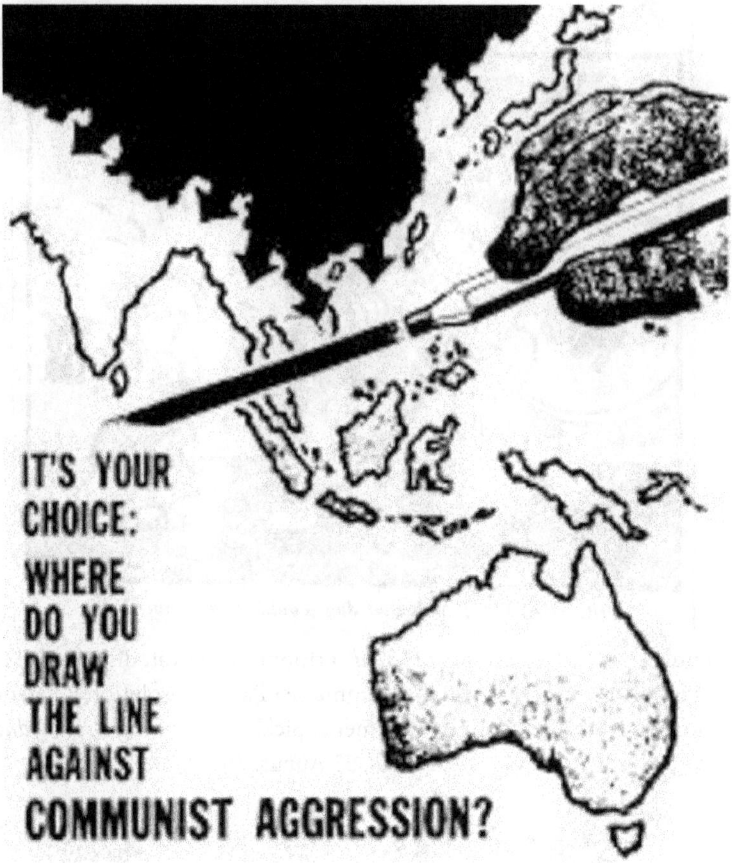
IT'S YOUR CHOICE:
WHERE DO YOU DRAW THE LINE AGAINST
COMMUNIST AGGRESSION?

WE DONT WANT FASCISM HERE!
VOTE NO
AND KEEP AUSTRALIA FREE
HOW TO VOTE
2 YES
1 NO

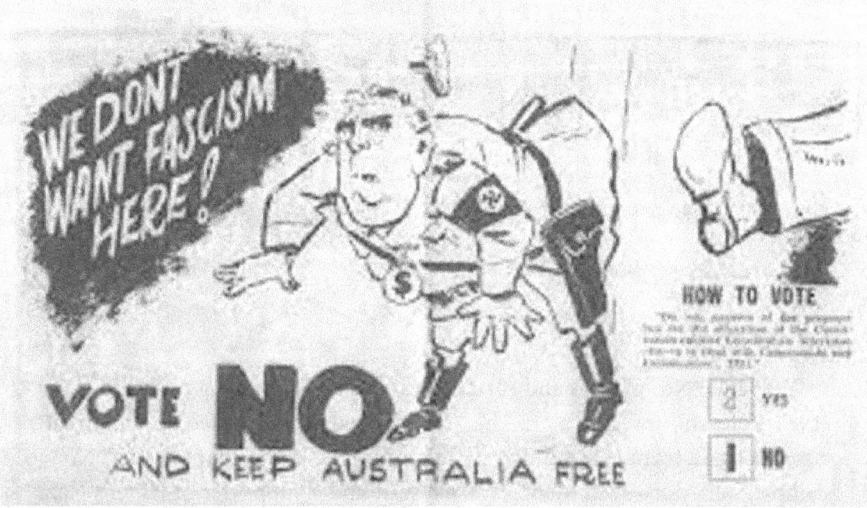

The August 1953 budget as seen by John Frith. A triumphant Menzies is carried off the football field by middle Australia as Arthur Calwell and Bert Evatt look on in frustration. The 1953 budget was evidence of the economic recovery which helped the Menzies government to its narrow victory over Labor in the May 1954 election. *The Herald* (Melbourne), 10 September 1953.

Cartoonist Ian Gall depicts Opposition leader Evatt's failure to cost Labor's promises in the 1954 election campaign. *The Courier Mail* (Brisbane), 19 May 1954.

7

Referendum Campaign 1951

Generalising from past referendums, one might say that a government has no chance of carrying a referendum proposal against party opposition unless it had, at the previous Commonwealth general election, a majority of total votes and a majority of votes in each of four states and unless there is a favourable electoral trend sufficient to counteract the inherent advantage enjoyed by the "No" case. By any such test as this, the Menzies Government had a poor chance of obtaining the powers it sought to deal with Communists and Communism. – Leicester Webb[1]

Over decades, the result of the 1951 referendum on the banning of the Australian Communist Party has been written up as a great victory for Labor leader Bert Evatt who led the campaign for the "No" case. In fact, the question to be asked is, rather, why was the win for the "No" case so close? In a high turnout of voters at over 95 per cent of all registered to vote, there was a total of 4,687,936 votes cast, of which 2,370,009 were for "No" (50.6 per cent) and 2,317,927 for "Yes" (49.4 per cent). New South Wales, Victoria and South Australia narrowly voted "No" and Queensland, Tasmania and Western Australia voted "Yes". Overall, the majority for "No" was just 52,082 votes. The highest vote for "Yes" was in Queensland where just under 56 per cent voted "Yes"; the highest vote for "No" was in New South Wales, Evatt's home state, with just under 53 per cent voting "No".

Undoubtedly, as the Morgan pollster reported, in early August there was an overwhelming majority for the "Yes" vote in all states. Six weeks later, that 73 per cent in favour had plummeted to 53 per cent. This left the Morgan pollster opining that, with such a trend continuing, the referendum result could be around 50:50.

Academic Murray Goot, analysing what happened, has argued that Morgan's early estimates were not wrong and, had the question at the referendum been put then, the result would have been a victory for the "Yes" campaign. But weeks of debate changed people's perspectives: "The shift reflected the way the framing of the issue was increasingly contested as the campaign unfolded. Support for banning the Communist Party remained widespread. But it was trumped by other considerations, from worries about taxation to concerns about the rights of individuals named as communists."[2]

Goot has also analysed the different styles of the two leaders' campaigns which were, he found, very different, arguing: "Menzies and Evatt campaigned with contrasting levels of intensity and self-discipline, travelled to different places, addressed dissimilar audiences deploying different approaches and used radio in quite distinctive ways."[3] In the mainstream press, Goot found that Menzies' speeches were widely reported in the dailies – newspapers which were overwhelmingly in favour of a "Yes" vote (13 to 2). But Evatt, in doing more stump speeches over a longer period and often in regional towns - over 30 of his speeches were reported in the dailies - this, even as the dailies disagreed with his case, was to his advantage overall. Menzies, meanwhile, delivered only ten speeches in the campaign.[4] This again raises the question, why was the result so close, especially when Australia's referendum failure record is taken into account?

As in all political campaigns, especially those for referendums, there was a great deal of hyperbole - exaggerated suppositions, some rational, many more emotive to tug at voter prejudice. Menzies had the "Red" menace; Evatt had the "totalitarian", loss of rights, threat. In a national broadcast on 12 September – 10 days out from voting day – Evatt emphasised the dictatorial nature of the legislation to ban the CPA and outlaw communists. Taking up his familiar line of argument that it would allow the government to not only define who was a communist but also widen that power to involve other groups, Evatt accused Menzies of seeking the powers of a "totalitarian" autocrat, all of which was an argument he used time and time again in his campaign against the referendum question. However, Evatt went further in this speech, addressing issues of more universal concern as if campaigning in a general election.

The referendum campaign, Evatt suggested in his broadcast of 12 September, was designed to distract voters from "vicious taxation" which the government was about to impose on salary earners as a result of the 1951 Budget to attack inflation. And there was the broken promise of putting value back into the pound. With this, how could voters believe in anything the government said. "What a wreck has been made of the stable Australian economy which they inherited from Mr Chifley," continued Evatt. He went on to condemn the Menzies/Fadden government for indirect taxation increases, the sacking of postal workers and increases in postal charges and in general making a mess of the economy, concluding, "What a government!! Almost intent on organising a depression in this country and forcing the states and private employers gradually to adopt a similar attitude. Even the ABC Band is threatened."

Judged from the wide range of condemnations in the Evatt broadcast, by mid-September, the contest over the Communist referendum question had broadened considerably. In his national broadcast, even the post war peace settlement or Treaty of San Francisco which Australia had just signed with Japan, along with 48 other nations, caused Evatt to decry the actions of the Menzies government. A government, he said, after Australia's war against Japanese Imperialism, that Menzies is "now so willing to receive with open arms".[5]

A report of the Evatt campaign on 9 September confirmed the Labor leader's interest in the referendum as being to make his mark as Labor leader. The correspondent travelling with Evatt wrote of how he had begun the campaign weeks earlier than the prime minister in order to "make contact with Labour leaders and trades union representatives in all states, and to make himself known to many Labor Party supporters who had not met him and were anxious to see the new Labor leader". The correspondent went on to confirm that Evatt agreed with the PM's criticism that he was fighting the referendum as if it were a federal election and he "made no excuses for doing so". However, some Labor Party supporters had confided to the correspondent on his travels with the Opposition leader that they were not happy with the campaign for "No" due to their "hatred of communism".[6]

Such was the heat and propaganda of the contest in the referendum campaign of 1951, alongside the personalities of the two leaders, within a couple of weeks of it beginning the political correspondent for the Fairfax *Sunday Herald* reported on 9 September that the campaign had become a "Menzies-Evatt duel". Menzies, the correspondent said, had become "stung by Dr Evatt's taunts about fascism and warmongering" so much so that, for the first time at a meeting in Brisbane on 8 September, Menzies had launched into "a bitter personal attack" on Evatt "far stronger than anything he had previously made". The correspondent continued, describing Menzies' use of his satirical phrase "the learned doctor" to refer to Evatt as losing its mocking tone, saying it had become more one where he was "not trying to raise laughs. He was not even being satirical. He was obviously hitting as hard as he could." [7]

Each leader had much at stake in the campaign. For Evatt, this was his time to convince party doubters that he was the leader they needed. He had dominated Labor's attack on the legislation in the House of Representatives, even as Chifley led the debate. Yet, elected to the leadership of the party, Evatt had worried some of the old hands at the top in this party of trade unionists and blue collar workers – this temperamental academic lawyer known for his fits of bad temper and egocentric spats, one who adhered to high minded legal principles of justice and the power of argument. While welcomed by the rank and file, his colleagues needed to see his ability to lead. At the Bathurst by-election following Chifley's death, Evatt came through even as his lack of diplomacy at times almost caught him out, such as his impatience at a Scottish piper playing him to the stage where he went from expletives to gracious thanks in a few minutes.[8]

Evatt was still an unknown quantity in August. The by-election for the seat of Balaclava (Melbourne) at the end of July had shown a slight drop in the Liberal vote in a safe Liberal seat. But, as the Melbourne *Herald* columnist E H Cox reminded readers, the by-election had not been fought on the communist issue as the federal election had been. Even so, Cox had observed that Labor figures were reflecting a confidence that the party could defeat Menzies' referendum proposals.[9] It was a referendum campaign where Evatt was on top of the arguments and the law. In anticipation of a dogged fight, Evatt began his campaign some two weeks ahead of Menzies on 17 August with a meeting in Cairns.

Meanwhile, Menzies had firmed in his belief that communism was a threat to a free society such as Australia, that the CPA's fifth column activities were designed to overthrow a democratic government in a quest for Soviet style socialism and, as his statement to the press on 19 August emphasised, communism had endangered Australia in actual war in East Asia.[10] Moreover, the federal election just months before had delivered a strong win and the Coalition had also won a majority in the Senate. There might be an expectation that inflation and the cost of living could threaten the government at the next election but the polls for the "Yes" case were strongly in favour.

Evatt was a new and untried Labor leader, whose advocacy in the law had not always proved convincing such as in the challenges to the Banking legislation that he had led. Menzies was also confident of his own persuasive abilities, and his fundamental grounding in the legal arguments supporting the proposal. He would let Evatt make a running and come in from behind. There was a lot happening in government – a Budget to bring down, the Korean War peace talks floundering, a new treaty with Japan and the curse of dogged inflation to counter. Menzies felt he had time on his side.

Menzies' biographer Allan Martin concedes that the "Yes" campaign did show something of complacency, in the campaigning - "Evatt outstripped Menzies in energy and dedication".[11]

As the campaign opened, seemingly with a disregard for the history of lost referendums and no doubt buoyed by the polls, the Prime Minister could not imagine losing to the "No" case. A day after launching the "Yes" campaign, however, Menzies might have paused in his confidence had he taken in the analysis of J A Alexander in the Melbourne *Herald*. In an article headed "Hard To Change The Rules", Alexander reminded readers of the many times referendums had failed to change the Australian Constitution, writing "The inelasticity of the Australian federal system, disclosed by 19 unsuccessful attempts in 40 years to amend the Constitution, has been the despair of non-Labor, as of Labor, governments." Citing one reason for referendum failure as the majority needed in a majority of states, Alexander pointed to the partisan, or party against party, nature of referendum campaigns as being another major reason for failure, adding: "Could prior agreement have been reached between governments and oppositions on the powers to be sought, no doubt amendments ... would have been secured long ago."[12] And so, another referendum campaign was about to go down in a divided party contest.

Before a large crowd, standing in the open air on Commonwealth Corner in Cairns on Friday 17 August, Evatt began making the fundamental points he would repeat over the coming weeks travelling across the country. Criss-crossing state borders, flying in and out of country centres, this was a man on a mission. And he was used to the hurley burley of meetings and journeying and making something of the chaos about him. In his years as External Affairs minister and Attorney-General, it had always been thus. He could flick his mood switches as the moments carried him forward. For a man who hated flying, Evatt's career as a foreign affairs minister and Labor leader suggested that whatever horrors he felt in the air, his overriding ambitions conquered all.

The Labor Party was "utterly opposed to communism", Evatt argued to a supportive crowd in Cairns, as the evening shadows lengthened, but that was not the question. The referendum was about accepting the Menzies Government's legislation to deal with communists, legislation that was "unnecessary, unjust and totalitarian and could threaten all minority groups". Invoking the name of a favourite Labor hero, Evatt called on people to heed the warning of Ben Chifley before he died that the powers the Menzies Government asked for would "injure groups and persons who had no connection whatever with Communism".[13] The following evening at another open air meeting, this time in Townsville at what locals called the "Tree of Knowledge" (not to be confused with the historic Labor site in Barcaldine), Evatt spoke in similar vein.[14] The message was plain, legally sound and worthy of notice. There was not, as yet, in Evatt's appeal any widening of the case against the government as a whole. Next stop was Melbourne, then Sydney. The referendum's voting day was still a month away.

In Sydney on Thursday 23 August, a crowd of some 2000 filled the Town Hall to listen to Evatt go through the "No" case arguments, technically and lucidly. It was a calm and appreciative crowd – there was no heckling as Evatt opened Labor's case for "No". The evening event caused little or no interest nationwide, with a respectful report in the local *Sydney Morning Herald* and only a brief mention in Brisbane's *Courier Mail* at the end of an article rebuffing rumours that deputy Labor leader Arthur Calwell was planning a challenge to Evatt's leadership. But reports of Evatt's earlier Melbourne referendum meeting in the South Melbourne Town Hall, on Tuesday 21 August, offered clues to where the rumours around a challenge to Evatt were coming from.

Anti-communist Grouper activity in Labor's Victorian division had split the Victorian party on the referendum with anti-communist Labor MPs avoiding any support for the "No" case. The anti-communist *News Weekly* was claiming that Calwell was hoping "to emerge as the 'non-extremist' who would lead the party back to public favour as a united body" should Evatt lose in his efforts against the referendum.[15] *The Herald*, before the meeting, had suggested that it would be a test of Labor unity if anti-communist Labor MPs did not appear at the opening of the "No" campaign in Melbourne. *The Herald* continued: "It has been claimed that a statement by any of them could have been used as a basis for a move to have them expelled from the party or from caucus."[16]

As all but predicted, two federal Labor MPs from Melbourne with anti-communist affiliations – Stan Keon and John (Jack) Mullens – did not attend Evatt's Melbourne meeting. For all that, as *The Argus* reported, Evatt was supported on the stage by a host of Labor heavies including "Mr A Calwell, deputy leader of the federal parliamentary party, Mr J Cain, state parliamentary leader, Messrs. Drakeford, Peters, Cremean, Crean, Bird and Bourke, MHRs and several Labor senators."[17] Labor, meanwhile, defended the two absent Labor MPs saying there was no compulsion on Labor operatives and members to attend. Arthur Calwell, protesting the rumours of a challenge to Evatt which he strongly denied, said that the two MPs were not "out of step" with Labor as their votes opposing the bill were recorded in parliament. In fact, when the vote on the bill was taken in parliament, both Keon and Mullens along with Cyril Chambers had been absent from the chamber.[18]

The challenge from anti-communist Labor to Evatt's campaign in Victoria continued in small bursts such as with former head of External Affairs John Burton, a doctrinaire left-winger, upset at having his appearance as principal speaker at a "No" rally, a week out from polling day, cancelled by the Victorian central executive. The reason given was that the Victorian party rule, introduced to keep out Eddie Ward at the federal election of 1949, banned interstate Labor speakers in Victoria without their own state executive's consent.[19] In John Burton's case he needed permission from the NSW executive. Burton protested that he had been cancelled because of the influence in Victoria of a section of the Victorian Labor Party that was "paying lip service to opposition to the referendum while secretly supporting its proposals".[20] The spat played out in local newspapers.

Victoria was not alone in having senior Labor figures divided over the referendum. *The Sydney Morning Herald* reported Evatt's meeting in Hobart on 24 August as his poorest with only the Minister for Lands, Eric Reece, in attendance for the state Labor government. There was no reason given for Labor Premier Robert Cosgrove's absence but it is possible Cosgrove had already sensed the mood of his state was apathy with regard to the referendum. He was a long serving premier in a small state, with authority in his own right. And, personally, he was opposed to the "No" case.[21]

On the Liberal side, Robert Menzies had his own dissenters. Even before his "Yes" campaign had been officially opened, a much publicised attack on the government's referendum proposal had been launched by young barrister Alan Missen, the Victorian Vice President of the Young Liberal and Country Movement. In an opinion piece published in *The Argus* on 22 August under the heading "The powers they seek are – totalitarian!", Missen said that while what he wrote was only an expression of his personal opinion, many members of the Young Liberal and Country Movement, the Melbourne University Liberal Club and other Liberal groups supported what he was saying.

While urging people to vote according to their consciences, Missen then proceeded to put arguments for a "No" vote, objecting to the proposals "from essential principles of democratic government". For Missen, a ban on the Communist Party such as there had been during the war years would only make martyrs of communists and be an "archaic and clumsy" weapon. He saw the triumph of Britain and the Allies in World War II as evidence that a democracy could "defeat the dictatorship without adopting dictatorial policies". And, sounding very much like the leader of the Opposition, Missen warned that the increase in Commonwealth powers gave the federal government "virtually unrestricted power to decide who are communists, what is a communist, what measures are necessary and what protection (if any) a person may have if unjustly declared a communist".[22]

At a meeting of the state executive of the Liberal and Country Party on 30 August, Missen was suspended from the party. The meeting of 40 Liberal and Country Party officials heard comments that both supported and condemned Missen's actions. Ivor Greenwood said, with some emotion, that a party with "liberal" to its name should be prepared to allow Mr Missen to think as he saw fit. Another said Missen was a "young bunny" who should be "rooted out of the pack".[23]

The divide in this referendum debate was developing to become a lot more than just a division along party lines. In a report in *The Argus* on 15 September, when the polls still favoured a "Yes" vote, divisions among university students said much about the emotions being stirred in the campaign. At a Students Representative Council meeting of 500 students during lunch hour the day before, at Melbourne University, the students voted 8 to 1 in support of a "No" vote. The meeting affirmed that the students rejected communism but considered the referendum proposals would "endanger the democratic rights of Australians". When a supporter of the referendum asked the meeting: "Do you honestly believe these powers will be abused?" he was answered by a loud chorus from the assembled students of "Yes".[24]

Former Liberal politician Michael Baume looks back on the debate as one that crossed all sorts of political divides. At the time, he had just graduated from Sydney University and was a member of the Labor Party. At university, he had been a follower of Philosophy's Challis Professor John Anderson who was a great promoter of free thought. "We were anti-communist," says Baume, "but also anti-authoritarian. ... Menzies who had appeared to be the rescuer from the authoritarian push – getting rid of petrol tax, getting rid of big government - was now banning the Communist

Party." Baume believes that Menzies' great mistake was to reverse the onus of proof for anyone "declared" a communist. This he felt solidified the violent opposition to the proposals, even for many anti-communists. He also believed a ban on the CPA would make it stronger, working from underground. Baume remembers attending rallies and handing out Labor leaflets. Twenty-five years later, at his Liberal Party pre-selection, when asked to explain his membership of the Labor Party he opined that in 1951 the Liberal Party seemed, to him, not all that "liberal" but over time it had changed.[25]

The Prime Minister opened the "Yes" campaign in the Canterbury Memorial Hall in Melbourne on the evening of Tuesday 4 September. Days before on 27 August, Evatt had arrived in Perth where correspondent Fred Coleman reported that the Opposition leader had already travelled to every state in Australia over some 11 days recording a distance of 9,000 miles or 800 miles a day.[26] Evatt's meetings were generally undisturbed by hecklers – and if anyone did try to heckle him they would be answered sharply by Evatt that interruptions only advanced the totalitarian cause. The entrance of the Prime Minister into the public campaign dramatically changed the mood. The meeting in the Canterbury Memorial Hall was a scene of chaotic demonstration.

As reported in an excited press the next day, headlines noted that some 30 men and six women had been ejected from the hall and Senator John Gorton had wrestled with one interjector, allegedly snatching at the man's collar and shouting. "Come outside, you yellow rat." Police were reported as dragging the senator away rather than the interjector.[27] In Brisbane, two days later, at another rowdy meeting, Menzies joked that he had brought the protestors with him from Sydney. Menzies' supporters cheered him as he began and well outnumbered the interjectors, but police were still needed, having found a shanghai on the floor – fortunately before it was used to attack the speaker. Police also broke up a fight between a communist and a supporter and removed a number of men and women from the audience, but no arrests were made.[28]

At a meeting of 2,000 listening to Menzies at Hurstville in Sydney on 17 September, the interjections continued from a hostile group among the largely supportive audience. Some 70 uniformed police lined the walls to keep order. Another 20 were present in plain clothes. Embattled and cheered, at the microphone Menzies fought on, saying: "At a time like this I wish to say to my occasionally doubting Liberal friends that to say to the Government it must have complete responsibility for the defence and security of our land and not have any power over the greatest enemy our country has is madness (Loud cheering)."[29]

Menzies had handled hecklers often in public meetings; but these scenes were well beyond his usual banter. He accused the protestors of trying to silence debate, he sometimes managed to keep the noise of the protests away from being heard on the radio broadcast, but nonetheless it was widely reported and observed that, on many occasions, whenever Menzies took to the stage a nasty exchange ensued. It certainly wore at him and ate away at his moods. These uproars at the PM's meetings could affect voters either way. They could have undermined Menzies' campaign as much as offered an illustration of the forces Menzies was trying to contain. Since many of the demonstrations were largely organised by radical unionists and their followers, no doubt the scenes could have been counter productive for the "No" vote. But in terms of promoting rational debate, as such, it was reasonable for Menzies to limit the rallies he spoke at. A third of his speeches were made in a studio and broadcast live, through radio.

As the campaign approached mid-point, the propaganda became more extreme. Especially in denigrating an imperious prime minister in the figure of Robert Menzies. Evatt had painted him as an authoritarian dictator using legislation to silence and ban his critics, turning Menzies' opposition to Communist and Nazi totalitarianism back on him. The man who said he opposed dictatorships was about to legislate his own. Both the legislation and Menzies' patriarchal presence encouraged this interpretation, however far-fetched. Former Australian PM John Howard recalled how his relatively conservative mother came to see Menzies in the referendum as wanting to take a sort of autocratic control.[30]

This then allowed the histrionic assertions of Evatt to take root. That Menzies was set on installing a jack boot dictatorship by reversing the safe guards of Australian law. Speaking in Perth on 27 August, Evatt reached for the Nazi analogy saying: "With Hitler, it was the Reds first and the Jews second, then the trade unions, then the Social Democratic party and, finally, the minority church groups. We should be warned in time lest the Police State appear in Australia."[31] Numerous Communist Party pamphlets picked up the theme depicting Menzies as a fascist or Nazi, a corpulent figure in a military uniform and heavy knee high boots giving Nazi salutes, in one as a shopkeeper offering a gun to a young boy with his mother while the shop has no food on its shelves. One leaflet picturing a Japanese soldier about to decapitate an Australian prisoner was captioned: "One of Menzies' friends … dealing a death blow to an Australian … don't let Menzies deal a death blow to Australia."[32]

Whether such Communist Party propaganda material found its way to the average Australian is hard to tell but, coming from the CPA, it could well have been a message too far and more likely to offend. But it did have ramifications for Labor. Before the campaign had begun, Lloyd Ross writing in the Melbourne *Herald* warned that CPA tactics were a danger for Labor. He opined that the CPA would use the referendum campaign to partner with Labor unless "Labor men consistently make clear that Labor opposes this referendum in the interests of liberal principles and not of communism."[33] A cartoon, titled "The Same Tune", in *The Sydney Morning Herald* on 22 August depicted the figures of Arthur Calwell (beating a huge drum marked "Vote No") and a shorter Evatt beside him (holding a bugle with a music sheet labelled "Referendum Blues") and a noisy dog – wearing a worker's cap with a communist hammer and sickle flag hanging from it - barking at them. The caption reads: DR EVATT: "I wish that dog would stop joining in!"[34] It was not surprising that in all his speeches, Evatt was at pains to stress that Labor was opposed to communism but that it could be tackled under the *Crimes Act* rather than the draconian legislation of the referendum proposals.

Australia in 1951 was a nation wedded to a Christian tradition, so much so that on page 2 of *The Argus* newspaper, in the last week of August 1951, a series called "I Believe" featured five Christian clergymen (albeit none Catholic) offering a column each day expressing a feature on each man's religious belief. The churches had great influence – not just with spiritual issues but with the everyday debates on politics and civil life. Significantly, in the 1951 referendum a few prominent clergymen might have had an impact.

Among Catholics, the somewhat revered Archbishop Daniel Mannix of Melbourne did not become part of the "No" campaign – as he had done in the conscription plebiscite of 1917 – but it was known that he was opposed to the referendum proposals. In Sydney, Cardinal Norman Gilroy said that it was up to Catholics to vote according to their conscience and acknowledged that both government and opposition were opposed to communism but differed in how to deal with it. He believed whatever the result of the referendum, the Government should take quick and effective action to deal with communism because "the people of Australia have clearly and repeatedly declared that that should be done".[35] Archbishop James Duhig of Brisbane, just days before the vote, came out with support for "Yes" – saying that he did not want to influence anyone but that was his personal preference. As he put it: "I do not think anyone who stands for communist principles can be loyal to Australia. I would not begrudge a government any powers it needed to curb the activities of communists."[36]

It was from among a small group of Anglicans that clerical comment on the referendum made most headlines. Begun by the Anglican Bishop of Canberra and Goulburn, the Right Rev E. H. Burgmann in his letter to the diocese at the end of August, his views stirred a sectarian spat that, looking back, was entirely without foundation. Burgmann, known for his soft left position on communism, argued that the referendum proposals had been pushed on the government by groups of "Roman Catholics". He was obviously referring to the Victorian (Catholic) Groupers, whom he described as "on the horns of a dilemma" with their church telling them to vote "Yes" and their political party to vote "No". He went on in the vein common to Protestant sectarians by referring to "Rome" when referring to Catholics, and saying Rome had "got both political parties on the spot". He cautioned that "Anglicans and others" needed to "awake in time and come to the rescue of our traditional British freedoms". If he was not heeded, he said, "Rome is likely to win a victory in this referendum that she will know how to use in the future".[37]

Burgmann was supported by Canon E J Davidson of St James church in Sydney and the debate took off in the letters pages of *The Sydney Morning Herald*. Sadly, the arguments were mostly about whether Rome would take control of Canberra rather than focusing on the real issues of the legislation. There was also considerable opposition from the Anglican hierarchy in Sydney to Burgmann's views. In Melbourne, Archbishop Mannix in an address given in the suburb of Bentleigh referred to "sectarians" who were asserting that Catholics had been instructed to vote "Yes". "If that is true," said the Archbishop, "They know more than I do." [38]

Across the nation, only *The Argus* of Melbourne among the major dailies supported the "No" case. Yet, reporting of the referendum debate was balanced and where Menzies made more front page news, this was as much because of the unruly meetings as the news interest of the Prime Minister's case. Editor Colin Bednall of *The Courier Mail*, writing to Evatt on 19 October well after the referendum result, assured Evatt that the *Courier Mail* had been even handed in reports on the referendum. Bednall wrote:

> *In the past Referendum campaign we actually provided in one issue 58 inches of editorial space for the presentation of your statement of policy, as opposed to 53 inches provided for the Prime Minister's statement. As for reporting of meetings addressed by you and by the Prime Minister, the division of editorial space was harder to handle because of the public interest in the unruly meetings of Mr Menzies. Most of the space taken up by the reportings of Mr Menzies' meetings, however, was concerned with descriptions of demonstrations, ejections, interruptions, etc. I do recall, however, that when you came to Brisbane, special action was taken to ensure that your much calmer meeting in the City Hall was prominently and fully reported on page one. I feel sure you will recall this report.*[39]

Radio was also important in the campaign and especially communicated with women. However, by far most people got their information on the referendum from newspapers. For all that, the front page headlines continued to be the issues of the day, both internationally and domestically, and these took precedence over a long running referendum campaign. Issues such as the Korean War, the Treaty with Japan, inflation and the price of butter, even Princess Margaret's 21st birthday and her father's ill health took precedence over those of the referendum campaign. Reports of the campaign, except for major moments, and its leaders were mostly column inches set further down on page one or later into the paper, along with an occasional editorial. But newspapers had saturation circulation. Three million papers a day went into the homes of a total population of five million voters.[40] Voters generally, well educated and not, were far more attuned to reading newspapers each day than they were in the audio-visual decades to come.

As in all political campaigns, the heat of the debate intensified during speeches and rallies in its last days. By the final week, Evatt was accusing Menzies of "hiding behind the capacious skirts of a few lawyers".[41] Just days earlier, at Griffith in NSW and taking up a bucolic theme, Evatt spoke of Menzies as "like a lazy neighbour who, to make his own job easier and to avoid the trouble of going along to the ordinary highway, demands from us a right-of-way through the middle of our homestead".[42] At Hurstville, on 17 September, as Menzies stood up to speak, an interjector shouted, "Heil Hitler." Menzies shot back: "You call me Hitler and Dr Evatt calls me Goebbels – make up your mind."[43] And so the campaign drew to an end with voters turning out in large numbers on Saturday 22 September and predictions of what had been a comfortable win for "Yes" by then a line ball outcome.

The referendum went down but strangely with a whimper rather than a grand announcement. The vote was so close it took days to conclude that indeed the "No" case had scraped home. *The Age,* announcing the win for "No" on its front page on the Monday morning after the vote, gave premature figures of the majority overall as more than double what it in fact became.[44] More important affairs quickly took the newspapers' interest – the King was ill and would emerge from surgery with a lung removed, inflation was the order of the day with the Budget under attack and the government strong in its defence.

Evatt had a new bounce in his stride. *The Argus,* the only prominent newspaper to support the "No" case, ran an editorial on Monday 24 September headed "Democracy Works". The editorial concluded: "… the referendum being over, the Government has no excuse for not getting right down to the economic and other tasks that have been waiting too long already".[45] The "No" case had won but the result being so close would leave any observer unclear on just what the message was. Australians were indeed split evenly, right down the middle, on the matter of how to deal with communists in their midst. Even the attempt of the Labor Opposition to make the last weeks an attack on the Menzies government as a whole had not delivered a clear message from the result.

The outcome also, ironically, saved Menzies from having to enact legislation which almost certainly would have been as divisive and unsettling to civic order as the hearings in the United States of America in the late 1940s and early 1950s, conducted to determine accused (declared) individuals' loyalty or otherwise to communism. Known as the McCarthyist hearings, they left a legacy that undermined the notions of liberty in a democratic community for decades. It had also cemented in Menzies the belief that a government should not go to the people for constitutional change via a referendum. Menzies would never again propose one, on any matter.

Meanwhile, Evatt had proved he could lead the Labor Party successfully. Except that he now risked being seen as soft on communist activity, even as he asserted that Labor had no time for communists. Moreover, with a win for the "No" case, Groupers such as Keon and Mullens, along with *News Weekly*, who had supported the case for "Yes", were viewed by Labor's federal executive as an enemy within, paving the way for serious friction and struggle within the Opposition. Added to this, elements of the union movement within the Labor Party continued to be active under the influence of the CPA. And, for all Evatt's reasoning that the means to overcome such influence was available to government, politics in the next few years would shake that argument. What followed would affect Evatt's career in ways he was yet to understand. All this in yet another round in his struggle with Menzies.

8

AN ELECTION WIN BY HOOK OR BY CROOK

Menzies stopped me outside Parliament House and said, "Thank you for that piece, I found it very interesting ... But you're wrong on one vital fact. Dr Evatt is not a great Australian, he's a great man for Evatt; he's not interested in power for Australia, he's interested in power for Evatt." I said, "What does that mean? Does that mean you're staying in politics a long time because you want to keep him out?" And, he said, "Most definitely. I would leave politics this 1954 but for Dr Evatt. He's a menace to Australia and he must be kept out of office by hook or by crook." The Menzies phrase which he used only when roused. – Journalist Frank Chamberlain speaking to Mel Pratt for The National Library of Australia[1]

The aftermath of the 1951 referendum saw Labor in an uplift of spirits marred only by recriminations from party headquarters over anti-communist Groupers in the Victorian and Tasmanian sections of the party who had aided the "Yes" campaign by opposing "No". Evatt had secured his leadership credentials, but division remained. In November, the Federal ALP executive censured members of the party who had defied the executive by refusing to campaign for a "No" vote in the referendum. Labor's anti-communist publication *News Weekly* – which had supported the "Yes" campaign - was proscribed, with members of the Labor Party who continued to assist with its distribution threatened with expulsion.

Around this time, tensions under any surface unity exploded in the House of Representatives in the early hours of 21 November when a row between Labor MPs Jack Mullens and Reg Pollard saw the Speaker Archie Cameron calling on the two men to settle their quarrels outside the House and ended with Pollard calling Mullens a "narrow-minded skunk" for any suggestion Pollard had defended communists.² While not obvious at the time, this was the division that would seal Evatt's fate a few years on - and that of the party.

For all that, Evatt was on a healing mission and determined to make peace with the anti-communist Groupers. After six months in the Labor wilderness, Evatt convinced the federal executive to lift the ban on *News Weekly*. Then, he began attempts to woo Bob Santamaria as a supporter. Looking back some three decades later, Santamaria reflected in detail how Evatt's behaviour made him uneasy. Santamaria was a unique combination of astute political player and a man of strongly held principles. He was not one to bend for a deal and, in 1954, he was by no means the well known name he would become but he had enormous sway within the Catholic anti-communist Groupers or Movement of which he was both a founder and organiser. Thus, he held great influence within anti-communist Labor cells, in Victoria especially.

In April 1953, Evatt had met Santamaria at a function in Melbourne's Exhibition Building and expressed a wish to make contact, which in February 1954 he did, arranging for them to meet at the Hotel Windsor. Santamaria had been wary of the move, but his mentor Archbishop Mannix encouraged him to go. In fact, Evatt met Santamaria on two occasions, one in Santamaria's Melbourne office, in the weeks leading up to the federal election. At the Windsor Hotel, in a discussion that continued for an hour, the "Doc" was sycophantic in his praise for Santamaria's writing and in pushing for Santamaria to work alongside him for a Labor victory at the coming federal election. As Santamaria put it, "The discussion in his suite began with the most outrageous flattery directed to the speech he had heard me give at the reception to the two Cardinals a year before ... that I had a knowledge of foreign affairs of which he would like to avail himself, as he expected to form a government. I suggested that one who had occupied his positions could learn little from me."³

Evatt continued to press Santamaria, even showing his complete support for The Movement's action to remove Pat Kennelly as federal secretary of the party, only offering reservations with regard to replacing Kennelly with Bill Colbourne. He further promised to expand immigration, make substantial funds available for land settlement programs, solve the financial problems of independent schools and make Keon a member of Cabinet. It was a shopping list to die for among Movement supporters but it did not fool Santamaria who felt it rather disgusting and went home and told his wife he had met a man without a soul. The second meeting in Santamaria's Gertrude Street offices a little later was much the same. A last request was for Santamaria to come to Canberra and assist with the preparation of his election policy speech – a request Santamaria declined.[4]

The anti-communist Groupers had won some important gains in the unions. Evatt knew that he needed to keep them onside if he was to maintain a sense of Labor unity and win the 1954 election. In 1951, the efforts of anti-communist union leader Laurie Short and his followers had seen him replace the CPA's E. W. Thornton, defeated as national secretary of the wealthy Federated Ironworkers Association - the Groupers were now in control. In Queensland, the Groupers had control of the Australian Workers Union, the Waterside Workers', Ironworkers' and Clerks' unions. Then, a combination of Groupers and the anti-communist AWU removed NSW state president Jack Ferguson. As John Murphy has written, "with substantial power in Victoria and New South Wales, and some in Queensland, the Groupers were in the ascendant in the ALP federally by late 1952".[5]

Commentators began to opine that Labor was set to win the next federal election. Prominent businessman and former financial journalist W. S. Robinson wrote to Evatt at the end of 1951, predicting a bright future for Labor, "You appear to have a comfortable grandstand seat from which to watch the mass suicide of your opponents." Robinson continued to feel the next election was Labor's to win a year later.⁶

Evatt did not attend the meetings in London following the death of King George VI in February 1952 - instead staying home, touring states and, later, adding his efforts to the state election campaigns in Western Australia, South Australia, Victoria and Queensland. In these state elections from December 1952 till March 1953, Labor increased its majorities, defeated its opposition to take government or, as in South Australia, wound back government numbers. In Victoria, the Cain Government won an outright majority, making this the first Labor majority in the state's lower house. Furthermore, two by-election results – the seat of Flinders on 18 October 1952 (Labor gain) and Werriwa on 29 November 1952 (huge Labor win for E. G. Whitlam) – saw the Liberal/Country Coalition fearful of losing its Senate majority in the half-Senate elections due in May 1953.

One reason for the Menzies Government's poor ratings in 1952-53 was undoubtedly the economy where inflation needed to be brought under control. And this, at a time when the government believed another world war seemed inevitable and had pushed forward the *Defence Preparations Act* to restore government powers to that of war time, if needed. War time, should it return, would also demand an increase in spending just when the government intended to squeeze back inflation. Thus, defence spending was increased in the 1951 Budget in line with government thinking regarding international tension.

The Budget of 1951, brought down days after the referendum vote on 26 September, was loosely described as the "Horror Budget". The Treasurer, Artie Fadden, said he made no apology for the increase in taxes – both direct and indirect – as inflation was a "whirlwind" sucking up income and jobs.⁷ The aim of the Budget stringencies was to create a surplus of more than £100 million to be paid into the National Debt Sinking Fund. In the year that followed, many voters were not happy. There were import restrictions, rising prices, unemployment at rates that, in 1951, seemed far too high and a crisis in Australia's balance of payments. Menzies forged on, travelling to Britain via the US in May 1952, ultimately to allay Britain's angst at Australia's import restrictions in its effort to stem inflation. Aside from that, there was debate over easing trading relations with Japan and the need to import more from its old enemy to address the trading imbalance. Evatt had much to attack the Menzies administration for and he did.

Menzies' biographer Allan Martin draws a portrait of a weary prime minister bearing up in the House of Representatives for its final sitting of 1952 while battling the effects of ill health to the extent that his departure for the Commonwealth Prime Ministers Economic conference in November-December, called by Sir Winston Churchill as an emergency over British economic and military decline and the United States' surging role in the world, had to be delayed. It was only Menzies' insistence that he go to Britain that saw off warnings against it from not only family and friends but the head of his own department, Allen Brown.[8] Meanwhile, as Evatt biographer Kylie Tennant writes, the "Doc" was at a new peak, having been labelled a "non-stop fighting machine" in Labor's *Century* magazine and going on to trim the Coalition's majority in the Senate to two in the May 1953 half Senate elections. As Tennant describes it, "Evatt was bringing Labour back to a position better than in 1943 under Curtin. In two years, this was an extraordinary achievement."[9]

With the Budget for 1953, however, a new tone entered the economic message. Good times were back. The 1953-54 Budget would be balanced, it was announced, with sales tax reductions to bring down prices and general relief for a nation having done the hard yards to beat inflation. The left leaning *Argus* in Melbourne her-alded the Treasurer's achievement in its editorial saying: "Hardly a home in the land can remain unaffected; hardly a business but must benefit in eased burdens." It added that it was "a much needed shot in the arm", except for its meagre handout to pensioners and war widows.[10] Menzies' first step to winning the federal election in 1954 had been taken.

The success of the Budget and its effect was not lost on journalist E. H. Cox writing in *The Herald* in Melbourne just above a cartoon labelled "Man of the Hour". The cartoon depicted a hugely happy Bob Menzies being carried from the field on the shoulders of a smartly dressed man and woman – representing happy voters. Under the PM's arm is a football marked "1953 Budget". Behind him, and scowling, are the figures of Evatt and Calwell as Menzies' defeated rivals, dressed in opposing colours. In E. H. Cox's comment, he acknowledged that the Budget would not be a quick fix for the government's popularity but that it would, in the months leading to the next election, do two things. It would confirm and accelerate a slow return of support for the Menzies Government while the full economic benefits from the Budget would be operating around the time of the election.[11] Menzies and his team had held strong through the economic punishment needed to curb inflation, even refusing numerous requests from British industry and government to remove the import quotas - all that, in order to offer financial thanks in time for the election campaign.

And so, federal election year 1954 opened. Popular consensus remained that the Menzies Government was on the way out. In spite of this, Labor anti-communist publication *News Weekly*, in its page 2 review of 1953, led with the following: "The year 1953 … saw a slow and steady shift of the political wind that looks like keeping the Menzies-Fadden Government in power in the federal election early this year."[12] This comment was encouraged by growing economic confidence generally, even before the visit to Australia between 3 February and 1 April of newly crowned Queen Elizabeth II which would give the Menzies Government two months of positive regal distraction bestowing beneficent feeling in the national mood. But even without the regal visit, *News Weekly*'s report pointed to the lack of sound economic policy in Labor's message. This would prove prophetic.

The 1953-54 Budget was having a good effect. And then there was the visit of Queen Elizabeth II and her good looking husband Prince Philip in days when the young couple were on a par with pop stars.

It is said that when the young Queen Elizabeth arrived in Farm Cove, Sydney on 3 February 1954 for a 58-day visit of Australia she stopped a nation. A million people watched from vantage points on and around the harbour from a city of 1.8 million inhabitants. Still more listened on their radios. The occasion was also filmed by AWA making it the first televised event in Australia, albeit just relayed to the Spastic Centre in Mosman. The tour marked the first

Queen Elizabeth II enters Parliament House accompanied by Prime Minister Robert Menzies on 15 February 1954. The tour of the then Princess and her husband Prince Philip, scheduled for March 1952, was postponed due to the death of George VI and her subsequent coronation. The rescheduled tour of the now Queen and Duke of Edinburgh ran from 3 February to 1 April 1954. It was followed by the federal election of 29 May 1954.
Photo: As depicted in Jane Connors' *Royal Visits to Australia* (National Library of Australia)

visit of a reigning British monarch to Australia – the couple visited 57 towns from Cairns in the north to Hobart in the south, Broken Hill in the arid inland and across to Perth where an outbreak of polio meant they could only eat and sleep on *The Gothic*, their personal ocean liner. In all states they travelled between regional towns and held gala events in the capital cities. The only major city they missed was Darwin.

They greeted crowds wherever they went, opening parliaments, unveiling the Australian-American Memorial in Canberra, circling showgrounds and parks in open cars where masses of schoolchildren assembled, performed or made massive welcome displays. They planted trees, waved to lined streets of well-wishers in capital cities and smaller settlements and carried out a hectic schedule from breakfast till way past dinner time. They were young and the nation was in love with them. Hosting their visit was a proud prime minister and six state premiers, most of whom were Labor. And while the PM had the front row position, to introduce and escort Her Majesty at major functions, the leader of the Opposition Bert Evatt was well in front of the crowds on numerous occasions.

So, it was not Menzies alone who basked in the bright lights of a royal tour. Labor leaders had their moments too. But the visit was a huge distraction from everyday concerns and pressing issues. It cast a joyous note over the stream of daily press reports, offered entertainment in glamorous photos of Her Majesty against an Australian backdrop while the bunting, streetlights and royal decorations captured the magic of the occasion, along with Movietone News at local cinemas. And it pumped millions into commercial coffers, whether it was producing the flood of souvenirs and publications, retail outlets making the most of the party going, or transport carriers, ice cream vendors and more besides. Australia had seen nothing like it.

As the glow of the visit subdued, commentators went back to hard-nosed assessments of the political play. E. H. Cox, in the Melbourne *Herald* could see Labor continuing to inch ahead of the Coalition but felt the field was still open, writing that the coming election was "likely to be to an unusual degree a personal struggle between the leaders". If the government was to win "the task will fall heavily on Mr Menzies during his 3½ weeks of whirlwind campaigning". He saw both Menzies and Evatt as successful campaigners – Evatt in the referendum of 1951 and Menzies in Queensland in the half Senate election of 1953 from where he saved his slim majority in the Senate.[13]

Over decades, disappointed Labor leaning historians and commentators looked back on the federal election of 1954 and claimed Menzies had "pulled a rabbit out of his hat" to gain advantage against Labor in an election campaign Labor had seemed likely to win. On 13 April, just weeks before voting day on 29 May, Menzies announced in the House of Representatives, that the Third Secretary and Consul in the Soviet Embassy in Canberra, Vladimir Petrov, had defected and had requested through ASIO to be given political asylum. Menzies made clear that he had only been informed of the development a few days earlier. The PM went on to announce that the government would immediately begin the process of setting up a Royal Commission to investigate espionage activities in Australia, stemming from surveillance by ASIO and information handed over by Petrov. The process would take time but the PM believed that the public was due this preliminary information, saying, "while it would have been agreeable for all of us to defer an appointment of such importance until after the new Parliament has been established, there can, as I am sure all parties here will agree, be no avoidable delay of investigation into what are already beginning to emerge as the outlines of systematic espionage and at least attempted subversion."[14]

Evatt was absent from parliament on the evening of 13 April, having left late that afternoon for Sydney where he was attending an annual reunion at his alma mater, Fort Street High School. Hearing of Menzies' announcement around 9 pm in Sydney, he was livid at not being informed in advance so that he could have stayed in Canberra to be in the House. Evatt's statement to the press the following day stressed that Labor stood shoulder to shoulder with the government and that if "any person in Australia has been guilty of espionage a Labor Government will see that he is prosecuted according to law".[15]

Evatt was certain the announcement of Petrov's defection had been timed in the last days of the parliamentary session before the election in order to boost the government's stocks as a strong force in protecting Australia's security. He wanted, as his private secretary for 20 years Alan Dalziel has written, to "be thought just as tough, just as ruthless, in dealing with spies and traitors as Menzies".[16] In hindsight, and after decades of research by historians of both the left and the right, it has been shown that Menzies had indeed not known of the defection until a few days before 13 April and, moreover, had little alternative than to go forward with a royal commission. As Menzies has written, only at the beginning of April did he learn of the defection and the name of the defector. He had been warned in February by head of ASIO Charles Spry that a defection was coming but ASIO gave no more information. The timing was entirely dependent on the Secret service. A meeting at the Lodge between the PM, Charles Spry, ASIO's Ron Richards who had handled the Petrov defection and an interpreter previewed the documents but as Menzies has written, "No attempt was made to conduct an exhaustive examination of the documents ... What I needed was a general understanding of the nature of the documents, and this I obtained."[17]

Having agreed to back the government over the setting up of a Royal Commission, Evatt believed there should be more than one commissioner appointed, to which Menzies immediately agreed. The terms of reference of the Royal Commission were approved without division of parliament. In the event, the election campaign would not be fought on the issue of Petrov, apart from a solitary mention by Fadden which was reported. The Petrov defection would be Evatt's post-election destiny and one which would cripple him. But in the campaign of 1954, Petrov was put aside.

What is important about Evatt's reaction to the announcement of Petrov's defection on 13 April, in Evatt's absence, is his anxiety to match the government in assuring voters he was as determined and capable as Menzies in dealing with espionage. However, after three days of strongly supporting the government's stand on Petrov and the commission, on Friday 16 April, Evatt launched an attack on Menzies in a statement to the press which accused the PM of "sly insinuations" and making a "crude attempt" to disparage the previous administration's Security service handling.

The *Sydney Morning Herald*'s Canberra correspondent waxed lyrical the following Tuesday, saying that, while restrained in public, Menzies and Evatt made no secret of their dislike for one another, but this personal attack by Evatt had "brought the old-world conventions of election campaigning to an end". It was the writer's belief that, with the Petrov defection announcement, Evatt had faced a "web partly woven by the blind workings of fate, partly by his political rival, Mr Menzies, and partly by himself". He went on to argue that Evatt had no doubt realised that by simply supporting the government "would probably make his defeat at the next election inevitable".[18] Thus he had put himself in the extraordinary position of agreeing with the government on the Royal Commission one day, while condemning it for setting it up a few days later. In fact, Menzies was true to his word in avoiding any reference to Petrov or the Commission in the election campaign. All Evatt did, at this early point in the campaign, was confuse electors and suggest he had ground to make up in his opposition to communism. Exactly what he wanted to avoid.

Well after the election, Evatt would allege conspiracies against him in the calling of the Commission. It begs the question whether the tag of being soft on communism, after leading the "No" vote campaign in the Communist Party dissolution referendum and his

High Court appearances for communist unions, had left a shadow Evatt wanted to avoid. In the press, as the Petrov defection became public, various commentators made predictions the Petrov affair was a gift for the Menzies Government. Their assumptions were that the drama would fill newspapers up to the election. But it did not. The serious revelations only came later; Evatt was mostly harmed by his intervention in the Commission well after the election.

One of the myths that has plagued the recorded history of the 1954 election has been the long held and over-stated belief that, somehow, Menzies stole his win from Evatt by using Petrov to push voters back to the Coalition. In fact, with the experience of elections over the next half century in Australia, it is possible to explain the voter shift in support from Labor to the Coalition in 1954 without any impact of the Petrov Royal Commission, as well as how the Menzies Government retained office, albeit with an estimated 49.3 per cent of the votes to Labor's 50.3 per cent. The 1954 election loss for Labor is comparable to the federal election in 1998 when Labor leader Kim Beazley managed a majority of the overall two-party preferred votes but failed to gain a majority of seats, at a time when the Howard Government was believed to be looking at defeat. So, how did Menzies defeat Evatt in 1954?

In the wash up of the publicity surrounding the Petrov defection, journalist Frank Chamberlain was one commentator who saw the affair advantaging Menzies. However, in one of his pieces he also noted that, even before the Petrov defection, government stocks were on the rise and the electoral mood had already been "moving ominously against Labor".[19] Evatt's strong suit on human rights, the law and social equality did not suggest experience in financial affairs. And, as the post war years of peace time development and expansion would demand, economics was coming into play with voter preference, in spite of concerns about global instability. Voters, faced with reconstruction in peace time around family life and employment opportunities, sought answers to inflation and the cost of living, a shortage of building materials and concerns about security, financial and otherwise, in the future. Menzies captured their hopes in his opposition to excessive government control with socialisation and his support for home ownership, alongside an appeal to women with his belief in solid family values and domestic harmony.[20]

On 4 May, at Melbourne's Canterbury Memorial Hall, Menzies opened his campaign before 1,000 supporters, with another 300 listening outside from amplifiers, saying that the government would stand on its record of combating inflation and strong defence with the added promise of government assistance for housing loans, an easing of the means tests for pensioners, tax reduction and an increase in pensions. He said he was "willing to be judged, not just upon new promises, but upon past promises faithfully performed."[21] He referred to the Labor Opposition as "destructive critics" and said that true development requires "private action" from people helping to build a great Australia. Leaving after the talk in his car, Menzies was mobbed by a crowd of 500.

Evatt opened his campaign on 6 May in Sydney's Hurstville before an equally enthusiastic crowd of supporters. It was a speech peppered with promises which he maintained could be paid for by using loans for development works rather than, as was the Coalition's way, using taxpayers' money. His government would end the means test for pensioners, increase pensions and child endowment, offer easy home loans with Housing Commission deposits as low as 3 per cent, abolish sales tax on household goods and furniture, abolish the property disqualification clause for aged pensions, use all petrol tax for road maintenance and much more. An editorial for *The Sydney Morning Herald* opined: "Dr Evatt's policy is not devoid of sound and progressive proposals. But they are overlain by the sheer bulk of the material designed to purchase Labor's entry to office."[22] The left leaning *Argus* added that Evatt had made "more promises to electors than any post-war Australian political leader"[23] The page 1 headline was "'Security for All' Labor's pledge, says Dr Evatt" It was a cute line.

Within days the debates had taken on a fiscal note. The Menzies team had costed Evatt's promises as double the figures Arthur Calwell had given in the hundreds of millions while Evatt argued back that conservative governments always haggled over the spending in peace time but were never worried about large expenditure in times of war.[24] He was correct about hefty government spending in war time but had forgotten that it was Labor which had had administered the treasury benches through most of World War II. Moreover, a Budget blowout was tempting inflation and money printing, at a time when the electorate was just beginning to recover from the consequences of that over the past two years. And so, the spending wars raged on in stump speeches from both leaders across the country. The *Canberra Times* editorialised five days out from election day that the campaign was drawing to a close "with attention almost entirely focussed on financial issues"[25]. Government spending was the key to the 1954 election so much so that one newspaper called it the "Gimme" election.[26]

Ten days out from election day, *The Courier Mail* ran a cartoon that captured much of the debate around uncosted Labor promises. It featured the "Doc" as an Aladdin genie holding up his big pot of money, the bank notes in the thousands falling from the skies around him. Headed "There's the Rub", a figure labelled "elector" looking on asked, "You wouldn't fall for this make-believe stuff, would you?" A signpost behind the genie figure indicates "This way to Aladdin's cave-in".[27] The election was close and tempers were sharp and edgy by the end of the campaign. But the debate was not over communism. The major divide in the 1954 election campaign was the economy. Menzies was standing on the government's record with more benefits to come; Evatt was promising a brighter government funded future that Labor maintained could be properly paid for by "using business methods and cutting out waste".[28]

The calculations for Labor's promises, however, did start to worry even those of a mind to support greater spending on government services and pensions. *The Argus* editorialised that "Dr

Evatt seems to be inexplicably reluctant to respond to the rising demand for information on what his social services programme will cost". The editorial went on to accept the need for Labor's attempt to increase the amount of social security but opined there was only one way to do it. That was to adopt a contributory scheme and no government could abolish the means test without such a levy.[29] On 10 May, opening his campaign in Melbourne's Prahran Town Hall, Labor MP for Fawkner Bill Bourke stated that Labor would have to revise its promises to abolish the means test. He was disciplined in a meeting at the Trades Hall shortly after and promised not to comment on the means test again.[30] But he had broken ranks and his views did not help his leader.

Five days before voting day, an editorial in the Melbourne *Age* crystalised the major question mark over Labor's promises. These, it said, were "a list of monetary increases which must inevitably lead to another burst of inflation". It added that the government could point to success in halting inflation and that there was plenty of evidence that costs and prices were under control. It had been government policy that had brought that about. The editorial concluded that the "increased spending power of the community which would flow from the Opposition's programme would cause immediate inflation."[31] The newspaper giant was undoubtedly for the government. It was a similar story in Sydney where *The Sydney Morning Herald* the following day editorialised in much the same way, going so far as to quote the late Labor hero Ben Chifley against Evatt when the former PM had said that it was "an illusion that social welfare and other benefits can be had by some easy method of finance. They must be paid for from taxation."[32] The leading newspapers of all the other states ran editorials backing the Menzies government and arguing that Evatt's promises would threaten Australia's economy. Moreover, Evatt had not explained how they would be paid for.

The Menzies Government was returned at the 1954 election but with a reduced majority. For all that, with a majority of seven in the House of Representatives and control of the Senate, this was a position governments seven decades on would have envied. The election count was slow owing to a number of seats hanging in the balance – there was no doubt the government had been returned, only by how much was uncertain. The Coalition picked up the seat of Flinders in Victoria from Labor, but Labor won five other seats from the Coalition – Bass (Tasmania), Griffith (Queensland), St George (NSW), Sturt (South Australia) and Swan (Western Australia) - to whittle down the government's majority. A young Malcolm Fraser, the future prime minister, failed to take the seat of Wannon by a matter of seventeen votes. Evatt, knocked by the result, took to saving face the Monday after voting day by arguing Labor had won a majority of the two-party preferred vote and he predicted a minority government.[33] His calculation of a swing to Labor of 2.5 per cent from the 1951 election, however, would prove to be optimistic. In fact, the swing was less than half a percentage point on the final count. It would take time for Evatt to register what had been lost.

Within a day, the Canberra correspondent in *The Sydney Morning Herald* was opining that Evatt had taken "calculated risks", but he was ready to face the first Caucus meeting after the election, nonetheless. He had much to explain, the correspondent argued, saying that Evatt as party leader, having often been criticised in the campaign for "trying to placate everyone" had then taken "complete charge, ignored party factions and sailed in an almost lone-handed policy". But he would survive. The piece ended with an assessment that now seems ironic, given what would follow for the Labor Party in 1955. The correspondent said that there was "no other leader in sight who could guarantee to take over and weld the party into unity".[34] Menzies for his part when questioned about the election results would simply say that he was waiting for the election to be over.

9

The Petrov Fallout

Labor-inclined historians are wrong to say the Petrov Commission was a creation, a manipulation, by Menzies. Menzies certainly would not have regretted it. But not even he could have expected the Labor Party to have played the issue as appallingly as Labor's leader at the time, Bert Evatt, did. – former NSW Labor premier Bob Carr[1]

It took some decades for Labor leaders and supporters to face the disappointing fact that Labor leader Bert Evatt had been his own worst enemy, and Labor's, in what happened to Labor during and after the Petrov Royal Commission. As with the legacy of former Labor Prime Minister Gough Whitlam years later, the tendency to revere such a brilliant mind among more mundane Labor operatives, clouded perspectives. For years Evatt's supporters lauded his brilliance and argued that his demise as Labor leader and loss in federal elections to Robert Menzies was all part of a devious conspiracy orchestrated by Menzies to bring the Labor leader down.

Allan Dalziel led the way, writing of his former boss as being a victim in the Petrov affair of "a carefully contrived political plot".[2] He went further, suggesting that the plot also involved the United States Central Intelligence Agency (CIA). As historians decades later would affirm, this was pure assertion on the part of such left leaning associates of Evatt, individuals who themselves would be caught up in the Petrov Commission. Later the Evatt fan club would add to such conspiracy theories. The aura around Evatt for these supporters came out of the belief that he was brilliant, far exceeding the ordinariness of his contemporaries. These Labor luminaries paid homage to Evatt who, as Dalziel has written, "was not one to be greatly moved by external evidence of supposedly great learning. He would laugh at the idea of Labor politicians like Kim Beazley with his B.A., and Gough Whitlam with his B.A. LL. B, being regarded as intellectuals. To him they were ordinary products of a comparatively minor university education; they had no distinguishing marks of true intellectualism".[3]

What all such supporters of Evatt had missed was that politics is not simply a game of intellectual prowess so much as the skill in managing both ideas and people and the system of government a political leader is selected to lead. Menzies could match Evatt in outstanding honours in his university studies, albeit not continuing, as Evatt did for a time, on an academic path, instead choosing work as a barrister and politician. Evatt, however, had been brought up by a mother who instilled in him a belief in the superiority of academic prizes. He conducted his career as a politician and minister very much in this vein. He was a sloppy manager, expecting his minders to clear up the messes he created – the eccentric genius who only needed to show he could persuade and argue with opponents in order to accomplish his ends. A performer on a political stage, enjoying a personality cult that took him forward. In the Petrov Commission, however, his political carelessness would be his stumbling block. Not least his naivety about the forces at play.

Menzies had set up the Royal Commission into Vladimir Petrov's defection just before parliament closed for the federal election on 14 April 1954. The defection brought dramatic headlines initially, only to be followed by even more sensational scenes on front pages of newspapers when Soviet embassy officials attempted to force Mrs Evdokia Petrov, who worked for the KGB, back to the Soviet Union, manhandling her onto a plane at Sydney's airport where she lost her shoe. At Darwin, she was given the opportunity to choose whether to defect and stay in Australia with her husband, or return to the USSR. She chose to stay. The saga of the Petrovs' defection, the Royal Commission and the fallout for the Labor Party would fill newspaper columns and historical articles and books for decades. The defection, we now know, brought important information to the West, unlocked Soviet secrets of significance and revealed the names of collaborators working for the Soviets.

The Petrovs were Soviet spies working as diplomats in Canberra. They had spent 20 years in Soviet security and intelligence. The defection was not brought about by any conspiracy on the part of ASIO or the Menzies Government but the fact that Vladimir Petrov was fearful of the change at the top in the Soviet Union. As supporters of Lavrentiy Beria, chief of the Soviet secret police who was arrested and executed in the chaos following Stalin's death in March 1953, the Petrovs' return to Russia was likely to see them eliminated. In a deal worked out over months with ASIO, which included a £5,000 payment for his living expenses and the assurance of political asylum, Petrov agreed to defect and hand over important documents on Soviet espionage occurring both in Australia and globally. The defection just happened to break the news as Menzies was about to call the 1954 election – a date the government had decided on long before, having chosen to go for a full term.

It was not until 17 May that the Royal Commission commenced its proceedings, having been delayed by the refusal of Labor's Cain Government in Victoria to allow a member of the Victorian judiciary to be part of the commission which was eventually presided over by justices W. F. L. Owen (Chairman), R. F. B. Philp and G. C. Ligertwood, judges of the New South Wales, Queensland and South Australian Supreme Courts respectively. References to the Commission in newspaper reports of opening remarks by Counsel Assisting Mr W. J. V. Windeyer QC referred to documents which "would show a general pattern of activities which were hostile to the Australian nation". Windeyer had added that recruits by the Soviet Union were sought among persons who were "ideological Communists", working as "junior civil servants, secretaries, clerks and in some cases journalists".[4] On the second day of the Commission's inquiry, Windeyer QC referred to the Petrov documents as identifying individuals who had been close to the Soviet embassy, even one Australian "who was prepared to sink in seeking to aid emissaries of a foreign power". What this person wrote for the Soviets, Windeyer said, was a "farrago of facts, falsity and filth".[5] On the third day, the Inquiry was adjourned until after the federal election. No names had been revealed. The election campaign, while occasionally raising the issue of communism in Coalition election ads, was devoid of debate about Petrov.

The investigation into the Petrov defection, and its Royal Commission, suffered initially from the denials of many of those named as collaborators with the Soviet Union along with Evatt's insistence the whole matter was a conspiracy hatched by the Menzies Government to bring down the Labor Party. Decades on, with the smokescreen of denial and conspiracy theories lifted by serious research, and the further release of crucial documents such as the Venona intercepts, official ASIO historian David Horner could write, "[as Robert Manne has shown] the royal commission was correct in its conclusion that the documents produced by Petrov were genuine, not forgeries … no further evidence has been found to suggest otherwise".[6] As to the timing of Petrov's defection, that had been Petrov's own decision and made to coincide with the arrival of his replacement from Moscow and before he had to return to the Soviet Union. As events unfolded, it had to be early April 1954.

Among the documents Petrov had surrendered to ASIO were papers that linked the Soviet embassy in Canberra with members of Dr Evatt's staff – his press secretary Fergus O'Sullivan, his private secretary Allan Dalziel and assistant private secretary Albert Grundeman. Information given by MI5 Liaison officer Derek Hamblen had also revealed that Petrov had made a strong suggestion that Australia's External Affairs department – of which Evatt had been Minister for many years – was thoroughly penetrated by a circle of Russian agents which appeared to include Allan Dalziel. Faced with this, Menzies immediately decided a Royal Commission was necessary. As Hamblen later reported, Menzies regarded the situation as "so serious that everything must be done in the national as distinct from political party interest to prevent Evatt becoming Prime Minister". Moreover, the government needed to pass the necessary legislation enabling the Royal Commission before parliament rose for the election campaign in case Labor won and "legal action would almost certainly be stilled".[7]

Evidence as it unfolded at the Petrov Royal Commission exploded across the front pages of newspapers, day after day, from Thursday 1 July. Election propaganda on the communist menace now found light of day and veracity as Petrov and his wife opened up about the espionage activities of the Soviet embassy in Canberra and its overarching Moscow headquarters. On the first day of hearings, Petrov spoke of the USSR's special directorate in Moscow for technical and atomic espionage, how officials serving overseas in official positions were watched by the Secret Police who sent reports back to Moscow, and then named a number of top Soviet officials with whom he had worked who had since been executed. The Commission had attracted a huge crowd in Melbourne with people queuing to seek admission more than half an hour before the doors opened. Photographers and journalists jostled on the pavement as each new car pulled up, but Petrov went through the Judges entrance flanked by security men and joined the courtroom almost unnoticed. When Windeyer QC asked for Petrov to be called, most people looked to the back doors while Petrov "slipped quietly from his seat" to take the stand.[8]

The revelations continued. Petrov spoke of the amounts he had paid for the fares of four Australian informers to travel to the USSR. At the request of the judges, he then wrote down the names of the individuals concerned. On viewing the names, the bench requested these not be made public at that stage. Agents had also been assigned to persuade former Russians living in Australia to return to the Soviet Union. The operation had not been very successful. Evdokia Petrov followed her husband to the stand. She had not known about his intention to defect and at first thought he had been kidnapped. Then she was imprisoned in the Soviet embassy and had been watched day and night while she feared for her life.[9] She was told that when she returned to the USSR she would be placed in a prison camp or executed.

One of the documents handed over by Petrov was labelled "Document J" – the document that Windeyer had referred to as containing a "farrago of facts, falsity and filth". This was believed to have been composed by communist journalist Rupert Lockwood. Evdokia Petrov, in a sworn testimony in the courtroom, revealed that the document had indeed been written by Lockwood and he had typed it in her husband's room in the Soviet embassy in Canberra. He had been paid £30 and given several bottles of brandy after he had finished the document.[10] For decades, Lockwood would deny he was the author of Document J and, at the Commission, even refused to answer the questions put to him. At one point he tried, through the High Court, to take a libel action against the Commonwealth about a matter put to the Commission by Windeyer QC. He would not die, however, without admitting the truth. In July 1995, during an interview with Australian academic Des Ball, at the Natimuk Bush Nursing Home near Horsham, Lockwood told Ball that he was the author of the complete text of Document J.[11]

A week after Evdokia's testimony about Lockwood writing Document J, the Commission heard that Document J had named three members of Dr Evatt's staff as the sources for some of the allegations it made – Dalziel, Grundeman and O'Sullivan. A series of denials would follow but Evatt was now part of the inquiry. Appearing before the Commission, having been dismissed from Evatt's staff a few days before, O'Sullivan denied being associated with Document J but admitted to being the author of another - Document H – which he said he had written to "help relationships between Australia and the Soviet Union". He admitted the document contained "untruths about the Canberra Press Gallery" but that his feelings about the document were "neutral" and that the issue had "assumed a sinister importance that was not intended".[12] As the names of Grundeman and Dalziel became public, Evatt wrote by telegram to the Royal

Commission attesting to the fact that his staff had strongly denied giving any information to the author of Document J and that the Commission in making their names public had made "defamatory and injurious imputations" about them. He went on to argue that the imputations had been made without evidence and he wanted his telegram embodied in the proceedings of the Commission".[13] While not advising his Labor colleagues immediately, Evatt had then decided he would appear for his staff before the Commission.

The tragedy of Evatt was that he firmly believed himself to be the "brilliant boy", that he was the master of a legal brief, indeed he had form if one forgot about the banking legislation. But, in 1954, as even sympathetic Evatt historians have observed, with his barrister brother ready to represent Evatt's staff before the Commission, "It would have been wiser to allow Clive to do a speedy job of clearing Dalziel and Grundeman, but Bert felt that his own future was at stake. So, H. V. Evatt confronted the Royal Commission for a considerable period of time in August."[14] The trap was set, but not by the Prime Minister. Evatt had set himself up.

The Petrov Commission and its effect was operating on two levels. There was the court and the testimony and then there was the political battle, as Evatt saw it, of bringing to light the devious plot Menzies had used to bring down the Labor Opposition. Evatt's firm belief was that the Government had staged the Petrov defection on the eve of the federal election, had gone on to win that election, stolen it in fact from Evatt, and now wanted to demolish the Opposition with smears from a couple of bolting Soviet spies out to gain what they could with fabricated documents. That's how Evatt saw it. And it was not a good frame of mind to be in when setting out on a brief before the three commissioners. Menzies just had to wait.

In the House of Representatives on the evening of Thursday 12 August, Menzies and Evatt tore at each other after Evatt asked four questions of Menzies over the payment to the Petrovs of £5000, information which Evatt had only just received. Menzies protested that he had no knowledge of the payment until 9 May during the election campaign and, as with all the other information he had on the Petrov defection – much of which was damaging to Evatt and his staff – he was acting as a generous campaigner by not disclosing what information he had. Had Menzies disclosed all he had known, he said, Dr Evatt would no longer be in his position as leader of his party. He described Evatt's statement and questions as not only "hysterical" but also as "containing, if I may borrow a term from another place, a farrago of ideas, closely following the normal Communist line about this royal commission". Going into more of Evatt's statement, Menzies held Evatt's view up for ridicule, throwing back his comments with, "[according to Dr Evatt] when the tangled skein of this matter is finally unravelled, the Petrov/Menzies Letters case will rank in Australian history as an equivalent to the notorious Zinoviff Letter which was used to defeat a Labour Government in the British election of 1924 or— and here is the cream of it — the burning of the Reichstag which ushered in the Hitler regime in 1933".[15]

Evatt returned fire, pointed, contemptuous and convinced, that Menzies had used the opening of the Royal Commission in the Albert Hall in Canberra to get maximum publicity during the election campaign, and that Petrov was more interested in the money and only handed over the documents after he got it – the implication being that the documents were fraudulent with an accusation the government had bought such documents "for the purpose of unduly influencing the people of Australia at the general elections". Evatt poured scorn on Menzies' notion that he had been generous in not revealing any of the Petrov information before the election – it had been his duty to share that information with the leader of the Opposition. And so it went.

Menzies held, strong and confident in the knowledge that he had not manipulated the defection of the Petrovs and that Evatt could only be manufacturing the scenario he posited to suit his delusions. Menzies had no doubt about the workings of the Soviet machine, its lies and its fifth column operations. He opposed it all and could never be as naïve about international demarcations as Evatt. As David McKnight has pointed out, Menzies' experienced political eye took in one important fact – "all the espionage trails led to or from the office of the man sitting opposite him each day at the despatch box of Parliament: Dr Herbert Evatt". And Evatt had been warned a year before by ASIO head Spry that some of his staff made "indiscreet remarks" and socialised with communists.[16]

It was as if Menzies was the cat playing with the mouse – his cautions to Evatt on a few occasions during their exchanges in the House on 12 August of "Be careful" might have been more than a caution over Evatt's choice of words. It was as if Menzies could see how Evatt was digging his own trench, bogged and muddy. That Evatt's demeanor was showing signs of losing the plot. After all, Menzies knew the documents were not false, that Petrov had brought significant information and that MI5 and other authorities beyond Australia were taking it very seriously. *The Age* reported on the debate of 12 August saying that, "For half an hour both party leaders indulged in unprecedently bitter and personal attacks."[17] In a packed chamber, Menzies had drawn loud cheers from his colleagues and jeers from the Opposition as the House debated the bill to strengthen the validity of the Petrov Royal Commission and provide penalties for certain listed contempts. On the day of the spat between Menzies and Evatt, the day after the bill was introduced, it passed both houses. Menzies was master of the parliament.

Evatt's appearance before the Commission on Monday 16 August as advocate for his two staffers caused a sensation in the press but disquiet in the Labor Party. Yet, as newspapers reported, a showdown would not happen until the full Caucus could meet, and the Senate was not sitting. The Caucus also wanted to assess Dr Evatt's intervention before any decision about it be made. From the outset, in a telegram to all Labor members, Evatt saw his role before the Commission as much more than a legal defence; it was a defence against Labor's political opponents – i.e., the Menzies Government.

It was an extraordinary beginning, not only because of the lack of consultation with party colleagues. During the first day before the Commission, Evatt demanded to be given extracts of Document J so that he could "see its physical composition and have it submitted for expert evidence tests". The report of his manner at the Commission referred to Evatt speaking excitedly, waving papers in the air and thumping the Bar table on two occasions.[18] A trusted source who was able to verify for David McKnight that Lockwood was the author of Document J also told him that "Evatt genuinely thought it was false and that O'Sullivan had written it".[19]

For three weeks Evatt was on leave from his duties as party leader as he appeared before the Royal Commission. The party continued to be divided over his intervention in the Commission as much because he had not consulted his colleagues as that his appearance at the Commission was seen by many as a bad move on his part. It had drawn attention to accusations his office was infiltrated by communist collaborators and his approach to his defence of the staffers increasingly took on political allegations beyond any support for their innocence.

Evatt's appearances ended abruptly when the Commissioners decided on 7 September that Evatt had exceeded his role as defence counsel in making political statements regarding the Commission outside in the public domain. This was the result of Evatt becoming hostile to the French Ambassador and the French government over their handling of one of their officers, a Madame Ollier, who had been named in the Petrov documents and whom they had removed for three months to New Caledonia. Aside from that, Evatt's dismissal most likely had much to do with the case he had developed in support of his two staffers which involved complicated tests he thought would prove that the Petrov documents were fabrications. Evatt had alleged that the Petrovs and Fergus O'Sullivan were parties to a conspiracy for "a local political purpose". In doing so, Evatt accused ASIO's Deputy Secretary for NSW Ron Richards of failing in his duty.

After hearing Evatt's evidence for his case, both Windeyer QC and J. A. Meagher (for O'Sullivan) criticised Evatt's logic – Meagher saying his case against O'Sullivan was "vague" and Windeyer that Evatt had not redeemed the "irrationality and incoherency of his allegations by the vehemence with which they were made".[20] At one point, as Evatt went on about his theories, Mr Justice Owen asked tersely: "Will you please answer our questions?" Later still, Evatt having accused Windeyer QC of making charges he had not made, Owen asked: "Will you please address us Dr Evatt?" Quite clearly, as with many of his other appearances before the bench over years, Evatt had worn out the Commissioners' patience. Then he overplayed his hand with the Madame Ollier case, and it was time to go.

Patience was wearing thin in the Labor Caucus as well. The election loss was a bitter pill. With the Petrov Commission and Evatt's distraction by it, not least his belief it had been the reason he had lost the election to Menzies, Labor was unable to sort out its strategy as an Opposition. Personal tensions surfaced from time to time in physical attacks. On 12 August, the press reported that at a Labor Party meeting in Canberra the evening before, Eddie Ward and Les Haylen came to blows and then went on to sit together later in the House of Representatives. At a similar party meeting in Canberra, on 8 September, Eddie Ward and Albert Thompson had to be pulled apart as they shouted at each other violently. At the heart of the agitation and fisticuffs was Eddie Ward, at the time convinced Evatt must go but not yet. The tussle in September had come after a long and emotional speech from Evatt about his appearance at the Royal Commission and Ward's attempt to move a vote of confidence in Evatt as leader. In his speech, Evatt had said he believed this was the greatest case of his career and that the Government would fall when the facts came out. He was reported as, at times, "trembling and almost tearful with emotion".[21]

The Petrov defection affair and the Commission's hearings had overtaken Evatt the politician. He had become obsessed by it. Following reports of the disorderly Caucus meeting on 8 September,

Evatt held a special press conference where he scoffed at the reports saying the meeting had been "one of the calmest he had ever attended". Sounding not so calm, however, he added that he was not attacking "you people" (the press) as he knew they got their information from "other people". Presumably he was suggesting paid informers. The report that appeared in the press was a "cooked report", he added.[22]

The press would have not been convinced. The same day, the Adelaide *News* carried an article headed "Is Dr Evatt facing a breakdown?" It reported that Evatt's press conference had been an "angry tirade" and that this was only one of the danger signs many had observed in his behaviour. It continued: "He seizes almost any opportunity to analyse the Petrov affair, shouting his conviction that the documents in the case are concoctions. Parliamentarians, officials, Pressmen and even House attendants report having been buttonholed by Dr Evatt."[23] It had also not gone unnoticed that during a parliamentary exchange in the House over the mundane matter of telephone services, a question from Eddie Ward to the Postmaster General had caused Evatt to interject twice with "Police state!" before the question was finished. When the Speaker asked him to withdraw, Evatt rebutted, "I suppose I ought to apologise to the police", before withdrawing unreservedly.[24]

The issue refused to go away. On 11 September, Evatt made a statement to the press that he wanted the Commission to be reconstituted on a broader basis with five justices not three. He must have known that this was whistling in the wind, but he was on a mission. He went on to accuse the commissioners of departing from the "safeguards of established judicial procedure".[25] Within days, with Evatt avoiding discussion in the weekly Caucus meeting, stories were breaking that he would return to the Commission and seek leave to appear further. Labor MPs were reported as being "staggered", others "incensed". The first they had heard of the move was from radio reports. He had not consulted any of his colleagues. By the time they heard of Evatt's plans, he had left Canberra for

Sydney. He had also cancelled his arrangements to fly to Darwin to join the Prime Minister for the opening of the Rum Jungle uranium ore treatment plant – another factor that angered his party colleagues.

On Thursday 16 September, Evatt presented himself at the Royal Commission on Espionage sitting in No 1 Court Darlinghurst Courthouse. He was cheered by supporters going in and coming out. His request to be reinstated as an advocate in the case for his two staffers was refused with the Commissioners saying that "nothing had occurred to change their opinion that Dr Evatt, as a politician, could not take the impersonal attitude they demanded from a barrister." He then asked permission to appear for himself, as a person on whom reflections were made in Document J. The Judges refused permission, Mr Justice Owen saying, "We cannot have anyone who holds certain views on the matter to appear at the Bar table and be allowed to represent himself. We would have half the population of Australia appearing at the Bar table and wanting to see Security documents."

During the course of the exchange between Evatt and the bench, Justice Ligertwood gave Evatt some plain speaking. He told Evatt he had spent the weekend going through the evidence and security documents connected to the Petrovs. He made clear he could not accept Evatt's assertion that the documents were fraudulent. He told Evatt his allegation was "fantastic" and went on to make that clearer saying: "I have read all the documents, the Moscow letters and any other relevant material and, I repeat, every one shows how fantastic is the allegation that they were forged for the purpose of injuring the Labor Party of Australia." The other justices immediately concurred.[26] While making it clear he protested strongly against the decision, Evatt stayed on in the court prompting his junior counsel Mr Sullivan and Mr Hill appearing for Lockwood.[27]

A week later Caucus, meeting in Canberra, was once more in heated discussion. Ted Peters from Victoria had put a motion to prevent Evatt as Leader of the Opposition from doing or saying anything about the Petrov defection without the party's approval. Victorian Bill Bourke, who had challenged the cost of Evatt's election promises during the campaign, declared that Evatt was "one of the Communists' greatest assets". West Australian Tom Burke accused Evatt of being "not a fit and proper person to be leader of the Labor Party". The charges and counter charges flew until reason prevailed and Peters withdrew his motion. It was generally accepted that if a vote had been taken Evatt had the numbers, but the discord and the accusations had shocked members.[28]

The Royal Commission on Espionage handed an interim report to Parliament in late October 1954. It found the Petrov papers to be legitimate, that the Soviet Embassy in Canberra had been used for espionage between 1943 and 1954, and that the only Australians who knowingly assisted Soviet espionage were communists. It recommended no prosecutions. On 28 October in the House of Representatives, Evatt spoke to his motion for the Report to be tabled and printed. Menzies allowed extra time for Evatt to make his case and sat back to hear the Leader of the Opposition restate the arguments he had put before the Justices of the Commission. Evatt was still arguing that the Petrov defection was a stitch up to bring down Evatt and his party, a conspiracy built around contaminated documents. He argued that in time it would be found Lockwood was not the sole author of Document J if he had written it at all – arguing "it was the Petrovs' story that he was, it is perfectly clear that they and the authors entered into an agreement for the purpose of producing this document".[29]

After 40 minutes of Evatt, it was time for Menzies to respond. On this occasion there were no sparks, just sardonic amusement. Menzies began by saying the House had witnessed a "very uncommon privilege". Its members had "heard counsel who has unsuccessfully advanced certain arguments before a tribunal have the opportunity to advance them for the second time before a tribunal which has not heard the witnesses and has not read the detailed evidence." In a mocking tone he added: "That is something I cannot remember in my fairly long experience of public affairs."[30]

Considering Evatt's complicated, conspiracy filled and unsuccessful arguments on the Petrovs, made before three senior justices, had gone down and with the indignity of being asked to stand down from being involved with the Commission, Menzies stood atop a diminishing opponent. His manner was superior and deprecating. He added to that by describing the impressive credentials of the three Commissioners who had decided against Evatt, their stature weighing heavily against the Opposition Leader's unproven allegations. But he stopped short of taking any of Evatt's bait, saying, "I am not re-arguing this case. This is not a court of appeal. This is a parliament." And he went on to make the point that the Parliament "has no material before it on which it could dare to disagree with those findings".

It was left for Menzies to luxuriate in a summary of what the Commission was set up to do and what its findings were. All of which gave the PM a chance to restate his role in bringing about the investigation into the Petrov affair, the soundness of the Petrovs' testimony and the conclusions of the Commissioners that Lockwood had been the author of Document J – even without needing to support that finding with the evidence from the Petrovs. The circle of Soviet friends had been spiked; Evatt had once employed one such friend as a press secretary. Menzies was also able to observe that the Commissioners had found that both Dalziel and Grundeman, in denying under oath their non-involvement with documents in the inquiry, could have pleaded their own innocence satisfactorily "but for the extraordinary course taken by Dr Evatt".[31]

Menzies finished by summing up Evatt's tragic part in the Commission and its outcome. Evatt had, Menzies said, been told by the Commission chairman "that if any other counsel appearing in the inquiry had made such statements about the Commission and about witnesses who gave evidence before it, the Commission would have committed that counsel for contempt". Menzies was on a roll. After years of being derided by Evatt for not being anywhere near the legal mind of the Doc, Menzies was taking revenge. Evatt, he believed, had confused – Menzies used the word "muddled" – his legal and political capacity. There was then just time to criticise Evatt's attack on the French in the Madame Ollier case which involved Australia's foreign relations and did not sit well for a former Minister for External Affairs. Which then left the PM to turn the screw. He described Evatt's motion as continuing his campaign of attack on the Commission and its justices, a campaign supported by the Communist press. Menzies finished by moving a motion, with half a minute to go for his allowed speaking time, that debate on the interim report be adjourned to the next sitting. To cries of "No!" from the Opposition, Menzies' motion was put to the House, overriding Evatt's, and passed on the numbers. Menzies and Evatt were still a sparing couple. But Evatt was now fetching much longer odds.

Postscript

The public debate over the Petrov Commission between supporters of Menzies and Evatt was for decades clouded by lack of incontrovertible evidence of the genuine nature of the Petrov documents and a myriad of conspiracy theories thrown at Menzies by opponents. For decades these theories persisted, so much so that in *Doc Evatt Patriot, Internationalist, Fighter and Scholar*, Ken Buckley, Barbara Dale and Wayne Edwards speculated that Menzies "could" have influenced the Commissioners in "unrecorded meetings or telephone calls". A suggestion that shows little knowledge of Robert Menzies who would never have breached the rules in such a way and who would, even so, have been cannily aware that any attempt to contact or influence a senior justice in a case would be completely counter-productive. They also argue that Evatt's not being allowed to continue to argue the details of his investigation of the documents, which he believed to be fraudulent, was "a travesty of justice" when the prosecution was permitted to attest to the documents' authenticity. This is drawing a very long bow. It was not a criminal trial. It also ignores the fact that Evatt was making the plight of his two staffers considerably more difficult by his actions rather than allowing them to just deny the allegations.[32]

The Petrov Commission, however, would continue to obsess Evatt and his supporters. So much so, that when the Royal Commission's final report was handed to Parliament in October 1955, many thought that there was still enough doubt over the findings of the Commission to allow Evatt to land a telling blow on the government. After all, the report had recommended no prosecutions. Some were now prepared to opine that this showed the defection was organised for political reasons. No doubt, such an atmosphere among his supporters in anticipating a revival for Evatt against Menzies encouraged him in what he then did.

There was no warning for those who helped Evatt prepare his speech. A speech that went for two hours in the House of Representatives on the evening of 19 October 1955. He told no one of his latest move. Leftist historian Brian Fitzpatrick had warned him not to get bogged down in details and to stick to the argument that the costly Royal Commission had all been a masquerade to exploit the defection and undermine Evatt and the ALP.[33] But Evatt believed he had a trump card up his sleeve. As reported on the front page of the left leaning *Argus* the following day the headline said it all – "I wanted to check the Petrov papers" EVATT WROTE TO MOLOTOV ... and he replied "They're false!" Telling this to a stunned House, a few minutes into his speech, Evatt explained that he did it because he "wanted to ascertain the truth of these grave matters".

Soviet Foreign Minister Molotov had given Evatt the answer he sought, replying that the documents handed over by the Petrovs "can only be, as it had been made clear at that time and as it was confirmed later, falsifications fabricated on the instructions of persons interested in the deterioration of the Soviet-Australian relations and in discrediting their political opponents." Whatever rationalisations followed from Evatt for the better part of two hours after this – amid interjections and laughter and a House the Speaker could barely control – nothing he said would prove his allegations about the documents. It mattered little. His case was lost with one false and manic move. Evatt had demonstrated not only his naivety and gullibility at believing anything the Soviet Foreign Minister might say about the Petrovs, he had now nailed his colours to the Soviet banner in being ready to believe a senior communist official in defence of his totalitarian government rather than the best of minds in Evatt's own country after viewing the evidence.

Menzies' reply to Evatt a few days later has been described by his biographer Allan Martin as not only one of his best speeches ever but also very cruel. Menzies held nothing back. Evatt had quite clearly lost Menzies' respect, not only as a politician but also as a lawyer and even as an opponent. Early on, Menzies asked "the House and the people to treat the whole of his [Evatt's] submissions as being either frivolous or offensive". He described Evatt's appearance before the Commission as a travesty saying:

> *He went through the motions of appearing before the commission as a lawyer. In reality, as the judges subsequently had to point out to him, he seemed to be appearing for himself, and to find it impossible to distinguish between his somewhat nominal functions as counsel for a couple of members of his staff, and his real function as the political exponent of points of view which, before the royal commission, made him the instant ally of Lockwood and Hill and all the other communists involved in the inquiry.*[34]

Writing of Evatt's Molotov "moment", biographer John Murphy opined, "... for many it was here Evatt's career ended."[35]

In his *Measure of The Years*, Robert Menzies reviewed the fateful episode of the Petrov defection. His description of the evening of the Molotov debacle noted it was "a dramatic occasion" with "gusts of laughter" from both sides of the House. And, as the derisive laughter continued, he noted the reactions of members of the Opposition, and concluded that it "boded ill for Evatt's future as their leader".[36]

From left: B.A. Santamaria, Minister for External Affairs Richard Casey, Bert Evatt, Cardinal Gregory Agagianian, Victorian Governor Sir Dallas Brooks, Cardinal Valerian Gracias and Archbishop Daniel Mannix during the reception for the visiting Catholic cardinals at the Exhibition Building Melbourne, April 1953. This was the first occasion when Evatt met Santamaria.

Photo: Melbourne Diocesan Historical Commission, taken from *The Advocate*

Evdokia and Vladimir Petrov in Australia in the mid-1950s. He was third secretary in the Soviet Union Embassy in Canberra. She was a highly skilled code breaker who had access to top-secret Soviet cables.

Photo: National Museum of Australia

Evdokia Petrov being escorted to a plane at Sydney's Mascot Airport on 19 April 1954 on her trip to Darwin on way to Moscow by two Soviet Union "couriers". She lost her right red shoe which was never found. Mrs Petrov asked for asylum at Darwin Airport and was freed from the Soviet operatives who were disarmed by Northern Territory police.
Photo: National Archives of Australia

Opposition leader Bert Evatt on the way to his ill-fated appearance at the Royal Commission on Espionage (the Petrov Royal Commission) circa mid-1954.
Photo: Bert Power

B.A. Santamaria, a brilliant orator, addressing a Sydney audience in the late 1950s. Evatt asked Santamaria to write Labor's foreign policy before the May 1954 election – the offer was declined. Photo: Australian Consolidated Press.

The Liberal Party's pitch for votes in the May 1954 election – a commitment to fight communism but no mention of the Petrov defection.

Dame Pattie and Sir Robert Menzies with granddaughter Edwina circa 1957. Photo: National Archives of Australia, A1200, 8363736

Bert Evatt and his American-born wife Mary Alice Evatt (née Sheffer). Mas, as she was called by some, was a loyal supporter of her husband until the end.

10

Endgame

In one of his histories, the late J L Hammond described how the speeches of Gladstone and Disraeli were listened to and discussed by working men in the industrial north with the passionate interest and criticism they now reserve for racehorses and football teams. It would be a gross exaggeration to suggest that Dr Evatt and Mr Menzies command the same interest and devotion in Australia, but when politics are discussed at all, their names are most frequently heard above the roar and argument in a public-house.
- John Douglas Pringle 1958[1]

While Evatt's Molotov moment in October 1955 was to mark his ultimate fall as Labor luminary, the destruction of Evatt as a Labor leader began well before. By 1954, Menzies had Evatt's measure, along with a sound reading and intuition of the mood and politics of the time. Conspiracy theorists might wrangle over the claim that Menzies exploited the communist menace, but communism was a real concern, regardless of the outcome of the Communist Party dissolution referendum. And, even here, the result was line ball to Evatt.

Chifley had been pushed to set up ASIO in the dying days of his government following perceived weaknesses on the part of Evatt and his department to guarantee secure management of confidential information. Menzies had reformed the fledgling service with the appointment of Charles Spry. The Petrov defection was encouraged by ASIO over many months. This was not a plot against the Labor Opposition but a security service doing its job. Had Evatt not been the captive of his theoretical leanings to soft left notions of liberalism, his suspicions about Menzies and the Petrov Royal Commission would not have happened.

That Evatt mishandled the Commission into Espionage had much to do with the fact that a number of his staff were inclined to a softness of approach with regard to the Soviet Union. This was certainly true of the Evatt staffers named in the Royal Commission but also of John Burton, Evatt's former private secretary and head of the External Affairs department from 1947 to 1951. Burton is regarded as having provided cover for Ian Milner's espionage activities with the Soviets while presiding over the External Affairs department. Burton's book *The Alternative*, published in the middle of 1954, argued that communist expansion in Asia should not be taken as aggression but had happened because of social circumstances. He believed communist influence in Asia could be solved by massive United Nations aid rather than containment through military deterrents.[2]

While knowing nothing of Ian Milner's nefarious activities and Burton's role in it, Evatt went along with Burton's soft left view of international affairs and tendency to mollify the actions of the Soviets from time to time. To some extent, as shown in his Molotov moment, Evatt saw the Soviets as just another part of the fabric of global government to be worked with. A United Nations approach. Order and world peace to be gained by negotiation rather than deterrence or the barriers of armed opposition.

Evatt's challenge to the government in the debate in the House of Representatives to ratify the Southeast Asian Treaty Organisation (SEATO) in November 1954 is reflective of his United Nations view of international relations. And it would not have gone unnoticed by his opponents, whether the Groupers or the government, that once again Evatt had singled out as unfair – as he saw it – the treatment of communism in the wording of the preamble. Tackling the wording, Evatt objected to the treaty's naming of "Communist aggression" as the fundamental force the treaty was designed to resist. Using the principles of the United Nations he argued:

> *Of course, if the regional agreement meant that it was to be opera-*

tive only against one type of aggression in the region, that is aggression where the aggressor is Communist, it would be contrary to the Charter of the United Nations because that Charter binds all members of the United Nations and it deals with regional arrangements. The Charter prescribes what such arrangements shall contain and provides that they must be concerned only with "the maintenance of international peace and security" in relation to the region. It only authorises regional agreements consistent with the "purposes and principles" of the United Nations.[3]

Significantly, in the debate on the treaty the following day, arch conservative MP Bill Wentworth accused the Opposition of putting two amendments to the treaty ratification legislation which he said would "give aid and comfort to the communists". He added a few moments later that he had seen "Dr Burton that notorious pro-communist … sneaking around the corridors of the Parliament" on the evening before.[4] Alan Watt in reviewing Evatt's stance on SEATO remarked that such was Evatt's disquiet at the reference on aggressors being only to communist aggression in the new treaty that he had suddenly "discovered considerable virtue in the ANZUS Treaty, which, when ANZUS was under discussion in Parliament, he had greeted without enthusiasm".[5] The Opposition amendments were defeated along party lines and the ratification of the treaty went forward.

Menzies saw Australia's strategic options quite differently from Evatt. For him, the world had dark areas that threatened democracy and the freedoms of the Western world. Those dark forces also threatened an old order that had been protected under the alliance between Britain and the United States. The colonial powers of Southeast Asia now faced radical dislodgement and Australia could be imperilled by a lack of allies in the region. From where Menzies stood, the only threat was from communism, already endangering stability in Indo-China which the Geneva Conference had just tried to resolve by division of Vietnam along the 17th parallel.

In his interview with Mel Pratt for the National Library of

Australia, journalist Frank Chamberlain threw light on the image Menzies wanted to convey of Australia to the world after taking office in December 1949. Chamberlain said that as he travelled with Menzies, he noted how in his early years as PM after 1949, he "courted" the press both at home and abroad because he wanted to "destroy what he called the Evatt image of Australia". Chamberlain, an old style Labor man who disliked Arthur Calwell intensely, believed Menzies was jealous that Evatt had received so much publicity in the United States and with the United Nations. Menzies had no interest in the UN and was inclined to scorn it.[6] Menzies was determined to leave a new imprint of where Australia stood internationally.

This division of perspective was not simply a gulf between Government and Opposition. With Evatt's reaction to the Petrov Commission, it was becoming a divide of an acrimonious nature within the Labor Party. Prior to the 1954 election, Evatt had conducted a charm offensive aimed at winning the support of what he thought of as Catholic Action around B A Santamaria's The Movement which largely backed Victorian Labor MPs like Mullens and Keon. The election lost, Evatt continued the goodwill with the Santamaria group for a time, in spite of being "incandescent with rage".[7] Then, friction stemming from Evatt's judgement over the Petrov Commission and his defence of his staffers named in the Petrov papers saw Victorian Bill Bourke (not a Santamaria friend) and West Australian Tom Burke take on Evatt in the Caucus over his associations with pro-communists, with details leaked to the press. The strain of the Commission's inquiries was to not only have a poor effect on Evatt's equilibrium, this was also starting to shake the Labor Caucus.

Where once the Groupers could rely on the support of Labor's leaders for their action in resisting communist activity in the unions, by 1954 most of the significant disruption had been overcome and the Industrial Groups no longer functioned as such. By 1946, the Groupers had taken control of the Melbourne Trades Hall

Council and by November 1946 the Trades and Labor Council in Sydney. By the time the Menzies Government had come to office, the CPA was well in decline even if still responsible for occasional disruption. For B. A. Santamaria, however, politics was about far more than preventing communist control of unions or parts of the Labor movement. Having set up his successful Movement, with its newspaper outlet and growing numbers of followers, Santamaria turned his attention to a broader program of influence over Labor in areas supported by Catholic teaching. To some Catholics this was merging religion and politics in dangerous ways, to others it was a reasonable expectation given the social justice principles enunciated by the church over decades. To these latter Catholics, Labor's promotion of fairness and opposition to the excesses of capitalism was a neat fit with Catholic social justice.

One of the features of John Burton's *The Alternative* was to make a direct attack on Catholic Action within the Labor Party, singling it out for having control over the pre-selection of candidates whom it would seek to ensure did not support socialist policies. Burton, the son of Methodist clergyman John Wear Burton, had been raised in a strong Protestant tradition. But it seems to have left him with somewhat prejudiced views and limited knowledge of the Catholic Church. In *The Alternative*, he seemed to be under the false impression that "Roman" Catholics – as he constantly called them – carried out their political activities under instructions from Rome as the communists did theirs from Moscow. Writing of Catholics in Australia as a major group of influence he drew parallels with the CPA: "… national Communist parties act in accord with the interests and even directions of Russia… This must apply equally to financial, religious and other groups which have close ties to with similar organisations in other countries."[8] His reference, in context, was "Roman" Catholics. He could not have been more wrongly informed but feeling along this line had become a growing sore within the Labor Party, as the influence of Catholic Groupers increased. It was, with Burton's influence, undoubtedly an influence on Evatt. The clash between Labor's socialisation ideals and anti-communism had become toxic.

In some ways, it was a battle of factions and personalities. But the smell of sectarianism also hung over the division. Labor's banning of any of its members being members of the Catholic Federation supporting state aid was not so far back in time. But the Groupers – Catholic Action and non Catholic – unlike the members of the Catholic Federation were, by the 1940s, a strongly supported part of the Labor Party, sponsored by Labor leaders. Certainly, there were Catholics in New South Wales who opposed the influence of Santamaria's Movement, such as Senator Jim Ormonde, but the strongest push back against the Catholic Groupers as they surged in success now came from members who distrusted a group of activists they saw associated with the Church of Rome. The old fear of permeation by an outside organisation took hold. Added to this was a sharply hitting speech made by Santamaria in early 1954 arguing for The Movement to take on the "Chifley legend" stance that opposed any position the Groupers put against anti-American positions. He called for a "Curtin legend" instead that was pro-American. As Robert Murray has written, "Within a few months, Santamaria was to be dubbed throughout the country as the man who had not only tried to subvert the Labor Party but, perhaps worse crime, the 'Chifley legend' as well."[9]

The history of what happened to Labor in the 1950s has been recorded in numerous books and articles. All interested parties now readily accept that the first shot – made by a press statement - in the internecine war that followed and led to the great Labor split was fired by Evatt on 5 October 1954.

The festering anger over Evatt's performance at the Royal Commission among the anti-communist MPs and supporters had spilled over at the Caucus meeting in Canberra on 22 September. An attempt to pass a motion to prevent Evatt from dealing with or making statements about the Commission without the parliamentary Labor Party's approval was put by Ted Peters from Victoria. The motion was aborted after Evatt "pleaded" with Peters not to go ahead with it and after assuring the Caucus he would not be appearing before the Commission again.[10] Tensions were extremely frayed with Bill Bourke of Victoria calling Evatt a "liar".

Parliament did not sit during the week beginning Monday 4 October. There was no Caucus meeting that week. Instead, on the evening of Tuesday 5 October, Evatt issued a statement denouncing a "subversive" element that was part of a minority group principally operating from Victoria. He would see to it that "appropriate action" was taken by the Federal Labor conference meeting in January 1955. He did not name any MPs but did single out *News Weekly* which immediately gave the mainstream press licence to argue that Evatt was referring to the Catholic groups centred on B. A. Santamaria.

The accusations Evatt made against these "traitors" was that they were organised much the same as communists or fascists, as if the way an organisation operates is the key to its threatening presence. Evatt's statement made no substantial charge as to how the aims of these groups were "subversive" except to have publicly contradicted their party leader over various policies. But, unlike activities of the communists, these secret meetings organised around Santamaria's Movement were not taking orders from any outside central headquarters such as the CPA did from Moscow, nor were the aims of The Movement at odds with democratic policy.

Evatt's statement concerned mainly the fact that the accused "element" he was attacking had not supported all of Labor's policies.[11] Viewed from seven decades later, in a world where opposing views are common in all political parties, and made public, Evatt's statement seems to have been hasty and badly advised. When Evatt had made contact with Santamaria in April 1954, Santamaria, as political historian Gerard Henderson has noted, "was not a public figure … and his influence on the outcome of any election would have been close to negligible".[12] In time, Evatt would blame Bill Bourke for Labor's loss of the 1954 election. During the campaign, on one occasion, Bourke admitted that some of Evatt's promises could not be funded.

It has always been former PM John Howard's argument that had the Labor Party operated under the administrative structure of the Liberal Party of Australia, the devastating 1950s Labor Split would not have happened. The Liberal Party's national executive does not have the power to dismiss a state division or branch. But Labor was different. And Evatt was ropeable. And in no mind to accept that his actions in the Petrov Royal Commission should be considered part of the problem.

So, Evatt, the leader who believed in liberalism and negotiated means to resolve disputes, was about to switch to an authoritarian stance against those whom he no longer could win over by argument. At his instigation, the Labor Party was about to go on a purge of dissidents much like what Evatt had argued was a breach of individual liberty during the 1951 referendum campaign. Members and branches would be named and expelled. In the case of paid operatives and eventually MPs, many individuals named would lose their jobs and livelihoods. Within days, the press was reporting that Evatt had begun a crisis for Labor, bigger than anything it had experienced in 20 years. Although, as it would transpire, that was nowhere near as bad as it became.

What followed Evatt's jaw dropping statement, as parliament resumed and Caucus met (explosively) on 13 October, was a motion proposed for a leadership spill. As the Caucus debated, emotions inflamed, the motion was held over until the following week's meeting on 20 October. This had given Evatt time to gather support but, when the Caucus met again, inflamed emotions became uproar. After Eddie Ward – now supporting Evatt strongly – called for a division, Evatt climbed on to a table so as to be seen and yelled "Take down their names".[13] This, according to Labor whip

Gil Duthie caused six MPs to change sides to the Evatt camp. The motion to declare the leadership position "vacant" had been proposed by West Australian Tom Burke. The vote went against Evatt's opponents 28 to 52. Fred Daly, in a graphic account of the meeting, concluded that what he saw of Evatt that day suggested he was enjoying the moment. As Daly put it, "It was Evatt and Ward at their hating best ... It was a degrading and disgusting spectacle – 28 members lined up like Japanese war criminals by colleagues with hate, vindictiveness and triumph written all over their faces."[14]

Peter Crockett has written that Evatt was not the best person to judge the effect of his move to remove the anti-communist elements in Labor. According to Crockett, "Evatt did not believe that a split would materialise, anticipating that dissent would be contained by eliminating disloyal elements so that the party's electoral popularity would be restored."[15] A difference of opinion between Evatt and Labor's Member for Eden-Monaro Allan Fraser made the front page of *The Canberra Times* on 11 October. Fraser believed that the Labor Party was in danger of disintegrating if the current disruption continued and warned against sectarianism in the party. Evatt responded assuring the public that Fraser was "wide of the mark" and that just because voters were troubled it was no help "to describe the disturbance as a hurricane". He continued, dismissing Fraser's anguish at the delight Labor had given its opponents, saying, "[the Government] may receive apparent temporary advantage from such a situation in the Labor Party but Labor must put its own house in order first". When this was done, the stocks of Labor would soar to remarkable heights.[16]

Murphy poses the question of whether any other leader might have held Labor together. A reasonable query. Murphy seems to think not and offers Fred Daly's opinion that when Chifley died the only man capable of preventing another Labor split had gone. But it does beg the question whether if Arthur Calwell had assumed the leadership, after the defeat at the 1954 election, he might have offered hope and a more likely patch up of differences. For the anti-communist Groupers, Evatt was anathema and his behaviour in the Petrov Royal Commission even more evidence of his failures as leader. Removed, there could have been some headway towards reason. With the next election scheduled for 1957, a new leader after the 1954 defeat could have brought Labor to a winning position, having been given almost three years to settle in. Menzies was not then the popular leader he was to become after years of success.

Stan Keon and George Cole had approached Arthur Calwell before the 13 October Caucus meeting to encourage him to stand if a spill was voted for. Calwell had the support of Allan Fraser who would stand as deputy. However, neither Calwell nor Fraser addressed the meeting and the spill was held over allowing Evatt to regroup. Gerard Henderson argues that "Calwell was not prepared to take on Evatt when Evatt was most vulnerable."[17] Fred Daly is more specific, from his vantage point at the time, writing: "Calwell played a pathetic part in those years; hesitant, uncertain and waiting for Evatt's job. He did so little when he could have done so much."[18] The moment gone, too many in the party were mesmerised by the reputation of the "Doc" as a great mind. They were not prepared to accept that he was a poor leader. As his colleague Kim Beazley senior, who could recognise his talents, put it, "… political leadership is an area in which character weaknesses are mercilessly exposed, and Evatt had his share of weaknesses".[19]

With Calwell as leader from the election defeat of 1954, there would not have been the fallout from the Petrov Commission – which Labor had supported. There would have been none of the pique associated with Evatt's vanity involvement on behalf of his named staffers at the Royal Commission which cruelled the Labor image. Calwell could have made concessions to the anti-communist Victorians who were from his home state, concessions that would not necessarily have upset Labor principles or mainstream policy. They were opposed to communism, not seeking to bring down the Westminster system. As Paul Strangio, after intense study of Victorian Labor, has pointed out, "the reality is that few of the major players were ideological warriors. Santamaria is an important exception".[20] It is worth noting that in the vote after the division on 20 October, both Deputy Leader Calwell and Deputy Leader in the Senate John Anderson voted with the 28 anti-communists.

What happened next has all been duly written about, analysed and recorded elsewhere. Labor's Victorian Executive and Labor members who supported the anti-communist Groupers were replaced by the instalment of a new Victorian executive. At the Hobart conference in March 1955 two Victorian executives arrived with the old executive hoodwinked into formal expulsion. Evatt continued to seek revenge long after the Hobart conference. In summary, six Victorian MHRs left the Caucus, joined later by Senator George Cole from Tasmania, while state legislatures were also affected.

On 7 April, the "new" Victorian executive began its purge, expelling councillors, endorsed candidates and parliamentarians. Eighteen state MPs were expelled along with six federal members who joined the already expelled Mullens. Then the "new" executive instructed that since a number of branches had failed to pledge complete recognition of the "new" executive, they were now regarded as having automatically forfeited membership. Seventy-eight branches were declared "bogus" with the remaining loyal members asked to rebuild them.[21] Revenge could not come quickly enough for the purged MPs. On 19 April, the expelled state Labor MPs sided with Henry Bolte's Liberal/Country Party coalition to bring down the Cain Government, what had been Labor's first majority government in Victoria.

Evatt had opened up wounds that could have been healed with the right leader. True, as many have recorded, the battle lines were many and complicated. But that is often the way of political parties; the role of leader is to manage them. Evatt was unable to separate his personal ambitions and pride from his party's needs. In his press statement on 5 October and in many that he would make later, the line of division was loyalty to him personally. His disastrous handling of the Royal Commission was his own doing, his conspiracy beliefs over the 1954 election result, again, were all about how the party had failed him.

Meanwhile, Menzies ended 1954 well pleased. The day before Evatt's statement to the press that would set off a barrel of dynamite under the Labor Party, *The Age* ran a "This Week in Canberra" column that complimented the Menzies Government on honouring most of its election promises already. There were increased pensions coming for invalids and war widows and another 65,000 new people about to qualify under the regulations. The PM had, the article opined, "weathered minor storms inside his own party and the Opposition is weak and disunited". This was before Evatt's explosive press statement about to be released that evening. Instead of tackling issues that concerned average Australians, in readiness for the next election, and building on the slight majority of two-party preferred votes at the 1954 election, Evatt had gone on a personal crusade against the Petrov defection and was about to begin a wrecking of the party he had so long served, and which had served him. Why his colleagues allowed him that indulgence is the great puzzle.

A divided Labor Party faced the government benches as federal Parliament opened on 20 April 1955. The previous day as parliament reassembled, Robert Joshua announced to the Speaker the names of his six colleagues who would "no longer recognise the leadership of the right honorable member for Barton". He told the House he had been selected to act as leader of the group which would be known as the Australian Labor Party (Anti-Communist). Menzies welcomed the group, leaving Evatt to respond snidely, "I note the congratulations expressed by the Prime Minister. It transpires that the secret alliance between the Government and the Santamaria group is now replaced by an open one."[22]

The following day, after Menzies proposed a motion that his recent statement on defence policy be printed, a stinging debate filled with accusations and acrimonious asides from both anti-communists and those still sitting with Evatt ensued. At last Labor was showing the public the enmity in its ranks it had till then kept private, with only snippets of the friction pieced together from leaked information reported in newspapers. Now voters could have listened to it all in full on the radio, as it happened. It shocked the House but offered the government a golden opportunity to sit back and let Labor demonstrate it was not fit to fill the government benches. After a stream of invective and accusations, added to by interjections from Evatt and some of his supporters, the Speaker allowed Stan Keon an extension of time.

Anti-communist Bill Bourke had led the charge, accusing Evatt of accepting £13,000 from the Communist Party in the campaign against the 1951 referendum. He quoted as his reliable source Kim Beazley MP, who was still sitting with Evatt and his Labor colleagues. This, said Bourke was a payment that had been held over Evatt by the CPA which pulled the strings and "made him dance". Moreover, Evatt had betrayed Labor by wiping out the Industrial Groups.[23] There were cries of "Judas" between Ted Peters and Jack Cremean with a young Gough Whitlam muttering "Why besmirch Judas?" after Peters said, "I object to being called a Judas by the greatest Judas of all time." When given the opportunity, Kim Beazley confirmed he had indeed passed on what was reported of his having been told about the £13,000 given by the CPA to Labor in 1951 but was prepared to accept Dr Evatt's denial that this was not true.[24]

With Labor's punch up out of the way, a debate followed over Australia sending troops to Malaya to help "preserve their present and future freedom", as Menzies put it, but which Evatt labelled "provocative". In the traditional Labor way, the party generally opposed sending Australia's soldiers abroad in peace time so the vote, as expected, was settled on party lines except that, on this occasion, the Liberal/Country Party MPs were enthusiastically supported by the seven anti-communist breakaway Laborites. The Split, what would become the greatest split Labor would ever know, had truly begun. Anti-communist Labor would support the Liberal/Country Party coalition in ways they had never imagined possible by preferencing the Coalition ahead of Labor in elections.

When Menzies was contacted by some of his prominent supporters after the Labor melt down in the House on 20 April 1955, they not only congratulated him on his speech over the new defence arrangements but also commented that the government could look forward to a long reign, after what had taken place between the Labor MPs in the House of Representatives. But it was the comment by J Macarthur-Onslow that came closest to an accurate prediction of what the debacle meant when he wrote to Menzies that he had "listened to the 'Donnybrook' between the Labor factions ... and felt certain now that you and your government can 'write your own ticket' for the next twenty years".[25]

Evatt's attack on the Santamaria Groupers, seen many decades on, is hard to understand for a party pledged to social justice and democratic values. How could a group of political activists, loyal members of the Labor Party, who had stood against communist disruption of commerce and government in the Chifley years, at the risk of their own promotion or livelihoods on many occasions, and which believed in Christian fundamentals that supported a society based on fairness for the working family and family-oriented policies be labelled as traitors inside the Labor Party?

That question leaves a significant shadow over Evatt's impulsive press statement of 5 October 1954. Evatt was an intense secularist. The values of Catholic activists were not part of his world view. He courted them when he needed them, in 1954 before the federal election, but he had no empathy with their fundamental opposition to communism as it operated in their perspectives. He could denounce the idea of communism, but when the deals were at play he was ever ready to bend and accommodate in the way of diplomacy. In the political reality of 1954 Australian federal politics, his moral equivalence had met its match – to the long-term destruction of the party which had given him political prominence.

On 26 October 1955, as Parliament was about to go into recess, the Prime Minister announced that he had been to visit the Governor-General and he was calling an election for the House of Representatives and half the Senate to be held on 10 December. The debate over the Petrov Royal Commission report had drawn to its last stages with Menzies' stinging words at Evatt haunting a battered Opposition. In responding to Evatt's long speech after revealing the reply to his Molotov letter, Menzies engaged with rancour, delivering an early riposte to Evatt that underlined Menzies' distrust of his rival and contempt for his cynicism, saying:

> *If the right honorable gentleman could get through ten minutes in this House without referring to McCarthy and smears, it would be a wonderful thing. However, as I propose to show with studied moderation, the right honorable gentleman, in this matter, has sought to smear every decent person associated with this inquiry. He has now thought fit, no doubt with the approval of those who sit behind him, to develop a series of charges, all of which he made directly or indirectly before the royal commission, and on all of which the commission has found against him.*[26]

In this poisoned atmosphere, Australia was to go to the polls.

The election campaign said much about the state of the major parties contesting it. The Labor Party (Anti-Communist) candidates and MPs for the House of Representatives went out to the hustings knowing they were likely to lose their seats. And they did. But, even as the Labor Party chose to give the anti-communists its second preferences, the ALP (AC) gave theirs to the Liberal/Country Party candidates. Mullens chose to stand against Calwell in the seat of Melbourne rather than recontest his own seat of Gellibrand, but Calwell prevailed.

Evatt's campaign, opening at Hurstville in Sydney on 9 November, was a rousing affair with wild cheers from a supporting audience of 2,000 giving a sense that this election could be a landslide moment for Labor. In fact, it would prove to be the rallying of the faithful at a time of unfortunate loss. Once again, Evatt outlined a costly financial program of promises, but also felt the need to spend considerable time defending his reputation saying, "I am not a communist." He was reported as trembling with emotion as he said, "It is all lies and slander to name me as a communist."[27]

Menzies, on the other hand, sensing an easy election win with Labor's loss of key MPs plus the Coalition's gain of their preferences, was quite different in his approach to his campaign opening. He was making no promises except "to maintain and increase Australia's prosperity". The Government would stand on its record. His only mention of the government and taxation was to say, "We all hate taxes." He did outline broad guidelines on where government policy would be directed – boosting trade, selling the Commonwealth Shipping Line if it brought a good price and arresting the run-down of Australia's overseas reserves in the following six months. But his main theme was an attack on Opposition leader Bert Evatt. He accused him of adding "touches of bewildering fantasy" to the campaign, proposing to increase taxation, destroying ASIO and attacking secret ballot laws designed to keep communists out of trade union posts.[28]

At the half-way mark in the campaign, George Kerr of *The Argus* summed up the two campaigns. With Menzies it was a quiet affair. He reported that Menzies was amazed at how apathetic voters seemed to be. His meetings were subdued with attentive, supportive audiences but also, for Menzies, boring. He was lacking real hecklers where he could fire back. Even the interjections of "Leave the poor old Doc alone" were omens in his favour. His constant reference to Evatt was to say to his audiences that the choice was between himself and "my learned opponent". Another put down after the Petrov Affair.[29]

Kerr had a very different take on the Evatt campaign. It was rushed, crowded, invigorated and noisy. Evatt was doing up to five speeches a day and seemed unstoppable. He was doing three times the meetings of Menzies and travelling into regional towns as much as major cities. It was as if he thought he could repeat the turnaround he achieved in the Communist Party dissolution referendum campaign. "The Doc leaves us all gasping" was the article's heading. Kerr's capture of "Saturday" gives the flavour:

> He flies to Sydney and, skipping breakfast, goes straight to work in his own suburban seat of Barton. It is a miserable wet morning, but he holds four street meetings before lunch without benefit of umbrella. He jams the hat more firmly on his head, and the water drips off it and down the back of his neck.[30]

Evatt's gamble was not to pay off. Menzies' taunt that Evatt brought touches of fantasy to the campaign was clear in the results. It was a landslide to the Liberal/Country Party with the Government increasing its majority in the House of Representatives from 7 to 28. Any punter watching the splintering of the Labor Party and its effect in the Victorian parliament on the Cain Government, along with the Labor (Anti-Communist) candidates delivering their preferences to the Government, could not have expected otherwise. And, while the preferential system in the Senate left the Coalition with a marginal 30 seats and the ALP with 28, the two cross benchers Frank McManus and George Cole as Labor (Anti-Communist) members – from 1957 to be called the Democratic Labor Party - were not likely to vote with Labor. The era of what became known as Democratic Labor Party (DLP) preferences had begun. Evatt had changed Australia but not the way he imagined.

Menzies would face Evatt across the despatch boxes in the House of Representatives for four more years. The Labor Caucus remained like creatures blinded by headlights unable to take the initiative and remove the Doc. Although he would manage to find form against Menzies in the Suez crisis in 1956, he had little effect on the politics of the day. At the 1955 election, Evatt had retained his seat of Barton by another narrow majority, dropping four per cent in first preference votes from the 1954 election when he had rallied. At this, instead of encouraging the Doc to hang up his political boots, the party found him the safer seat of Hunter to contest in the 1958 federal election.

Labor carried Evatt to the next election like a mascot. In the 1958 election, the two-party preferred vote for Menzies and the Coalition increased largely due to the preferences they received from the breakaway Laborites known in most of Australia as the Democratic Labor Party or in Queensland at that time as the Queensland Labor Party (QLP). The Queensland seats of Griffith and Herbert both changed from Labor to Liberal with the support of QLP preferences. The QLP had received over 14 per cent of first preferences that, in a disciplined way, mostly went to the Coalition. Labor in Herbert dropped some 9 per cent of first preferences and the Liberals a very small number while, in Griffith, the Labor vote dropped 5 per cent and the Liberal vote dropped some 9 per cent. QLP preferences were crucial for the Coalition to win those seats. In the seat of Kalgoorlie in Western Australia, DLP preferences also helped the Liberals win narrowly from Labor. In February 1959, Eddie Ward challenged Evatt for the leadership of the party and lost 32 votes to 46. It was not until the NSW Heffron Labor Government narrowly voted to offer Evatt the Chief Justice position that Evatt left politics and the Labor leadership in January 1960.

Epilogue

No two contestants in Australian political history could be said to have affected each other as much as Robert Menzies and Bert Evatt. In personality and political stances, they were direct opposites. In professional achievements they were uniquely balanced in many ways. Born a few years before debates over federating Australia moved to a final outcome, each was to ride high as part of the institutions those debates would engender. One to crisscross global capitals, helping to establish a workable platform to bring nations together in the cause of peace. The other to establish himself as Australia's longest serving prime minister and become acknowledged globally as the leader who made steadfast Australia's alliances in the Pacific.

From the time Bert Evatt entered federal parliament, Menzies had reason to dislike his overweening ambition. Then, in the war years and soon after, Menzies would languish as a leader who had failed, while Evatt sat at the top of the federal government. Menzies would get a second chance at the prime ministership and thrive, while Evatt would come to resent Menzies' ability to outplay him at politics in the age of the Cold War. Evatt would come to believe Menzies had cheated him out of becoming prime minister.

When Evatt died on 2 November 1965, Robert Menzies led the pall bearers with Arthur Calwell. Evatt was buried at Canberra Memorial Parks cemetery in Woden where his wife Mas had his tomb

Prime Minister Robert Menzies (left), a Protestant, and Opposition leader Arthur Calwell (right), a Catholic, lead the pallbearers at Dr Evatt's burial at the Woden cemetery in Canberra following his state funeral at St John's Anglican Church in the Canberra suburb of Reid. The date was 4 November 1965.

Photo: As depicted on Peter Crockett's *Evatt: A Life*

include a large stone proudly embossed with the United Nations emblem and the words "President of the United Nations 1948-1949". In fact, he was President of the United Nations General Assembly. In Evatt's mind, it had been his long lasting achievement.

Menzies would retire unbeaten as Australia's prime minister in January 1966. A year before, at the funeral of Sir Winston Churchill in London, Menzies had given the Eulogy. He would enjoy another decade in political retirement, travelling and writing and lecturing and enjoying sojourns in the UK as Warden of the Cinque Ports. He would die at home in Melbourne in May 1978 and be buried with great honours.

Both men had left historians much to ponder.

Endnotes

Chapter 1

[1] Peter Crockett, *Evatt A Life,* Oxford University Press, 1993, p. 93.

[2] *The West Australia,* 22 September 1951, p. 1.

[3] *The Argus,* 24 September 1951, p. 7.

[4] The Hon John Howard in an interview with Anne Henderson, Sydney, 15 July 2022.

[5] Email to Anne Henderson from Penelope Seidler, 7 July 2022.

[6] Justice Michael Kirby in an interview with Anne Henderson, Sydney, 22 June 2022.

[7] Amirah Inglis, *The Hammer, The Sickle and The Washing Up,* Hyland House, 1995, p. 104.

[8] The Hon Justice Michael Kirby, "H. V. Evatt Libertarian Warrior" in *Seeing Red – The Communist Party Dissolution Act and Referendum: Lessons for Constitutional Reform,* Evatt Foundation, 1992, p. 7.

[9] Ibid.

[10] Sir John Bunting, *R. G. Menzies A Portrait,* Allen & Unwin, A Susan Hayes book, 1988, p vii.

[11] Anne Henderson, *Menzies at War,* New South Publishing, 2014, p. 183.

[12] Cameron Hazlehurst, *Menzies Observed,* George Allen & Unwin, 1979, pp. 236-239.

[13] John Murphy, *Evatt: A Life,* New South Publishing, 2016, p. 267.

[14] Howard Beale, *This Inch of Time,* Melbourne University Press, 1977, pp. 34-35.

[15] Bunting, op. cit., p. 7.

[16] Ibid., pp. 19-20.

[17] Crockett, op. cit., p. 80.

[18] P. G. Edwards, *Prime Ministers and Diplomats,* Oxford University Press, 1983, p. 168.

[19] Sir Robert Menzies, *The Measure of The Years,* Cassell, London, 1970, p. 187.

[20] *Seeing Red – The Communist Party Dissolution Act and Referendum: Lessons for Constitutional Reform,* Evatt Foundation, 1992, Foreword.

[21] Clem Lloyd, "Evatt, Menzies, Latham and the Anti-Communist Crusade" in *Seeing Red*, p. 97.

[22] Arthur Geitzelt, "Principle Before Power" in *Seeing Red*, p. 66.

[23] Troy Bramston, "The double allegiance of a secret communist operative" in *The Australian*, 19 February 2022; see also Mark Aarons, *The Family File*, Black Inc, 2010, p. 106 and pp. 299-300.

[24] Kirby, op. cit., pp. 16-17.

[25] George Williams, "Reducing the Judicial Mind; Appellate Argument in the Communist Party Case", in *Sydney Law Journal*, Vol. 15, No. 3, 1993

Chapter 2

[1] Paul Hasluck, *The Chance of Politics*, Text Publishing, 1997, p. 221.

[2] Murphy, op. cit., p. 26.

[3] David (ed) Furse-Roberts, *Menzies: The Forgotten Speeches*, Jeparit Press, 2017, p. 65.

[4] B. A. Santamaria, *Against the Tide*, Oxford University Press, 1981, pp. 140-149.

[5] Murphy, op. cit., pp. 7-10.

[6] Letter C. Moodie to P. Crockett, 15 March 1987, quoted in Crockett, op. cit., p. 2.

[7] Hasluck, op. cit., pp. 80-81.

[8] Gideon Haigh, *The Brilliant Boy: Doc Evatt and The Great Australia Dissent*, Scribner, 2021, p. 191.

[9] K. Buckley, B. Dale & W. Reynolds, *Doc Evatt - Patriot, Internationalist, Fighter and Scholar*, Longman Cheshire, 1994, pp. 25-26.

[10] C. Hartley Grattan, "Australian Labour Leader" in *The Australian Quarterly*, Vol. 12, No. 3 (September 1940) pp. 69-81.

[11] Allan Martin, *Robert Menzies A Life, Volume 1 - 1894-1943*, Melbourne University Press, 1993, p. 14.

[12] Martin, op. cit., pp. 55-56.

[13] Bunting, op. cit., p. 60.

[14] Percy Spender, *Politics and a Man*, Collins, Sydney, 1972, p. 154.

[15] H. V. Evatt, *Liberalism in Australia - An Historical Sketch of Australian Politics Down to the Year 1915*, The Law Book Company of Australia Limited, 1918, p. 71.

[16] Kylie Tennant, *Evatt Politics and Justice*, Angus & Robertson, 1970, p. 25.

17 Murphy, op. cit., p. 66.
18 Paul Hasluck, *Diplomatic Witness*, Melbourne University Press, 1980, p. 36.
19 Haigh, op. cit., pp. 179-181.
20 Michael Pelly, *Murray Gleeson – The Smiler*, The Federation Press, 2014, pp. 29-30.
21 Furse-Roberts, op. cit., p. 14.
22 Ibid., p. 47.
23 Ibid., p. 19.
24 CPD, House of Representatives, 5 August 1954, p. 66.
25 Kim E. Beazley, *Father of The House*, Fremantle Press, 2009, p. 94.
26 *The Sun*.
27 Speech dealing with National War Council – delivered by Dr Evatt at Gosford, 16 September 1940, Evatt Collection, Flinders University.
28 *The Sydney Morning Herald*, 25 September 1940, p. 12.
29 Philip Ayres, *Owen Dixon*, The Miegunyah Press, 2003, p. 170.

Chapter 3

1 Fred Daly, *From Curtin to Kerr*, Sun Books, 1977, p. 58.
2 L. F. Crisp, *Ben Chifley*, Longmans, 1963, p. 328.
3 Menzies, op. cit., p. 109.
4 C. B. Schedvin, *Australia and The Great Depression*, Sydney University Press, 1988, pp. 94-95.
5 Crisp, op. cit., p. 167.
6 David Day, *Chifley*, HarperCollins Publishers, 2001, p. 323.
7 *The Argus*, Tuesday, 15 July 1947, p. 1.
8 Geoffrey Blainey, *Gold and Paper – A History of The National Bank of Australasia Ltd*, Georgian House, Melbourne, 1958, pp. 362-363.
9 A. L. May, *The Battle of The Banks*, Sydney University Press, 1968, p. 8.
10 Tony Blackshield, Michael Coper, George Williams (ed), *The Oxford Companion to The High Court of Australia*, Oxford University Press, 2001, p. 471.
11 Tennant, op. cit., p. 216.
12 David Marr, *Barwick – The Classic Biography of a Man of Power* Allen & Unwin, 1992, p. 56.
13 Allan Martin, *Robert Menzies A Life Volume 2 1944-1978*, Melbourne University Press, 1999, p. 66.

14 *The Argus*, Monday, 18 August 1947, p. 6.
15 *The Sydney Morning Herald*, Tuesday, 26 August 1947, p. 1.
16 *The Argus*, Friday, 29 August 1947, pp. 1 and 7.
17 *The Argus*, Tuesday, 19 August 1947, p. 1.
18 Martin, op. cit., p. 76.
19 CPD, House of Representatives, 15 October 1947, p. 798.
20 CPD, House of Representatives, 14 October 1947, p. 687.
21 *The Sydney Morning Herald*, Tuesday, 18 November 1947, p. 1.
22 Murphy, op. cit., p. 241.
23 Marr, op. cit., p. 63.
24 Martin, op. cit., p. 90.
25 Ibid., p. 97.
26 CPD, HoR, 15 February 1949, pp. 266-265.
27 Murphy, op. cit., p. 265.
28 Tennant, op. cit., p. 254.
29 Blainey, op. cit., pp. 370-71.
30 *The Argus*, 11 November 1949, p. 1.
31 *The Argus*, 15 November 1949, p. 1.
32 David Day, *Chifley*, HarperCollins, Sydney, 2001, p. 468.
33 Tennant, op. cit., p. 254.

Chapter 4

1 Peter Edwards, *Prime Ministers and Diplomats*, Oxford University Press, Melbourne, 1983, p. 176.

2 Keith McEwan, *Once a Jolly Comrade*, Jacaranda Press, 1966, pp. 24-25.

3 Aarons, op. cit., pp. xii and 37.

4 Helen Rappaport, *Joseph Stalin: A Biographical Companion*, ABC-CLIO, p. 53.

5 Aarons, op. cit., p. 46.

6 Katharine Susannah Pritchard, *Why I am a Communist*, Current Book Distributors, Sydney, p. 8.

7 Richard Hall, *The Rhodes Scholar Spy*, Random House, Australia, 1991, pp. 30-31.

8 Bernie Taft, *Crossing The Party Line*, Scribe Publications, 1994, p. 57.

9 L. L. Sharkey, *An Outline of The History of The Australian Communist Party*, Australian Communist Party, 1944, p. 12.

10 David Lovell & Kevin Windle, *Our Unswerving Loyalty – a documentary survey of relations between the Communist Party of Australia and Moscow, 1920-1940*, ANU E Press, 2008, p. 50.

11 Stuart Macintyre, *The Reds – The Communist Party of Australia from origins to illegality*, Allen & Unwin, 1998. pp. 221-223.

12 Eric Aarons, *What's Left*, Penguin Books, 1993, p. 41.

13 *The Sydney Morning Herald*, 19 December 1942, p. 8.

14 Taft, op. cit., p. 64.

15 Alastair Davidson, *The Communist Party of Australia*, Hoover Institution Press, 1969, p. 99-100.

16 Eric Aarons, op. cit., p. 118.

17 *The Sydney Morning Herald*, 18 February 1946, p. 4.

18 *The Sydney Morning Herald*, 5 September 1946, p. 3.

19 Davidson, op. cit., p. 130.

20 Taft, op. cit., p. 55.

21 CPD, House of Representatives, 5 June 1947, p. 3336.

22 Ric Throssell, *My Father's Son The Last Knot Untied*, William Heinemann Australia, 1997, p. 245.

23 David Lowe, *Menzies and The Great World Struggle: Australia's Cold War 1948-1954*, UNSW Press, 1999, pp. 14-15.

24 Beazley, op. cit., pp. 104-105.

25 Ibid., p. 105.

26 CPD, House of Representatives, 9 February 1949, p. 91.

27 CPD, House of Representatives, 15 February 1949, p. 265.

28 Ibid., p. 272.

29 Cecil Sharpley, "I was a Communist Leader", Melbourne Herald Publication, p. 2.

30 Taft, op. cit., p. 61.

31 Ibid., p. 63.

32 A. W. Fadden, *They Called me Artie – The Memoirs of Sir Arthur Fadden*, Jacaranda Press, 1969, p. 99.

33 https://electionspeeches.moadoph.gov.au/speeches/1949-robert-menzies

Chapter 5

[1] Beazley, op. cit., p. 95.

[2] David Horner, *The Spy Catchers: The Official History of ASIO 1949-1963*, Allen & Unwin 2014, p. 97.

[3] Ibid., p. 134-135.

[4] Ibid., p. 66.

[5] Ibid., pp. 56-66.

[6] Desmond Ball and David Horner, *Breaking The Codes Australia's KGB Network*, Allen & Unwin 1998, pp. 150-153.

[7] Lowe, op. cit., p. 17.

[8] Horner, op. cit., pp. 56-64.

[9] Ball and Horner, op. cit., p. 212.

[10] Mark Aarons, op. cit., pp. 2, 103-104.

[11] Bunting, op. cit., p. 132.

[12] A. W. Martin, *Robert Menzies: A Life Volume 2 1944-1978*, p. 135.

[13] CPD, House of Representatives, 9 March 1950, p. 623.

[14] *The Argus*, 17 April 1950, p. 3.

[15] *The Age*, 28 April 1950, p. 1.

[16] CPD, House of Representatives, 27 April 1950, p. 1995.

[17] Ibid, p. 2004.

[18] *The Argus*, 28 April 1950, "What The Bill Does to The Communists", p. 1.

[19] Martin, op. cit., p. 146.

[20] CPD, House of Representatives, 4 May 1950, p. 2219.

[21] CPD, House of Representatives, 9 May 1950, p. 2273.

[22] *The Age*, 29 April 1950, p. 1.

[23] *The Sydney Morning Herald*, 4 May 1950, p. 1v.

[24] CPD, House of Representatives, 9 May 1950, p. 2274.

[25] Martin, op. cit., p. 147.

[26] Murphy, op. cit., p. 267-268.

[27] CPD, House of Representatives, 9 May 1950, p. 2289.

[28] Ibid., p. 2287.

[29] Ibid., p. 2290.

[30] Martin, op. cit., p. 171.

[31] Murphy, op. cit., p. 275.

Chapter 6

[1] *The Canberra Times*, 14 June 1951, p. 1.

[2] Robert Menzies, "The Communists" in Furse-Roberts (ed), op. cit., p. 79.

[3] Gerard Henderson, *Santamaria: A Most Unusual Man*, The Miegunyah Press, MUP, 2015, pp. 133-134.

[4] Robert Murray, *The Split: Australian Labor in the Fifties*, Cheshire, 1970, p. 15.

[5] Ibid., p. 15-26.

[6] Santamaria, op. cit., p. 125.

[7] Murphy, op cit, pp. 270-274; D. Day, *Chifley*, HarperCollins, 2001, pp. 508-510.

[8] CPD, House of Representatives, 25 October 1950, pp. 1391-1393.

[9] CPD, House of Representatives, 26 October 1950, p. 1548.

[10] Ibid., pp. 1550-1551.

[11] W. J. Brown, *The Communist Movement in Australia*, Australian Labor Movement History Publications, 1986, p. 190.

[12] *Daily Telegraph*, Tuesday, 24 October 1950, p. 1.

[13] Marr, op. cit., p. 85.

[14] *The Argus*, 10 March 1951, p. 3.

[15] *The Sydney Morning Herald*, 10 March 1951, p. 1.

[16] *The Argus*, 14 March 1951, p. 1.

[17] Daly, op. cit., p. 104.

[18] *News Weekly*, 14 February 1951, p. 2.

[19] *The Age*, 4 April 1951, p. 1.

[20] *The Sydney Morning Herald*, 24 April 1951, p. 2.

[21] *The Sydney Morning Herald*, 2 April 1951, p. 2.

[22] *The Sydney Morning Herald*, 5 April 1951, p. 3.

[23] *The Age*, 26 April 1951, p. 2.

[24] *The Sydney Morning Herald*, 11 April 1951, p. 3.

[25] *The Sydney Morning Herald*, 27 April 1951, p. 3.

[26] Paul Hasluck, *The Chance of Politics*, Text Publishing, 1997, p. 220.

[27] *The Sydney Morning Herald*, 30 April 1951, p. 1.

[28] *News Weekly*, 2 May 1951, p. 1.

[29] Daly, op. cit., p. 105.

[30] Ibid., p 113

31 *News Weekly,* 27 June 1951, p. 2.

32 Leicester Webb, *Communism and Democracy in Australia,* Cheshire/ANU, 1954, p. 46.

33 CPD, House of Representatives 10 July 1951, pp. 1213-1218.

34 Murray Goot, "Referendums, Opinion Polls, and Public Relations: The Australian Gallup Poll and the 1951 Referendum on Communism" in *International Journal of Public Opinion Research,* Vol. 26, No. 4, 2014, pp. 424-426.

35 *The Sydney Morning Herald,* 6 July 1951, p. 1.

36 *The Sydney Morning Herald,* 7 July 1951, p. 1.

37 J. Boyd & N. Charwat (2014) "Ideology and the Economy: Capital Issues Controls, Inflation and the Menzies Government, 1950-51", *Australian Journal of Politics & History,* 60, pp. 503-517.

38 *The Sydney Morning Herald,* 12 July 1951, p. 1.

39 CPD, House of Representatives, 11 July 1951, pp. 1402-1403.

Chapter 7

1 Webb, op. cit., p. 52.

2 Murray Goot, "Referendums, Opinion Polls, and Public Relations: The Australian Gallup Poll and the Referendum on Communism" in *International Journal of Public Opinion Research,* Vol. 26. No. 4, 2014.

3 Murray Goot, "Party Leaders, and Political Persuasion: The Campaigns of Evatt and Menzies on the Referendum to Protect Australia from Communism", in *Australian Historical Studies,* March 2013, p. 72.

4 Ibid.

5 Text of a broadcast, "Dr H V Evatt's National Broadcast on the Referendum", 12 September 1951, Evatt Collection, Flinders University.

6 *The Sydney Morning Herald,* 9 September 1951, p. 7.

7 *Sunday Herald,* 9 September 1951, p. 7.

8 Tennant, op. cit., p. 281.

9 *Herald,* "Capital Talk" – "Labor forecasts a big gain", 10 August 1951, p. 4.

10 *Canberra Times,* 20 August 1951, p. 5; *The Sydney Morning* Herald, 20 August 1951, p. 3; Webb, op. cit., p. 60.

11 Martin, op. cit., p. 194.

12 *Herald,* 5 September 1951, p. 4.

13 *Cairns Post,* 18 August 1951, p. 5.

14 *Townsville Daily Bulletin,* 20 August 1951, p. 2.

15 *Herald*, 23 August 1951, p. 3.
16 *Herald*, 21 August 1951, p. 2.
17 *The Argus*, 22 August 1951.
18 Murray, op. cit., p. 87.
19 Ibid, p. 88.
20 *The Age*, 14 September 1951, p. 1.
21 Murray, op. cit., p. 89.
22 *The Argus*, 22 August 1951, p. 2.
23 *The Argus*, 31 August 1951, p. 5.
24 *The Argus*, 15 September 1951, p. 5.
25 Interview with Michael Baume, Sydney, 13 April 2023.
26 *The West Australian*, 27 August 1951, p. 2.
27 *The Argus*, 5 September 1951, p. 1.
28 *The Sydney Morning Herald*, 7 September 1951, p. 1.
29 *The Age*, 18 September 1951, p. 1.
30 Comment by The Hon John Howard AC launching *The Young Menzies*, Peter Cosgrove Centre, ACU Sydney, on 21 February 2023.
31 *The West Australian*, 28 August 1951, p. 3.
32 Webb, op. cit. p. 75.
33 Lloyd Ross, "Communists set Trap for Labor", *Herald*, 11 August 1951, p. 2.
34 *The Sydney Morning Herald*, 22 August 1951, p. 2.
35 *The Sun* (Sydney), 17 September 1951, p. 7.
36 *The Age*, 19 September 1951, p. 4.
37 *The Sydney Morning Herald*, 1 September 1951, p. 1.
38 Webb, op. cit., p. 94.
39 Letter to H. V. Evatt from Colin Bednall of *The Courier Mail*, 19 October 1951, Evatt Collection, Flinders University.
40 Murray Goot, "Party Leaders, and Political Persuasion: The Campaigns of Evatt and Menzies on the Referendum to Protect Australia from Communism", in *Australian Historical Studies*, March 2013, p. 76.
41 *The Age*, 19 September 1951, p. 9.
42 *The Sydney Morning Herald*, 15 September 1951, p. 2.
43 *The Sydney Morning Herald*, 18 September 1951, p. 1.
44 *The Age*, 24 September 1951, p. 1.
45 *The Argus*, 24 September 1951, p. 2.

Chapter 8

[1] Frank Chamberlain, interviewed by Mel Pratt for the National Library of Australia, nla:obj-221556016; 0.50.45– 0.51.42

[2] *The Sydney Morning Herald*, 21 November 1951, p. 1.

[3] Santamaria, op. cit., p. 141.

[4] Ibid., pp. 140-143.

[5] Murphy, op. cit., p. 298.

[6] Ibid, p. 297.

[7] *The Sydney Morning Herald,* 27 September 1951, p. 1.

[8] Martin, op. cit., p. 217.

[9] Tennant, op. cit., p. 288.

[10] *The Argus*, 10 September 1953, p. 2.

[11] H. E. Cox, *The Herald*, 10 September 1953, p. 4.

[12] *News Weekly*, 6 January 1954, p. 2.

[13] H. E. Cox, *The Herald*, 2 April 1954, p. 4.

[14] CPD, House of Representatives, 13 April 1954, p. 326.

[15] Murray, op. cit., p. 149.

[16] Allan Dalziel, *Evatt The Enigma*, Lansdowne Press, 1967, p. 79.

[17] Menzies, *The Measure of The Years*, pp. 162-163.

[18] *The Sydney Morning Herald*, 20 April 1954, p. 2.

[19] Murphy, op. cit., p. 308.

[20] Lowe, op. cit., p. 103.

[21] *The Argus*, 5 May 1954, p. 4.

[22] *The Sydney Morning Herald*, 7 May 1954, p. 2.

[23] *The Argus*, 7 May 1954, p. 1.

[24] *The Argus*, 12 May 1954, p. 1.

[25] *The Canberra Times*, 24 May 1954, p. 2.

[26] *The Sun-Herald*, 16 May 1954, p. 20.

[27] *The Courier Mail*, 19 May 1954, p. 2.

[28] *The Argus*, 15 May 1954, p. 5.

[29] *The Argus*, 13 May 1954, p. 4.

[30] *The Argus*, 12 May 1954, p. 1.

[31] *The Age*, 24 May 1954, p. 2.

[32] *The Sydney Morning Herald*, 25 May 1954, p. 2.

33 *The Sydney Morning Herald*, 31 May 1954, p. 1.

34 *The Sydney Morning Herald*, 1 June 1954, p. 1.

Chapter 9

1 Bob Carr, "Communism and The Labor Movement", in *The Sydney Papers Online*, 18 August 2011.

2 Dalziel, op. cit., p. 76.

3 Ibid.

4 *The Sydney Morning Herald*, 18 May 1954, p. 1.

5 *The Sydney Morning Herald*, 19 May 1954, p. 1.

6 Horner, op. cit., p. 318.

7 Ibid., p. 342.

8 *The Sydney Morning Herald*, 1 July 1954, p. 1.

9 *The Age*, 8 July 1954, p. 1.

10 *The Age*, 9 July 1954, p. 1.

11 Desmond Ball, "I believe Lockwood lied to Petrov commission to save his family's honour" in *The Australian*, 23 April 2011.

12 *The Sydney Morning Herald*, 16 July 1954, p. 4.

13 Murray, op. cit., p. 159.

14 Buckley, Dale & Reynolds, op. cit., p. 377.

15 CPD, House of Representatives, 12 August 1954, p. 283.

16 David McKnight, *Australia's Spies and Their Secrets*, Allen & Unwin, 1994, p. 58.

17 *The Age*, 13 August 1954, p. 1.

18 *The Sydney Morning Herald*, 17 August 1954.

19 McKnight, op. cit., p. 68.

20 *The Sydney Morning Herald*, 2 September 1954, p. 1.

21 *The Sydney Morning Herald*, 9 September 1954, p. 1.

22 *The Canberra Times*, 10 September 1954, p. 1.

23 *News*, 10 September 1954, p. 1.

24 CPD, House of Representatives, 8 September 1954, p. 1031.

25 *The Sydney Morning Herald*, 11 September 1954, p. 1.

26 *The Sydney Morning Herald*, 17 September 1954, p. 5.

27 *The Age*, 17 September 1954, p. 1.

28 *The Sydney Morning Herald*, 23 September 1954, p. 1.

[29] CPD, House of Representatives, 28 October 1954, p. 2472.

[30] Ibid., p, 2475.

[31] Ibid., p. 2478.

[32] Buckley, Dale & Reynolds, op. cit., p. 378.

[33] Murphy, op. cit., p. 347.

[34] CPD, House of Representatives, 25 October 1955, p. 1858.

[35] Murphy, op. cit., p. 348.

[36] Menzies, Sir Robert, *The Measure of The Years* Cassell London 1970, pp. 186-187.

Chapter 10

[1] John Douglas Pringle, *Australian Accent*, Chatto and WIndus, London, 1958, p. 62.

[2] John Burton, *The Alternative*, Morgans Publications, Sydney, 1954, p. 63-64.

[3] CPD, House of Representatives, 3 November 1954, p. 2576.

[4] CPD, House of Representatives, 4 November 1954, pp. 2691-2692.

[5] Alan Watt, *The Evolution of Australian Foreign Policy 1938-1965*, Cambridge University Press, 1967, p. 157.

[6] Mel Pratt interview with Frank Chamberlain, National Library of Australia, *nla.obj-221555740*

[7] Brian Costar, Peter Love, Paul Strangio, *The Great Labor Schism: A Retrospective*, Scribe Publications Melbourne, 2005, p. 12.

[8] Burton, op. cit., p. 96.

[9] Murray, op. cit., p. 177.

[10] *The Age*, 23 September 1954, p. 1.

[11] *The Argus*, 6 October 1954, p. 1.

[12] Henderson, op. cit., p. 256.

[13] Costar, Love & Strangio, op. cit., p. 13.

[14] Daly, op. cit., p. 128.

[15] Crockett, op. cit., p. 288.

[16] *The Canberra Times*, 11 October 1954, p. 1.

[17] Henderson, op. cit., p. 263.

[18] Daly, op. cit., p. 131.

[19] Beazley, op. cit., p. 92.

[20] Paul Strangio, *Neither Power nor Glory – 100 Years of Political Labor in Victoria, 1856-1956*, Melbourne University Press, 2012, p. 284.

21 Ibid., p. 337.
22 CPD, House of Representatives, 19 April 1955.
23 *The Canberra Times*, 21 April 1955, p. 1.
24 Ibid.
25 Martin, op. cit., p. 301.
26 CPD, House of Representatives, 25 October 1955, p. 1858.
27 *The Argus*, 10 November 1955, p. 1.
28 *The Argus*, 16 November 1955, p. 1.
29 *The Argus*, 28 November 1955, p. 4.
30 *The Argus*, 29 November 1955, p. 4.

Select Bibliography

Aarons, Mark, *The Family File*, Black Inc, 2010

Aarons, Eric, *What's Left*, Penguin Books, 1993

Atkin, Elsa & Evans, Brett (eds), *Seeing Red – The Communist Party Dissolution Act and Referendum: Lessons for Constitutional Reform*, Evatt Foundation 1992

Ayres, Philip, *Owen Dixon*, The Miegunyah Press, 2003

Ball, Desmond and David Horner, *Breaking The Codes: Australia's KGB Network*, Allen & Unwin, 1998

Beale, Howard, *This Inch of Time*, Melbourne University Press, 1977

Beasley, Jack, *Red Letter Days – notes from inside an era*, Australasian Book Society, 1979

Beazley, Kim E., *Father of The House*, Fremantle Press, 2008

Bialoguski, Michael, *The Petrov Story*, William Heinemann Ltd, 1955

Blackshield, Tony, Coper, Michael, Williams, George (eds), *The Oxford Companion to The High Court of Australia*, Oxford University Press, 2001

Blainey, Geoffrey, *Gold and Paper – A History of The National Bank of Australasia Ltd*, Georgian House Melbourne, 1958

Brown W. J. (ed), *The Petrov Conspiracy Unmasked*, Cedric Ralph, 1973

Brown, W. J., *The Communist Movement in Australia* Australian, Labor Movement History Publications, 1986

Brown, W. J. (ed), *The Petrov Conspiracy Unmasked*, Current Book Distributors, 1958

Brown, W. J., *The Communist Movement in Australia*, Australian Labor Movement History Publications, 1986

Buckley, K., Dale, B & Reynolds, W, *Doc Evatt – Patriot, Internationalist, Fighter and Scholar*, Longman Cheshire, 1994

Bunting, Sir John, *R. G. Menzies A Portrait*, Allen & Unwin: A Susan Hayes Book, 1988

Burgmann, Meredith (ed), *Dirty Secrets Our ASIO Files*, New South Publishing, 2014

Burton, John, *The Alternative*, Morgans Publications Sydney, 1954

Burton, Pamela & Edwards, Meredith, *Persons of Interest: An Intimate Account of Cecily and John Burton*, ANU Press, 2022

Calwell, Arthur, *Be Just and Fear Not*, Lloyd ONeil Pty Ltd, 1972

Colebatch, Hal G. P., *Australia's Secret War: How unionists sabotaged our troops in World War II*, Quadrant Books, 2013

Colvin, Mark, *Light and Shadow: Memoirs of a Spy's Son*, Melbourne University Press, 2016

Costar, Brian, Love, Peter, Strangio, Paul, *The Great Labor Schism: A Retrospective*, Scribe Publications Melbourne, 2005

Crisp, L. F., *Ben Chifley*, Longmans, 1963

— *The Australian Labour Party 1901-1951*, Hale & Iremonger, 1978

— *The Federal Labour Party 1901-1951*, Longmans Green and Co, 1955

Crockett, Peter, *Evatt: A Life*, Oxford University Press, 1993

Curthoys, Ann & Merritt, John, *Australia's First Cold War Vol 1 Society, Communism and Culture*, George Allen & Unwin, 1984

Curthoys, Ann & Damousi, Joy, *What Did You Do in the Cold War, Daddy?* NewSouth Publishing, 2014

Daly, Fred, *From Curtin to Kerr*, Sun Books, 1977,

Dalziel, Allan, *Evatt: The Enigma*, Lansdowne Press, 1967

Davidson, Alastair, *The Communist Party of Australia*, Hoover Institution Press, 1969

Day, David, *Chifley*, HarperCollins, Sydney, 2001

Deery, Phillip, *Spies and Sparrows ASIO and The Cold War*, Melbourne University Press, 2022

Edwards P. G., *Prime Ministers and Diplomats*, Oxford University Press, 1983

Evatt MP, H. V., *Australia in World Affairs*, Angus and Robertson, 1946

Evatt, H. V., *Liberalism in Australia – An Historical Sketch of Australian Politics Down to the Year 1915*, The Law Book Company of Australia Limited, 1918

Evatt, Herbert Vere, *Australian Labour Leader*, Angus and Robertson, 1942

Fadden, A. W., *They Called me Artie – The Memoirs of Sir Arthur Fadden*, Jacaranda Press, 1969

Fahey, John, *Traitors and Spies: Espionage and Corruption in High Places in Australia, 1901-1950*, Allen & Unwin, 2020

Ferrier, Carole, *Jean Devanny: Romantic Revolutionary*, Melbourne University Press, 1999

Freudenberg, Graham, *A Figure of Speech*, Wiley, 2005

Furse-Roberts, David (ed), *Menzies: The Forgotten Speeches*, Jeparit Press, 2017

Gibson, Ralph, *My Years in The Communist Party*, International Bookshop, 1966

Gibson, Ralph, *The People Stand Up*, Red Rooster Press, 1983

Golding, Peter, *They Called Him Old Smoothie: John Joseph Cahill*, Australian Scholarly Publishing, 2009

Gollan, Robin, *Revolutionaries and Reformists Communism and the Australian Labour Movement 1920-1955*, Australian National University Press, 1975

Grattan, C. Hartley (ed), *Australia*, University of California Press, 1947

Haigh, Gideon, *The Brilliant Boy: Doc Evatt and The Great Australia Dissent*, Scribner, 2021

Hall, Richard, *The Rhodes Scholar Spy*, Random House Australia, 1991

Hasluck, Paul, *The Government and The People 1939-1941*, Canberra, Australian War Memorial, 1965

— *The Government and The People 1942-1945*, Canberra, Australian War Memorial, 1970

— *Diplomatic Witness*, Melbourne University Press, 1980

— *The Chance of Politics*, Text Publishing, 1997

Hazlehurst, Cameron, *Menzies Observed*, George Allen & Unwin, 1979

Henderson, Anne, *Menzies at War*, New South Publishing, 2014

Henderson, Gerard, *Menzies' Child: The Liberal Party of Australia*, HarperCollins Publishers, 1994

— *Santamaria: A Most Unusual Man*, The Miegunyah Press, MUP, 2015

Heydon, Peter, *Quiet Decision: A Study of George Foster Pearce*, Melbourne University Press, 1965

Hobby, Nathan, *The Red Witch: A Biography of Katharine Susannah Pritchard*, The Miegunyah Press, 2022

Horner, David, *The Spy Catchers: The Official History of ASIO 1949-1963*, Allen & Unwin, 2014,

Inglis, Amirah, *The Hammer, The Sickle and The Washing Up*, Hyland House, 1995

Joske, Sir Percy, *Sir Robert Menzies 1894-1978: A New Informal Memoir*, Angus and Robertson, 1978

Kane, Jack, *Exploding The Myths: The Political Memoirs of Jack Kane*, Angus & Robertson, 1989

Kiernan, Colm, *Calwell: A Personal and Political Biography*, Nelson, 1978

Lee, David & Waters, Christopher (eds), *Evatt to Evans: The Labor Tradition in Australian Foreign Policy*, Allen & Unwin, 1997

Lockwood, Douglas, *Fair Dinkum*, Readers Book Club, 1960

Lovell, David & Windle, Kevin, *Our Unswerving Loyalty – a documentary survey of relations between the Communist Party of Australia and Moscow, 1920-1940*, ANU E Press, 2008

Lowe, David, *Menzies and The Great World Struggle: Australia's Cold War 1948-1954*, UNSW Press, 1999

Macintyre, Stuart, *The Reds – The Communist Party of Australia from Origins to Illegality*, Allen & Unwin, 1998

— *The Party: The Communist Party of Australia From Heyday to Reckoning*, Allen & Unwin, 2022

Mandel, Daniel, *H. V. Evatt and The Establishment of Israel: The Undercover Zionist*, Frank Cass Publishers, 2004

Manne, Robert, *The Petrov Affair: Politics and Espionage*, Pergamon Sydney, 1987

Marks, Ken, *In Off the Red*, Schwartz Publishing, 2005

Marr, David, *Barwick – The Classic Biography of a Man of Power*, Allen & Unwin, 1992

Martin, Allan, *Robert Menzies: A Life Volume 1 – 1894-1943*, Melbourne University Press, 1993

— *Robert Menzies: A Life Volume 2 – 1944-1978*, Melbourne University Press, 1999

May, A. L., *The Battle of The Banks*, Sydney University Press, 1968

McEwan, Keith, *Once a Jolly Comrade*, Jacaranda Press, 1966

McKinlay, Brian, *A Documentary History of the Australian Labor Movement 1850-1975*, Drummond, 1979

McKnight, David, *Australia's Spies and Their Secrets*, Allen & Unwin, 1994

Menzies, Sir Robert, *The Measure of The Years,* Cassell, London, 1970

Milliss, Roger, *Serpent's Tooth,* Penguin Books, 1971

Milner, Lisa, *Swimming Against The Tide: A Biography of Freda Brown*, Ginninderra Press, 2017

Monteath, Peter & Munt, Valerie, *Red Professor: The Cold War Life of Fred Rose*, Wakefield Press, 2015

Murphy, John, *Evatt: A Life*, New South Publishing, 2016

Murray, Robert, *The Split: Australian Labor in the fifties*, Cheshire, 1970

— *Labor and Santamaria*, Australian Scholarly, 2016

Pelly, Michael, *Murray Gleeson – The Smiler*, The Federation Press, 2014

Pringle, John Douglas, *Australian Accent,* Chatto and WIndus, London, 1958

Rappaport, Helen, *Joseph Stalin: A Biographical Companion*, ABC-CLIO, 1999

Romerstein, Herbert & Breindel, Eric, *The Venona Secrets: Exposing Soviet Espionage and America's Traitors,* Regnery Publishing Inc, 2000

Santamaria, B. A., *Against the Tide,* Oxford University Press, 1981

Sawer, Geoffrey, *Australian Federal Politics and The Law 1929-1949*, Melbourne University Press, 1963

Scarff, Wendy & Allan, *No Taste For Carnage: Alex Sheppard, a portrait 1913-1997*, Seaview Press, 1998

Schedvin, C. B., *Australia and The Great Depression*, Sydney University Press, 1988

Sendy, John, *Ralph Gibson: An Extraordinary Communist*, Ralph Gibson Biography Committee, 1988

Sendy, John, *Comrades Come Rally! Recollections of an Australian Communist*, Nelson, 1978

Sharkey, L. L., *An Outline of the History of the Australian Communist Party*, Australian Communist Party, 1944

Sharpley, Cecil, "I was a Communist Leader", A Melbourne *Herald* Publication, 1955

Sheridan, Tom, *Australia's Own Cold War The Waterfront Under Menzies*, Mebourne University Press, 2006

Short, Susanna, *Laurie Short A Political Life*, Alan & Unwin, 1992

Smith, Bernard, *Noel Counihan Artist and Revolutionary*, Oxford University Press, 1993

Spender, Percy, *Politics and a Man,* Collins, Sydney, 1972

Strangio, Paul, *Neither Power nor Glory – 100 Years of Political Labor in Victoria, 1856-1956,* Melbourne University Press, 2012

Stubbs, John & Whitlam, Nicholas, *Nest of Traitors: The Petrov Affair*, The Jacaranda Press, 1974

Taft, Bernie, *Crossing The Party Line*, Scribe Publications, 1994,

Tennant, Kylie, *Evatt: Politics and Justice*, Angus & Robertson, 1970

Throssell, Ric, *My Father's Son: The Last Knot Untied*, William Heinemann, 1997

Thwaites, Michael, *The Truth Will Out: ASIO and The Petrovs*, Collins, 1980

Trahair, Richard C. S. & Miller, Robert, *Cold War Espionage, Spies and Secret Operations,* Enigma Books, 2012

Uren, Tom, *Straight Left*, Random House, 1994

Ward, Russell, *A Radical Life*, Macmillan Australia, 1998

Watt, Alan, *The Evolution of Australian Foreign Policy 1938-1965*, Cambridge University Press, 1967

Pamphlets

Burton, John, *The Light Grows Brighter*, Morgan's Publications, 1956

Crawford, R. M., *The Real Facts About Russia*, Australia-Soviet House, 1946

Dixon, R., *The Trial of L. L. Sharkey*, Current Book Distributors, 1949

Lockwood, Rupert, *America Invades Australia,* Current Book Distributors, 1954

Mortimer, Rex, *The Great Crime,* Coronation Press Pty Ltd

Pritchard, Katharine Susannah, *Why I am a Communist*, Current Book Distributors, Sydney, 1956

Ryan, Rev P. J. MSC, *Dean Hewlett Johnson's Socialist Sixth of the World*, St Vincent Boys Home, Westmead

Sharkey, L. L., *A Reply to Father Ryan*, Communist Party of Australia, 1943

Sharkey, L. L., *Democracy For Whom?* Modern Publishers, Communist Party of Australia, 1941

Articles/Papers/Theses

Carr, Bob, "Communism and the Labour Movement", *Sydney Papers Online*, no. 12, 24 May 2011

Colebatch, Hal G. P., "Treachery: the Communist Party and the Labor Party", *National Observer*, no. 59, Summer 2004, pp. 52-66

Cottle, Drew, "How Australia failed to destroy communism", pp. 13-28, *Australian Society for the Study of Labour History*, vol. 10, issue 1 2015

Goot, Murray, "Referendums, Opinion Polls, and Public Relations: The Australian Gallup Poll and the Referendum on Communism", *International Journal of Public Opinion Research*, vol. 26 no. 4, 2014

— "Party Leaders, and Political Persuasion: The Campaigns of Evatt and Menzies on the Referendum to Protect Australia from Communism", *Australian Historical Studies*, March 2013

Gordon, The Hon Justice Michelle Gordon AC, "Communist Party Case: Core Themes and Legacy", *Public Law Review*, vol. 432, no. 4, 2021

Grattan, C. Hartley, "Australian Labour Leader", *The Australian Quarterly*, vol. 12, no. 3, September 1940

Williams, George, "Reducing the Judicial Mind: Appellate Argument in the Communist Party Case", *Sydney Law Journal*, vol. 15, no. 3, 1993

Winterton, George, "The Significance of the Communist Party Case", *Melbourne University Law Review*, vol. 18, issue 3, pp. 630-58

Woodhouse, Fay, *The 1951 Communist Party Dissolution Referendum Debate at the University of Melbourne*, Fourth Year Honours Thesis, Faculty of Arts, Victoria University of Technology, October 1996

Select Primary Sources

Papers of H. V. Evatt, Flinders University, South Australia
Papers of Sir Robert Menzies, National Library of Australia, Canberra

Interviews

The Hon Michael Baume AO
The Hon John Howard OM AC
The Hon Michael Kirby AC CMG
Penelope Seidler AM (née Evatt) (by email)

Newspapers

The Age
The Argus
The Australian
The Cairns Post
The News (Adelaide)
Canberra Times
The Courier Mail
Daily Telegraph (Sydney)
The Herald (Melbourne)
The Mercury (Hobart)
News-Weekly (Melbourne)
Sunday Telegraph (Sydney)
Sydney Morning Herald
Townsville Daily Bulletin
The West Australian

Acknowledgements

This book has been a long time evolving. Work I have done over decades on books on Joseph and Enid Lyons and Robert Menzies has contributed immensely not only to background for the history covered in the political lives of these two men but also added context and detail. Those who assisted me in those histories, I thank again.

It was a great advantage to be able to talk with some prominent Australians who could recall the 1951 referendum on the Dissolution of the Communist Party of Australia and its effect on their communities and family life. In this, I am grateful for interviews with The Hon John Howard OM AC, The Hon Justice Michael Kirby AC CMC and The Hon Michael Baume AO, along with a generous email exchange with Penelope Seidler AM (nee Evatt).

In accessing the Evatt Collection of papers at Flinders University in Adelaide, I was assisted over some hours by Library officer Mary Clare O'Brien who generously provided me with a selection of papers and supervised my time there. Her fresh Irish approach to Australia also offered perspectives on the contrasts to be found in contemporary Australia with some of the sectarian conflict my book would reflect.

At home, I have been advantaged for decades by living among a vast collection of books, journals, magazines and primary sources from the 1920s to modern times, collected by my long time partner, political analyst and commentator Gerard Henderson. His dedication to a life of examining and analysing Australia politics, especially the Labor Split of the 1950s, contributed invaluable resources – on tap – as well as offered critical fact checking and pertinent evaluations. He also was the inspiration for the work I have done on the 1951 referendum on the Communist Party Dissolution referendum, as well as urging me to believe I could complete the manuscript.

In the typing of interview transcripts, compiling the manuscript and collecting and processing illustrations, The Sydney Institute team of Paige Hally and Naomi Killin has been an heroic backup. Their professional capacity was impressive, as always. Special thanks also to Paige Hally for the cover. For the work on typesetting and layout of the book, thanks to Michael Gilchrist, and many thanks also for his suggestions and assistance in small essentials. For the index, a special thanks to Richard McGregor.

In recent pandemic times, the availability of historic online newspapers and magazines was wonderful. Hats off to Trove and all online services in this regard. Lastly, over years, I am grateful for the support and encouragement of The Sydney Institute's senior administrator and great friend Lalita Mathias.

Index

Note: Page numbers in *italics* refer to images or captions.

Aarons, Eric, 56, 57, 61, 62–63
Aarons, Laurie, 56, 57, 76
Aarons, Mark, 56, 57
The Family File, 15, 76
Agagianian, Cardinal Gregory, 163
Alexander, J. A., 116
Anderson, Prof. John, 120
Anderson, John (senator), 177
ANZUS Treaty, 169
Asia
    communism in, 168; as threat to Australia, 115, 169
    independence movements, 77, 169
Armstrong, Mick, *54*
ASIO, 74, 75, 137, 138
    Department of External Affairs under scrutiny, 55
    established, 55, 167
    and Western intelligence network, 55
    see also Petrov
Atyeo, Sam, 27
Australia
    economy postwar, 6, 7–8, 132; improvement, *110*; inflation, 64, 94, 132, 142; strikes, 7, 8, 9, 27, 47, 64, 70; unemployment, 133
    Christian tradition, 124; and sectarianism, 125
    Federation and government, 17
    Great Depression, 5, 28, 55; and banks, 35
    and relations with France, 154, 155, 160
    relations with United States, 75–76
    World War I and conscription issue, 24
Australian Labor Party (Anti-Communist), 178, 181
    supports Liberal/Country Party, 180, 183

Ball, Des, 150
Barwick, Garfield, 96, 97
    leads defence for banks against *Banking Act*, 44
Baume, Michael, 120–21
Beale, Howard, 9–10
Beria, Lavrentiy, 147
Beasley, Jack, 32
Beazley, Kim jr
    leads Labor to narrow loss, 140
Beazley, Kim snr, 30–31, 66, 146, 179
    on Evatt, 176
Bednall, Colin, 125–26
Belloc, Hilaire, 91
Bernie, Frances, 76
Bolte, Henry, 177
Bourke, Bill, 143, 158, 170, 173, 174, 179
Breaking the Codes (Ball and Horner), 76
Broadhurst, Henry, 27
Brooks, Sir Dallas, *163*
Brown, Allen, 133
Bunting, Sir John, 10, 77
Burgmann, Right Rev E. H., 124–25
Burke, Edmund, 28
Burke, Tom, 94, 158, 170, 174

Burton, John, 9, 46, *53*, 74–75, 118–19, 169
  The Alternative, 168, 171; on the Catholic Church, 171
  on communism, 75, 171
  and Milner, 168
  US and UK mistrust of, 74

Cain, John snr, 118
Cain Labor Government
  election win in 1952/53, 132
  forced to an election, 42; defeated, 43
  loses power in split, 177, 183
Calwell, Arthur, 2, 20, 175
  as deputy Labor leader, 102, 103, *110*, 117, 118, 123, 142, 177;
  approached about leadership, 176; lacks courage, 176
  pall bearer at Evatt's funeral, *185*
Cameron, Archie, 129
Carrington, Lord, 6
cases
  Chester v Waverley Corporation, 29
  Communist Party Case, 15
  Engineers case, 24
Casey, Richard, 41, *54*, *163*
Catholic Church, 14
  Catholic Action, 91, 92
Catholic Church in Australia, 14, 171
  Catholic Federation, 172
  social justice principles, 171
  see also Santamaria
Chamberlain, Frank, 140, 171
Chambers, Cyril, 118
Chesterton, G. K., 91
Chifley, Ben
  death, 8, 102
  hubris and pique towards banks?, 38
  in Opposition, 36, 102; and bills to ban Communist Party, 82, 83, 84, 85, 88, 90, 94; and Evatt's brief to challenge the legislation, 95; and 1951 election campaign, 100, 101; and referendum on Communist Party, 114; opinion of Evatt as potential leader, 102
  as prime minister and treasurer, 6, 7, 33, 35–37, 38, 41, 49, *53*, *167*; response to communist inspired strikes, 9, 47, 64–65, 69, (coal), 70
Chifley Government
  dealing with communist-inspired strikes, disruptions, 64–65, 70, 75, 85–86, 180
  and international affairs post war, 65, 75
  and referendum on social services, 36
  and socialism, 72
  and Soviet agents, 74
  stance on Cold War, 66; and allies, 66; and departments, 66
  see also nationalisation of trading banks; politics
Childe, Vere Gordon, 22
China
  under communism, 5, 6, 47, 67, 70, 75, 77, 78, 98
  and Korean War, 96
  treaty with Soviet Union, 77
Churchill, Sir Winston, 33–34, 133, 186
  and the "iron curtain", 75
Clark, Manning
  Meeting Soviet Man, 57
Clayton, Wally. *71*, 76
Colbourne, Bill, 131

Cold War, 5, 6
    communism as growing threat, 8, 30, 66; in Australia, 80–82, 94; as disrupter in twentieth century, 91; rise of in South-East Asia, 77
    defined as new kind of war, 80
    international tensions, 46, 65, 67; fears of new world war, 79, 105
    and nuclear weapons, 5, 73, 77
    espionage, 73; US Venona Project and communist infiltration, 15, 74, 75, 76, 146
    NATO established, 79
    see also Soviet Union/Russia
Cole, George, 176, 177, 183
Coleman, Fred, 121
Communist Party of Australia (CPA), 3
    and Cominform post war: front organisations, 64, *71*, *89*
    communism and representative government, 59
    communist unions, 7, 9
    CPA and politics, 15, 24; denies war aims, 79; elections, 61
    declared illegal in 1940, 61, 80; ban lifted in 1942, 61; continues to function, 76; goes underground, 60; infiltrates the military, 76
    in decline by 1949, 171; demise, 58
    and directives from Stalin's Soviet Communist Party, 56, 60, 65, 96, 173; role of Moscow Comintern, 60
    and the Labor Party, 59, 60
    members, 3, 15, 58, 59, 69, 70, *71*, 76, *89*, 95, 131, 150, 158; under attack, 4
    membership and a new direction in life, 55–56; blinkered attitude to Soviet realities, 57, 58
    and Nazi–Soviet Pact, 61
    postwar challenges, 62; allegations of union election rigging, 69; changes name, 62; divisions, defections, 69; opposing dissolution referendum, *108*, 123
    raids on offices, 95
    repression and totalitarian methods, 60–61
    stated aim, 81, *89*
    takes shape in 1920s, 24, 59; divisions, 59; subservience to Moscow, 60, 62
    and the war effort, 61
    see also Soviet embassy; trade unions
Communist Party dissolution referendum, 1, 6
    campaign posters, cartoons, *107*, *108*, *109*
    debate, 112; clerics join in, 124–25; Evatt broadens debate, 113; leaders and dissimilar audiences, 112
    defeated, 1, 2, 14, 16, 93; benefit for Menzies, 12, 127; close result, 127
    divisions in community, 119, 120, 127
    Evatt's stance and campaign as Labor leader, 2, 3, 4–5, 9, 14, 103, 104, 117, 123, 139, 174; link with "power grab" in defence preparations legislation, 105–06; labels Menzies a dictator, 122–23; making a mark as leader, 113–15, 128; meetings in Melbourne, 117, 118; narrow win, 111, 167; and radio, 112–13; reports in newspapers, 112, 117, 125–26; says Labor opposed to

communism, 117; sequence of meetings, speeches, 112, 116, 117, 121, 126–27

and history of referendum failure, 116

impact on Labor and communist sympathisers, 2, 4

Menzies' "Yes" campaign, 1, 4, 104, 115; communism as a danger, 115; and Communist Party pamphlets, 123; complacency, 115; few speeches, 112, 122; meetings, 121–22; newspapers and radio, 112, 122, 126; opposition, rowdy scenes, 119–21, 122, 125, 126

nature of campaign, 1, 2; bitter, 4, 104; hyperbole, 112–13; rhetoric, 4

polling: narrowing, 111, 127; support for "Yes", 2, 104, 111, 112, 115, 116, 120

Cosgrove, Robert, 119

Country Party, 31, 70

Cox, E. H., 115, 134, 136–37

Crawford, Max, *89*

Cremean, H. M., 92

Cremean, Jack, 179

Curtin, Daniel, 104

Curtin, John, 77

in opposition: rejects national government, 33; uniting caucus, 31, 32, 33

as prime minister in wartime, 5, 6, 7, 33, 34

Curtin Government, 93

Daly, Fred, 98, 175

on Calwell, 176

on Evatt as leader, 102, 174

Dalziel, Allan, 138, 145–46, 148, 151, 159

Davidson, Alastair, 62, 64

Davidson, Canon E. J.

Day, David, 49

Deakin, Alfred, 26

Democratic Labor Party, 183, 184

Denning, Esler, 74

Dixon, Owen, 24, 29, 33, 43

Doc Evatt (Buckley, Dale, Edwards), 160–61

Dougherty, Tom, 93

Duhig, Archbishop James, 124

Eastern Europe

communist control in Poland, Czechoslovakia, Hungary, 79

and Soviet encroachment, 5, 9, 48, 63, 67, 75, 79

Edwards, Peter, 11, 55

elections: federal

1929, 28

1931, 28

1934, 25

1940, 6, 31, 33

1943, 6

1946, 36, 39, 63

1949, 5, 6, 8, 34, 48–50, 75, 78–79, 85; Senate: proportional voting, 87

1951, 6, 8, 98, 101, 115

1954, 13, 14, 19, *110*, 140, 170, 176

1955, 181, 183

1958, 184

1998, 140

state elections

NSW: 1925, 22; 1927, 22

South Australia: 1952/53, 132

Queensland: 1952/53, 132

Victoria, 1929, 25; 1952, 132
Western Australia: 1952/53, 132

Elizabeth II
Coronation, 66
tour in Australia, 134, *135*, 136; brings lift in mood, 136; crowds, 135, 136

Evatt, Clive (brother), 151

Evatt, H. V. (Bert), *166*
abilities, 11, 21; as scholar, intellectual, 18, 21, 26, 146

afterlife as Labor man of principle, 13, 14

as Attorney General, 9, 34; as barrister on banking cases before High Court, Privy Council, 44, 48, 53, 90, 115, (erratic behaviour), 44–45; during strikes of 1947–49, 27, 31, (and communism), 65; and former court colleagues, 44, 45; lifts ban on CPA in 1942, 61; opinion on bank nationalisation, 38–39, (drafts legislation), 40, 151, (returns from overseas), 43

biographers: Peter Crockett, 11, 19, 20, 175; Gideon Haigh, 21, 28; John Murphy, 20, 43, 84–85, 131, 162, 175; Kylie Tennant, 19, 38, 50, 133

career in the law, 11, 18, 26–27; activist judge, 29; acts for Labor governments, 27; High Court justice, 22–23, 28, 29, 44, *51*, (stands down), 31; NSW Chief Justice, 12, 184; and the labour movement, 18; supporting the oppressed, 27

cast as soft on communism, the left, 12, 30–31, 47, 67–68, 75, 95, 97, 99, 128, 139–40, 168–69; alleges conspiracies, 139

character, 9, 10, 19, 20–21, 176; ambition, 6, 8, 18, 20, 116, 177; bad temper, 114, 174; brilliant to supporters, 145, 176; disliked in United States, 9; doesn't trust others, 102; fails to consult, 151, 156; gullibility, 31, 162; hates flying, 116; his view of colleagues, 145–46; lacks management skills, 10–11, 146; lacks networking skills, 26; public persona, 10, 11, 146; resilience, 11; soloist, 22, 34, 144; as speaker, 11; as viewed by colleagues, 20, 32–33, 176

death, 185; funeral, *185*

education: Fort Street School, 18; Sydney University, 18, 22, 26

entry to federal politics as MP for Barton, 6–7, 31–32, 33; campaigning, 33; contrast with Menzies, 32; making a difference, 34; problem for party leaders, 33–34, 94

as External Affairs minister, 8–9, 11, 20, 31, 34, 41; aligns with left, 66; department as a source of leaks, 75–76, 168; focus on, belief in work of UN and Security Council, 65, 66–67, 68, 74, 75, 168, 186; neutralist in international affairs, 65–66, 67; and new state of Israel, 43; role in formation of the UN, 8, 11, 38, 43, 65; US mistrust of, 74; on the world stage, 43, *52*, *53*

family and early years, 17–18

friendships, 22

interests, 27–28

lacks political acumen, 21, 139; unable to heal wounds in party, 177

letters to Menzies, 7

marriage, home life, 21, 32, *166*

mental deterioration, 44; strain, 170

in opposition: accepts brief on High Court challenge to the Act, 90, 94, 95, (wins), 96–97, 140; as acting leader, 103; on bills banning Communist Party, 47, 84, 85, 88, 90, 94; close loss in 1951 election, 101; considers leaving parliament, 84; win in court doesn't improve support for ALP, 98, 101

as Opposition leader, 1, 8, 9, 102, 167; blames party for 1954 loss, 178; and budget 1953, *110*; and the Catholic vote, 90; determined to make peace with Groupers, Santamaria, 130–31, 180; early tests, 114–15, 128, (challenge to maintain unity), 131; focus on communism ban rather than economic issues, 94–95; ignoring advice, writes to Molotov, 161, (loses respect), 162; leads ALP to election defeats, 8, 13, 14, 19, 143–44, 178; misjudges the times, 11–12; at new peak, 133; obsessed by Petrov royal commission, 155, 156, 157, 161, (retains supporters), 161; questions over mental health, 156; remains leader after split, 183, (defeats challenge), 184; seeks revenge after split, 177, 180; tours Australia, campaigns in elections, 132, 182–83; wins *Communist Party Case*, 15

re-evaluation of his place in Australian politics, 15

as state Labor MP for Balmain: develops political views, 22–23; as "Independent" Labor member, 22

values, inspirations, 11, 26; clash with realities, 27; human rights, civil liberties, 19, 27; interest in labour causes, 26, 27; liberalism, 26–27; secularist, 180; social change, 29

as a writer, 11; *Australian Labor Leader* (on William Holman), 22–23; *Injustice within the Law*, 22; *The King and His Dominion Governors*, 42; *Rum Rebellion*, 22

see also Communist Party dissolution referendum; Labor Party; (Petrov) Royal Commission on Espionage

Evatt, Jeanie (mother), 17–18, 146

Evatt, John (father): early death, 17

Evatt, Mary Alice (née Sheffer, wife), 6, 27, *166*, 185–86

Evatt Foundation
conference on Evatt's referendum campaign, 14
Seeing Red (book of essays), 14

External Affairs Department, 8, 9, 46, 74
attention from ASIO, 55, 167
suspected as source of leaks to Soviets, 75, 138, 145–46, 148, 150, 151, 159, 168

Fadden, Arthur, *54*, 70, 132
fascism, 29
Fitzpatrick, Brian, 161
Fleming, Ian, 73
Frith, John, *110*
Forde, Frank, 33
Fuchs, Klaus, 4
Ferguson, Jack, 85
Fraser, Allan, 175, 176
Fraser, Malcolm, 144
Furse-Roberts, David, 29

Gall, Ian, *110*
Gietzelt, Arthur, 15
  in praise of Evatt, 14–15

George VI, 127, 132
Germany in WWII, 61, 62, 63
Gilroy, Cardinal Norman, 124
Goot, Murray, 112
Gorton, John, 121
Gracias, Cardinal Valerian, *163*
Grattan, C. Hartley, 22–23
Green, Frank, 90
Greenwood, Ivor, 120
Grundeman, Albert, 148, 150, 159

Haigh, Gideon
    The Brilliant Boy, 21
Hall, Jim, 76
Hamblen, Derek, 148
Hanlon, Ned, 100
Hasluck, Paul, 10, *54*, 101
    on Evatt, 21, 27
Hayes, Gil, 93
Healy, Jim, 90
Heffron Government
    appoints Evatt as NSW Chief Justice, 184
Henderson, Gerard, 173–74, 176
Hitler, Adolf, 24, 48, 61, 87
    targets, 123
Higgins, H. B., 26
Holt, Harold, 95
Hollway, Tom, 40, 42, 43
Horner, David, 148
Howard, John, 2, 123, 174
Howard Government, 13, 140
Hughes, W. M. (Billy), 11
    bans International Workers of the World party, 80
    as PM, leaves Labor Government with followers, 24

Indo-China, 169
Inglis, Amirah, 4
Isaacs, Isaac, 26

Japan
    atomic bombs dropped on Hiroshima and Nagasaki, 73
Johnson, Dean Hewlett, *71*, 79
Jordan, Mick, 93
Joshua, Robert, 178

Kennelly, Pat, 93, 131, 170
Kent Hughes, Wilfred, 25
Keon, Stan, 118, 128, 131, 176, 179
Kerr, George, 182
King, R., 93
Kirby, Michael, 3–4
    on Communist Party dissolution referendum, 15
    on Menzies, 5
Kisch, Egon, 29, 60
Korean War, 6, 88, 93, 96, 100, 105, 115, 126

Labor Party (ALP), federal
    attitudes to Soviet Union, 9
    and communist influence, 30
    conferences, 33, 173, 177
    and economic policy in mid 1950s, 134
    factions in 1940, 32
    Federal Executive: on Communist Party ban, 94; sees Groupers as an enemy within, 128; votes to oppose referendum, 103
    in government, 1929–31: divisions; defections, 28; 1941–49, 5, 33

in 1920s: challenges, 24; activists, 25

post-split: Labor Caucus fails to move against Evatt, 183–84

and socialisation of industry, 7, 8

split in 1950s, 13, 15, 23, 144, 178; accusations against Evatt, 179; benefits Menzies, 62, 178; breakaway group, 178, 179; Caucus members leave parliament, 177; disquiet then anger over Evatt's appearances at Petrov commission, 153–54, 155, 157–58, 172, 174, 176; disappointment at 1954 election loss, 155; divisions over communism, 8, 64, 83–84, 88, 93, 94, 102, 103, 114, 117–18, (after referendum), 128, 129–30, 171; enmity revealed, 179; Evatt denounces "subversive" element – the Groupers – in party, 13, 15, 62, 172, 173, 175, 176, 178, 180, (authoritarian stance), 174; and industrial Groupers (opponents of Evatt), 62, 64, 83, 93, 103, 125, 130, 168, 170, 175–76, (influence increases), 171, (opposition from some Catholics, other Labor MPs), 172; leadership spill motion defeated, 174, 175, 176, 177; members, MPs, branches expelled, 174, 177; party lacks a strategy, 155; possibility of election win in 1952, 94, 131–32; and ratting, 23; smell of sectarianism, 172; split leads to years in Opposition, 15, 62, 130, 180; tensions, friction, 155–56, 170, 172, 173, 174–75, (become public), 179–80; what ifs, 175–76

in WWI, 59; split over conscription, 5, 24

see also (Petrov) Royal Commission on Espionage; trade unions

Labor Party in NSW

bars communists, 60

groupers in, 93

Lang Government, 22

Lang Labor, 32

State Executive, 35–36

Labor Party in South Australia, 132

Labor Party in Tasmania

Groupers, 129; recriminations, 129

little support for Evatt in referendum meeting, 119

Labor Party in Victoria, 40, 42, 43, 92, 132

divisions, 103, 117–19; expelled MPs help bring down Cain Government, 177, 183; Groupers, other anti-communists, 93, 103, 117, 118, 129, (replaced), 177

executive supports Communist Party referendum legislation, 103

new executive, 177; begins purge, 177

Labor Party in WA, 94, 132

Lang, Jack, 22, 26, 28, 60

Latham, John, 96

Lauritz, Norm, 92

Lawler, Adrian, 28

League of Nations, 92

legislation

Approved Defence Projects Protection Act, 65, 75, 85–86

Banking Act 1945/1948, 36, 37; challenged in High Court, 38, 43, 44

Communist Party Dissolution Act, 90; challenged in High Court, 90,

94, (overturned), 96–97, 105
Crimes Act 1932, 60, 85; invoked in 1950, 79
Defence Preparations Act 1951, 104–05, 132
Lenin, Vladimir, 56
Liberal/Country Party (Vic.), 119, 120, 177
Liberal Party, 5
   administrative structure, 174
   formation, 10, 25, 28, 34
   renewed interest in, 13
Lockwood, Rupert, 89, 150, 154, 158
   junior counsel for, 157
Lodge, the: renovation, 77
Lovegrove, D., 93
Lovell, David, 60
Lowe, David, 66
Lowe Royal Commission into Communist Party, 69
Lyons, Joseph, 25, 28, 31
Lyons Government, 25, 28
   and banks, 36
   and CPA, 60

Macarthur-Onslow, J., 180
McConnan, Leslie, 37, 41, 48
McEwen, John, *54*
McEwan, Keith
   as member of the CPA, 55–56, 57
Macintyre, Stuart, 60–61
   The Party, 15
McKell, Sir William, 98
Mackinnon, Donald, 49
McKnight, David, 153, 154
McManus, Frank, 183
Malony, J. A., *89*

Manne, Robert, 148
Mannix, Archbishop Daniel, 92, 93, 99, 125, 130, *163*
Mao Zedong, 70
Marr, David
   Barwick, 44, 45, 96
Martin, Alan
   Robert Menzies: A Life (2 vols), 24, 77, 88, 116, 133, 162
Marx, Karl, 56
Meagher, J. A., 155
Menzies, Frank (brother), 45
Menzies, Heather (daughter), 45
Menzies, James (father), 18
   member of Victorian Legislative Assembly, 19
Menzies, Kate (mother), 18
Menzies, Pattie (wife), 6, 45, 77, *166*
Menzies, Robert
   admirers, 1, 7
   career in the law, 11, 21, *51*; wins Engineers case, 24
   education, 18; University of Melbourne, 18; Wesley College, 18
   family and early years, 18–19, 24, 25; father as guide, 18; Scottish heritage, 24
   with granddaughter, *166*
   historians on Menzies years, 13
   as Opposition leader: approach to defence and foreign policy, 68–69; critical of UN, 68–69; election campaign in 1949, 48–49, 50, (pledge to ban Communist Party), 72, 77; languishes, 185; opposes communism and socialism, 47, 70, 72; rumblings in party, 39; six month break, travel, 44, 45, 47, 70; solidifies leadership, 39; view of Soviet Union, 45, 46–47

personality, 10; aloof,
intimidating, 25–26, 39; as
authoritarian, 122; public
appearance, 10; as speaker, 10

and politics (federal): as Attorney
General, 29; and Kisch, 60; natural
leader, 25, 28; master at collective
action, 34; role in formation of
UAP and Liberal Party, 25, 28, 34;
wins seat of Kooyong, 1934, 25

and politics (state): as Attorney
General and Minister for
Railways, 1932, 25; elected to
Victorian Parliament in 1928, 25;
joins Nationalist Party, 24

as prime minister 1939–41, 25–26,
31; declaration of war against
Germany, 31; loss of ministers in
aircraft crash, 31; in minority, 33;
stands down, 34

as prime minister 1949–66, 1,
6, 7, 77, 176, 184, 186; attends
Commonwealth Prime Ministers
conferences, 96, 133; benefits
from Labor split, 13, 62, 181;
calls early election in 1955, 181;
dominant political figure, 12, 78;
ends 1954 well pleased, 178; fights
1951 election on communism,
Coalition wins majority in
House and Senate, 98, 101;
governing style, 10; ill health, 133;
justifications for banning CPA, 15,
74, 76, 78, 80, 91, ("fanaticism"),
88; in the Lodge, 77; as pallbearer
at Evatt's funeral, *185*; and Petrov
defection, 14, 137; with the
Queen, *135*, 136; saves slim Senate
margin, 137; travel overseas, 88,
133

radio broadcasts, 29, 91–92, 122

in retirement, 13, 186; *Measure of
the Years*, 162

values: liberalism, 29–30; opposed
to communism and fascism, 28,
29–30; religious faith, 19, 29, 30;
sense of service to democracy, 19,
30

see also Menzies government

Menzies and Evatt: similarities,
differences, rivalry, 6, 7, 16, 17

achievements as students:
both win scholarships, obtain
professional success, 18, 19, 26,
146

careers in the law, 11, 21, 24, 27,
51, 184

contest over two decades, 1, 2, 14,
16, 32, 34, 43; battle over banks,
34; clashes in parliament, 34,
46–47, 73, 88, 133, 153, 181

differ over strategic options for
Australia, 169

different personalities, 9–10,
33–34, 184

liberalism as core belief of both,
11, 20, 26–27, 28, 30, 174

Menzies in the ascendant, 12, 162,
167, 185; sets out to destroy the
"Evatt image of Australia", 170

mutual dislike, 9–10, 14, 68, 100,
185; cruelty, 162; personal attacks,
114, 139, 153, 159–60, (after Labor
split), 181

same age, 17

and WWI, 23

see also Communist Party
dissolution referendum

Menzies Coalition Government
1949–66, 5, 186

banking legislation, 77

calls double dissolution, 98

and economic conditions, 6, 115,
127, 132–33; improvement in
1953, 133–34

foreign affairs focus: Asia and Pacific, 78, 115; external threats, fears, 5, 6, 78, 132; intelligence gathering, 74; trade with Japan, 133; Soviet spies in Australia, 74; and the UN, 78

legislation to ban Communist Party, 8, *54*, 77–78, 79–82; demonstrations, 79–80; and dividing Labor, 88, 94; and rights, 80, 82, 83, 84, 85, 88

and Petrov defection, 31

poor ratings in 1952–53, 132–33; and Budget of 1951, 132; increased defence spending, 132; loses seats in half Senate election, 133

return of support in 1953–54, 134

treaty with Japan, 115

see also Cold War

Mill, John Stuart, 28

Milner, Ian
 glowing report on Russian system, 58
 agent, informer, 75, 76, 168

Missen, Alan, 119–20
 expelled from Liberal and Country Party, 120

Molotov, Vyacheslav, 31
 claims Petrov documents fabrications, 161

Muggeridge, Malcolm, 20
 Winter in Moscow, 58

Mullens, Jack, 118, 129–30, 170, 181
 expelled, 177

Murray, Robert, 172

nationalisation of trading banks, 7, 8, 35, 36–37, 70
 High Court challenge to *Banking Act 1945*, 37; upheld, 38, 40, 40
 Banking Act 1948, 39; High Court,

Privy Council challenges, 41, 43, 44, (upheld), 48

Menzies leads campaign of opposition, with banks, 8, 35, 41, 42–3, 44; maintaining momentum for the election with banks, 48–49; rhetoric, 39–40

objections, dismay, 37–38, 40; huge rallies, 39–40, 41; petitions, 41

Nationalist Party, 24–25

National Labor Party (anti-ALP), 24

newspapers, journals
 Age, 80, 83, 143, 153, 178
 Argus, 6, 39, 49, 50, *54*, 82, 119, 120, 124, 133–34, 141, 142–43, 161, 182, 183; supports "No" case in referendum, 125, 127
 Australian Quarterly, 22–23
 Canberra Times, 142, 175
 Catholic Worker, 92
 Century (Labor magazine), 133
 Courier Mail, *110*, 117, 125–26, 142
 Daily Telegraph, 69–70
 Daily Worker (UK), 100
 Guardian (communist), 55
 Herald (Melbourne), 69, *89*, *110*, 115, 116, 117, 123, 134, 137
 News (Adelaide), 156
 News Weekly, 93, 94, 98, 102, 118–19, 128, 129, 134, 173; compliments Evatt, 103; ban lifted, 130; proscribed by Labor, 129
 saturation circulation, 126
 Smith's Weekly, 27
 Sunday Herald, 114
 Sydney Morning Herald, 33, 40, 49, 99, 100, 101–102, *107*, 117, 119, 123–24, 125, 139, 141, 143, 144
 Women's Weekly, 32

Nunn May, Alan, 4

Ollier, Madame, 154, 155, 160
Ormonde, Jim, 172
O'Sullivan, Fergus, 148, 150, 154–55

Page, Earle, 31
Patton, George, 82
Peters, Ted, 157–58, 173, 179
Petrov, Evdokia, 146, 149–50, *163*, *164*
  seeks asylum, *164*
  as Soviet spy, 147
Petrov, Vladimir, 147, *163*
  defection, 12, 14, 31, 47; and ASIO, 137–39, 167; husband and wife at risk, 147; sensational scenes, 146; timing, 148
  Menzies doesn't advise Evatt, 152
  revelations after 1954 election, 140; intelligence gained, 147, 153
(Petrov) Royal Commission on Espionage, 137
  adjourned for election campaign, 148
  "collaborators" mainly deny accusations, 148
  documents genuine, 148; Evatt's approach, 154; link Soviet embassy with members of Evatt's staff, 148, 150, 153, 159; show hostile intent, 147–48
  Document H, 150
  Document J, 150, 151, 154, 158, 159
  Evatt: appearances at commission, defending staff, 13, 150–51, 153–54, 155, 161, *164*, 168, 176, 178, (end abruptly), 154, (error of judgement), 151, 177–78; claims commission is a conspiracy against Labor, 148, 151; and disquiet, criticisms in Labor Party, 153–54, 155–56, 157–58; impact on public standing, 13; leads to political ruin, 11, 14, 15; manner, 154, 155; political carelessness, naivety, 146; refused permission to appear again, 157; supports commission, 138, (then criticises Menzies), 139
  Evatt a subject of inquiry, 150
  fallout of events for Labor Party, 146–47; Evatt his own worst enemy, 145; Evatt's demise as a conspiracy, 145; political battle, 151–53
  information indicates External Affairs penetrated by Russian agents, 148; prompts Menzies to establish royal commission before election, 148–49
  led by three judges, 147, 155, 157; final report, 161; interim report: findings, 158
  Petrovs give evidence about Soviet espionage in Australia, 149, 150; Australian informers, 149
  public interest in, 149
  and Venona intercepts, 148
  W. J. V. Windeyer, Counsel Assisting, 147–48, 149, 150, 155
Philip, Duke of Edinburgh, 135
politics, federal
  budget of 1953: "triumphant" Menzies, *110*
  by-election wins for Labor, 132
  Cold War and Australian politics, 12, 14, 67–69; and socialism, 72
  Communist Party activities, aims, 25
  Country Party and Menzies, 31
  debate on bills to ban Communist Party, 82–83, 84–87, 88; aftermath

of successful challenge, 97–98; in committee, 87; Labor does not defend communists, allows bill to pass, 84–87, 90, 94; second reading, 87

debate on Communist Party referendum legislation, 103; Evatt leads opposition to bill, 103–04, 114; government seeks to amend the invalidated Act, 103; Menzies' third attempt at a ban, reverses onus of proof, 104, 121

debate on Petrov royal commission, 151–52; bill strengthening commission is passed, 153; Evatt implies documents are fraudulent, 152, 158, (seems to be losing plot), 153; Evatt's approach to Molotov, 161, (and loss of credibility), 162, 167; Menzies: dismisses Evatt's accusations, restates commission findings, 158–60; holds firm, 152–53; Menzies' cutting riposte to Evatt's charges, 181; public debate continues for decades, 160–61

debate on SEATO treaty, 168–69

defence preparations legislation, 104–05; Evatt labels it a "power grab", 105

election campaign of 1949: Chifley and Labor, 49; Menzies and the Coalition, 48–9, 50; satire, 49, *54*

election campaign of 1951: dominated by issue of communism, numbers in Senate, 98, 99, 100; and the economy, 99; Evatt a weak link, 101; Labor on the defensive, 100–101; Menzies' campaign, 98–99, 100

election campaign of 1954: electoral mood improves for Coalition, 140; Evatt's suite of policies, *110*, 134, 139, 140–41, (and arguments over costings), 142–43, 174; Menzies' campaign: home ownership, family values, 139, 141, *165*; narrow win for Menzies Government, 140, 143–44; Petrov defection and timing of announcement, 137–39, 140, 147, 148, (not part of campaign), 148, 152

election campaign of 1955: ALP (Anti-Communist) candidates preference Liberal/Country Party, 181; Evatt's campaign and program, 181–82, (has to defend his reputation, works hard), 182–83; impact of Labor split, 183; landslide Coalition win, 181, 183; Menzies campaigns with confidence, 182, (taunts Evatt), 183; poisoned atmosphere, 181; voters apathetic, 182

election campaign of 1958: breakaway Laborites preference Coalition, 184; increased vote for Coalition; 184; Labor loses seats, 184

in Great Depression, 28; implosion of Scullin Government, 35; radicalisation of right and left, 29; rise of UAP, 28

and Labor Split: benefits Liberal/Country Party in parliament, 179–80; debate on sending troops to Malaya, 179, 180

non-Labor side: division in government, 31; fragmented, 28; inspirations in 1920s, 24–25; loses government, 34

parliamentary debates over banking bill, 41; Chifley's justification for legislation, 41; second reading, 42, 43–44

rents and prices referendum campaign, 44

see also elections

politics in NSW
  1920s, 22
politics in Victoria
  1920s: Nationalist Party and tensions with radicals in Country Party, 25
  1947: election campaign, 42–3; supply blocked, election forced over federal banking issue, 42
Pollard, Reg, 129–30
Pratt, Mel, 169
Prichard, Katharine Susannah
  belief in communism, 58; informer, 76
  impressed on visit to Soviet Union, 58
  Why I Am a Communist, 58, 71

Reece, Eric, 119
Reed, Geoffrey, 74
Reed, John, 27
Reed, Sunday, 27
Richards, Ron, 138, 154
Robinson, W. S. 131–32
Rose, Fred, 76
Rosenberg, Ethel, 4
Rosenberg, Julius, 4
Ross, Lloyd, 123

Sampson, John, 24
Santamaria, B. A., 13, *165*, 177
  Against the Tide, 19, 20, 93
  critics, 20
  edits *Catholic Worker*, 92; *News-Weekly*, 93, 171
  and Evatt, 19, *165*, 170, 173; meetings with, 130, *163*; uneasy feeling, 130, 131
  and Catholic Action (ANSCA), 19–20, 92; attacked within Labor, 171; and Industrial Groups: in Curtin years, 93; Groupers gain substantial power in the ALP, 131; fighting communist unionists in Melbourne, 14, 62, 64, 92–93, 125; in Sydney, 93
  links with anti-communist cells in Victorian Labor Party, 92, 130
  and the Movement, 92, 130, 131, 170; backs some Victorian Labor MPs, 170; copies Communist Party, 93; opposition from some Catholics, other Labor MPs, 172; secretive network, 93, 173; strong Grouper protagonist, 92–93, 130; towards broader influence over Labor, 171
  provocative speech on "Chifley legend", 172
  support of Archbishop Mannix, 92
Saunders, Cheryl, 38
Scullin Labor Government, 22
  and the banks, 3, 35–36
  schism, 35
Seidler, Penelope (née Evatt)
  and dissolution referendum campaign, 2, 4
Sharkey, Lance, 59, 60, 69–70, 81
  convicted of sedition, 70, *71*
Sharpley, Cecil, 69, *89*
Shedden, Sir Frederick, 75
Simpson, Jack, 3, 4
Solzhenitsyn, Aleksandr
  The Gulag Archipelago, 57
Short, Laurie, 131
Soviet embassy in Canberra
  attempted kidnapping, 146
  communist agents, network of

informers, 75–76, 81
intelligence sent to Moscow, 74
and espionage, 158
Soviet Union/Russia, 30
   atomic tests, 77
   blockade of Berlin, 45–46, 47, 67, 69
   Cominform: dividing world into two, 63–64
   Comintern: influence, 92
   as enemy of the West, 4, 5, 45, 47, 66, 69
   Great Terror of 1936–38, 57
   Krushchev's secret speech denouncing reign of terror, 58, 62
   massacre of Polish officers, 66
   Moscow Comintern and foreign communist activities, 60, 171; dissolved, 62
   and Nazi–Soviet Pact, 61
   reign of terror, 56–57; the Cheka and forced collectivisation, 57; death toll, 57
   and satellite states, 5
   and Stalinism, 4
   territorial expansion in Europe, 9, 46, 63; post war, 62, 70, 75
   uprisings and civil war, 56
   visits by foreigners controlled, sponsored, 57–58; refugees reveal grim reality, 58
   WWI and rise of Bolsheviks, 59
   in WWII, 61
Spender, Percy, 26, 54, 78, 84
Spry, Col. Charles, 76, 138
   warning to Evatt, 153
Stalin, Joseph, 56–57, 61, 62, 77, 81
   death, 147

Stout, Vic, 92
Strangio, Paul, 176–77

Taft, Bernie, 58, 61–62, 64, 70
Thompson, Albert, 155
Thornton, E. W., 131
Throssell, Ric, 65–66
trade unions, 3–4, 24, 92
   and communist members, influence, 24, 59, 61–62, 64, 81–82, 128; disrupting industry, civil society, 64–65, 69; Maritime Union, 89; coal strike, 70, 86
   industrial "Groupers" (anti-communist), 14, 62, 64, 83, 92, 93; control Trades Hall Council in Melbourne and the council in Sydney, 171–72; important wins with unions, 131
   push for nationalisations, 41
   strikes on waterfront, 79
Trotsky, Leon, 56

United Australia Party, 25, 26
United Kingdom
   decline, 133
   intelligence services, 74; MI5, 148, 153
United Nations, 8, 11, 31, 38, 43
   in the Cold War, 46; and communism, 68
   Evatt's support for, 46, 65, 66–67, 68
   view of international affairs, 168
United States
   the CIA, 145
   McCarthy-inspired witch hunts, 12, 127–28
   mistrust of Evatt, Labor, 74, 75
   nuclear weapons, 73

rise of, 133
see also Cold War

Vietnam, 169
as communist threat, 30, 77, 78

Wake, Nancy, 101
Ward, Eddie, 49, 82, 83, 84, 118, 155, 156, 174, 175
challenge for Labor leadership in 1959, 184
Ward, Russel, 2–3
Watt, Alan, 169
Webb, Leicester, 103
the Webbs
visit to Soviet Union, 57

Wentworth, Bill, 97, 169
What We Saw in Russia (Bevan, Strauss, Strachey), 57
Whitlam, Gough, 145, 179
enters parliament, 132
Williams, George, 15
Windle, Kevin, 60
World War I
death toll and global consequences, 23–24
World War II
and Australia, 31, 55; troops overseas, 31
ends with atomic bombs, 73
undermines democracy, 30

www.ingramcontent.com/pod-product-compliance
Lightning Source LLC
Chambersburg PA
CBHW070735160426
43192CB00009B/1446